The Administration

and Supervision

of

Special Programs

in Education

Gwen Schroth

Mark Littleton

 KENDALL/HUNT PUBLISHING COMPANY
4050 Westmark Drive   Dubuque, Iowa 52002

Introduction

Schools of today are more sophisticated and offer a vaster array of programs than ever before. A single individual is unlikely to possess a complete understanding of every program that is delivered in the typical public school. *The Administration and Supervision of Special Programs in Education* is designed to provide school personnel—particularly school administrators and teachers who share in the leadership of the school—with the necessary knowledge base and concepts needed to successfully manage the various school programs. For some readers, this book will be the first contact they make with programs such as Title I, TRIO, migrant, or other special programs offered by schools. For others, this book will be an excellent resource for understanding the purposes and intricacies of programs with which they interact daily.

Each chapter of the book begins with a list of objectives and ends with thoughtful questions that highlight some of the important points of the chapter. We felt that each chapter should include a section on the history of the program so that the reader can better understand the programs' background and purposes. Concluding each chapter is a case study that is designed to enable the reader to apply the concepts in a typical school setting.

The first chapter, "Special Education," is intended to be a concise overview of the most complicated special program in our schools. While this chapter is not intended to replace a well-written text, treatise or basic introductory course on special education, it is designed to provide a concise, yet thorough understanding of special education. Prospective school administrators and teachers are well advised to carefully read the text regarding federal and state laws and regulations. Special education programs are very sophisticated and require a great attention to detail; consequently it is not uncommon for a principal to delegate special education responsibilities. A section on school leaders' roles in special education is included to provide guidance to novice and experienced administrators alike.

The chapters on Title I, TRIO, migrant, and bilingual and English as a second language focus on federally-funded programs for special student populations. With the plethora of federal regulations that accompany funding, it is easy to become confused about which guidelines are applicable to each program. Purposes and guidelines can easily become blurred, and the application of the right guidelines can be made to the wrong program. These chapters provide a ready resource for the reader.

Vocational and career education, early childhood education, and gifted and talented education programs are more distinct, and probably easier understood by most school personnel. Often, however, school officials, particularly school administrators, have little experience working with these areas. These chapters provide an insight to these programs that educators generally obtain in a piecemeal manner after a period of time on the job.

The school counselor has become a necessary and vitally important member of the school community; consequently we include a chapter on what constitutes an effective counseling program. Few school administrators (and even fewer teachers) have a formal counseling background. Furthermore, the role of the counselor is not well defined, generally with the job description varying from school to school.

The chapter on central administration reviews central office and building level structures that facilitate and obstruct information regarding the knowledge and skills building that school leaders need to help their personnel. Special programs and services generally spawn a rich array of program specialists and administrators, many of whom are located at the central office level. The expertise of these individuals can help building principals and teachers meet and even enrich the instructional and legal requirements of various programs and services.

Schools that operate according to the belief that a community of leaders is preferable to a bureaucratic model are schools where responsibilities are shared. Consequently the final chapter highlights the critical point that teachers are vital to the successful implementation of special programs and particularly to the students themselves.

We are deeply indebted to those who spent many hours preparing their contributions to this book. The names of the contributors are listed at the beginning of each chapter, yet it is apropos to mention them once again. Our very special thanks to:

Carol S. Anderson	Richard E. Lampe
Reba J. Criswell	Rafael Lara-Alecio
Ana M. Decious	Doris J. Meyer
David Drueckhammer	Leeann Moore
Beth Anne Dunavant	Anita Pankake
Beverly J. Irby	Jerry Trusty
Holly Lamb	Judy T. Walker

Putting this book together has been challenging, yet enjoyable. We certainly hope that you find it helpful to you.

Gwen Schroth and Mark Littleton

About the Authors and Contributors

Gwen Schroth is Associate Professor of Educational Administration at Texas A&M University-Commerce, Commerce, Texas. Her email address is: Gwen_Schroth@tamu-commerce.edu.

Mark Littleton is Professor of Educational Administration at Tarleton State University, Stephenville, Texas. His email address is: Mlittleton@tarleton.edu.

* * * * *

Carol S. Anderson is Director of Gifted Education at Mount Pleasant Independent School District, Mount Pleasant, Texas.

Reba J. Criswell is a doctoral student in the Department of Counseling at Texas A&M University-Commerce, Commerce, Texas.

Ana M. Decious is Director of Bilingual/ESL/Migrant Programs at Mount Pleasant Independent School District, Mount Pleasant, Texas.

David Drueckhammer is Professor and Head of Agricultural Services and Development at Tarleton State University, Stephenville, Texas.

Beth Anne Dunavant is a teacher in the Gifted and Talented Program at Mount Pleasant Independent School District, Mount Pleasant, Texas.

Beverly J. Irby is Professor and Director of the Center for Research and Doctoral Studies in Educational Leadership at Sam Houston State University, Huntsville, Texas.

Holly Lamb is Professor of Curriculum and Instruction at Tarleton State University, Stephenville, Texas.

Richard E. Lampe is Professor of Counseling at Texas A&M University-Commerce, Commerce, Texas.

Rafael Lara-Alecio is Associate Professor of Educational Psychology at Texas A&M University, College Station, Texas.

Doris J. Meyer is Director of Strategic Planning and Resource Development at Aldine Independent School District, Houston, Texas.

Leeann Moore is Associate Professor of Elementary Education at Texas A&M University-Commerce, Commerce, Texas.

Anita Pankake is Professor of Educational Administration at Texas A&M University-Commerce, Commerce, Texas.

Jerry Trusty is Professor of Counseling and Assistant Dean of the College of Education at Texas A&M University-Commerce, Commerce, Texas.

Judy T. Walker is Principal at Annie Sims Elementary School at Mount Pleasant Independent School District, Mount Pleasant, Texas and a doctoral student in the Department of Educational Administration at Texas A&M University-Commerce, Commerce, Texas.

Table of Contents

Chapter 1

Special Education

Mark Littleton and Gwen Schroth

*Special education is now me, and my classroom. Now
we are all special and perhaps all irregular, too!*
A. M. Lamb

Objectives:
- Discuss the historical evolution of special education.
- Identify legislation related to special education and its impact on public schools.
- Discuss components of the Individuals with Disabilities Education Act that are relevant to the public school principal.
- Outline the referral, admission, placement, and dismissal of students in special education.
- Discuss the uniqueness of programs designed for students with disabilities.
- Discuss actions related to disciplining students with disabilities.

American public schools provide students with relatively standard services. What is taught, how instruction is delivered, and even the physical arrangements in Ohio, for example, closely resemble those in California, Texas, or Vermont. While considerable effort is expended to create a high quality education for all students, the needs of some students require additional accommodations. Students with disabilities are among those whose educational needs obligate teachers, principals, support staff, and superintendents to closely scrutinize what is offered and how it is delivered.

Presented here is a basic description of special education services mandated for students with disabilities, information which educators should have at their fingertips in order to knowledgeably and legally supervise and implement special education services. The historical background, requirements for referral and placement of students in special education, disciplinary guidelines for special education students, and the role of the building administrator in this process are discussed.

Historical Background

Until the early 1970s, educating students with disabilities was not primarily the responsibility of public schools. More often than not, parents of students with disabilities were expected to educate these children at home or find alternative arrangements. If the students did attend school, they were frequently segregated from other children. Osborne (1996) describes public schools in colonial America as places where students with disabilities were virtually excluded.

The only education and training they received, if any, was provided by the family. However, in the nineteenth century special schools and classes began to emerge for the visually impaired, hearing impaired, and individuals with physical disabilities. Toward the end of that century and early in the twentieth century classes were developed for students who were mentally retarded. Unfortunately, these programs were segregated from the mainstream and often were taught by insufficiently trained personnel. (Osborne, 1996, p. 1)

Attitudes about the education of students with disabilities began to change as a result of the civil rights movement in the United States. Through the landmark 1954 desegregation case, *Brown v. Board of Education of Topeka*, "The U.S. Supreme Court unknowingly laid the foundation for future right to education cases on behalf of students with disabilities" (Osborne, 1996, p. 4). Writing for the majority, Chief Justice Warren stated:

In these days, it is doubtful that any child may reasonably be expected to succeed in life if he is denied the opportunity of an education. Such an opportunity, where the State has undertaken to provide it, is a right that must be made available to all on equal terms. (*Brown v. Board of Education, 1954*)

Given support from the courts and advocacy groups, parents of children with disabilities began to demand the same rights to an equal educational opportunity for their children that had been gained by other minority groups. Educators, however, were uncertain about how to serve children with special needs and many students went without help altogether.

In the 1970s, advocacy groups worked to improve the rather haphazard manner in which students with disabilities were being educated (Underwood & Mead, 1995). In concert with the advocacy movement, two landmark court cases established the basis for special education legislation that was soon to follow (Tucker, 1998). According to Rothstein (2000), *Pennsylvania Association for Retarded Children (PARC v. Commonwealth* and *Mills v. Board of Education* approved consent decrees that enjoined states from denying education to children who were mentally retarded and children with other disabilities without due process procedures for labeling, placement, and exclusion. The *Mills* consent decree went so far as to set out an elaborate framework for what that due process would entail. Rothstein (2000) describes the conditions of those times.

Of the more than eight million children with disabilities in the United States, more than half were receiving either inappropriate or no educational services. ....Identification and placement of children with disabilities was haphazard, inconsistent, and generally inappropriate. African-American, Hispanic, and some other ethnic groups were often stereotyped and disproportionately placed in special education programs. Parental involvement was generally discouraged. (p. 12)

Much-needed regulations, however, did emerge and continue to be refined even today. Initial clarification was furnished in 1970 with the passage of the Education of the Handicapped Act (EHA). This act provided minimal educational guidelines so that states could require—and schools provide—a truly free and appropriate public education to special needs children. Until the passage of this act, special education placement did not center on formal assessments, parents were not always informed of decisions regarding their child, and segregation was the norm. "The EHA was a congressional response to findings that children with disabilities historically received inadequate educational services, were improperly identified and evaluated, and were often needlessly segregated and excluded from regular school populations" (McEllistrem, Roth & Cox, 1998, p. 2).

More permanent and far-reaching legislation was passed in 1975 when Congress amended EHA and voted into law—and President Ford signed—Public Law 94-142, the Education of All Handicapped Children Act (EAHCA). Public Law 94-142 contained most of the significant legal protections for students with disabilities by obligating states to provide free and appropriate public education (FAPE) for all disabled children and youth, regardless of severity. FAPE means that education is "provided at public expense, under public supervision and direction, and without charge (920 U.S.C. § 1401[8]). Procedural and substantive due process protections were also given to those with disabilities at this time.

Public Law 94-142 also required that American children with disabilities receive their education "in the 'least restrictive' (that is, the most normal) environment in which an appropriate education can be delivered to them....This law explicitly creates the expectation that teachers will work with pupils who in the very recent past would have been excluded from regular classes"(Lakin & Reynolds, 1983, p. 13). The least restrictive environment (LRE) is often referred to as *mainstreaming*. The wording of the statute is such that many debates have ensued over its precise meaning.

> To the maximum extent appropriate, children with disabilities, including children in public or private institutions or other care facilities, (should be) educated with children who are not disabled, and that special classes, separate schooling, or other removal of children with disabilities from the regular educational environment (should occur) only when the nature or severity of the disability is such that education in regular classes with the use of supplementary aids and services cannot be achieved satisfactorily.... (20 U.S.C. § 1412[a][5][B])

In 1990, P. L. 94-142 was amended and renamed the Individuals with Disabilities Education Act (IDEA) to clarify the minimum federal education standards. The language, as well as the title, of IDEA emphasized Congress' preference for the term "disability" as opposed to "handicap." Additionally, the amendment created substantive rights (Rothstein, 2000) as well as procedural due process rights, an area the courts and legislators typically leave to the education establishment (Kemerer & Walsh, 2000). Categories for eligibility were more clearly delineated. As used in this part, the term child with a disability means a child evaluated in accordance with Sections 300.530-300.536 as having:

- Mental retardation.
- A hearing impairment including deafness.
- A speech or language impairment.
- A visual impairment including blindness.
- Serious emotional disturbance.
- An orthopedic impairment.
- Autism.
- Traumatic brain injury.
- An other health impairment.
- A specific learning disability.
- Deaf-blindness.
- Multiple disabilities.

When IDEA was reauthorized in 1997, states were given the option to expand this list of eligible conditions to include children aged three through nine experiencing developmental delays (34 CFR §300.313).

Even with this delineation of disabilities, substantial disagreement continues over how some of the categories are defined. Particularly troublesome for educators is identifying students with learning disabilities. Essex (1999) notes that "No single test should be used as the sole criterion for determining disabilities; rather a battery of tests...should be used" (p. 75).

To be eligible for federal funding under IDEA, states are required to provide special education to all disabled persons aged 3 through 21 (20 U.S.C. § 1412[a][1][A]). If a district does not have a pre-school program to satisfy these requirements, the district must pursue other alternatives such as Head Start, private school programs, or classes in regular elementary schools (Tucker, 1998, pp. 393-394). The duty to find students with disabilities lies with the school.

Implementing IDEA placed new pressures on school personnel. Disabilities were identified by category, detailed educational plans were written at least yearly, and protection from spurious placements was supplied. The eligibility of students with learning disabilities for special education services impacted schools considerably. The number of students for whom the schools now had to provide services increased significantly (Rothstein, 2000).

In 1997 IDEA was reauthorized, bringing some changes that impacted educators. These changes called for increased parent involvement, clarification of who is to participate in meetings, mandated transition plans from school to work for students age 14 and older, provided for student discipline concerns, and addressed private school issues (Walsh & Gallegos, 1997). Additionally, for the first time schools were required to provide FAPE for special education students who were suspended or expelled from school.

Some students, however, have disabilities that fall outside of special education eligibility guidelines. These children also require special accommodations for which the schools are responsible under Section 504 of the Rehabilitation Act of 1973. Section 504, as it is commonly known, is discussed later in this chapter.

Identification and Referral of Students for Special Education

Who should receive special education services? A child does not qualify for special education services merely by exhibiting a disability. "The disability must translate into an educational need for services not provided by the conventional classroom" (Underwood & Mead, 1995, p. 65). While this process might differ somewhat from state to state, the law is clear that the student must have an educational need for services in order to be placed in special education.

What determines an educational need? Underwood and Mead (1995) note that for an educational need to exist,

> ...a child must demonstrate that his or her disability hinders educational progress. Therefore, although many children may require accommodations to be successful in regular education, not all of them will receive services...because they do not exhibit needs exceptional enough to meet all the eligibility requirements... (pp. 63-64)

Modifications

IDEA requires local education agencies to provide for students with disabilities an appropriate program of special education and related services that is individualized and "reasonably calculated to confer educational benefits upon the student" (McEllistrem, Roth, & Cox, 1998, p. 39). The key words in IDEA are "educational benefits." The most common demonstration of an educational need is a child's failure to learn even when a teacher attempts to intervene by modifying instruction and/or altering classroom arrangements. Hence the initial focus is on teachers' efforts to work with the student in the regular education setting.

Additionally, referrals to special education are intended to be a last resort, not the first intervention considered. "Prereferral interventions are used in the general education classroom to attempt to ameliorate the problem prior to referral to special education" (Yell, 1998, p. 224). Modifications to the regular curriculum may sufficiently address a student's educational difficulties, making referral for special education services unnecessary. (In some cases, the student is assessed and found to qualify for special education services but classroom modifications are deemed to adequately address the educational need.) If efforts to modify fail to meet the child's educational need, the process of assessment, evaluation, and an IEP Team decision about eligibility may begin. Understandably, simple classroom modifications will not suffice for students with severe disabilities (such severe cases of autism or mental retardation) and the referral for special education may be otherwise expedited.

Some commonly used techniques teachers use to modify instruction are:

- Shortened assignments.
- Oral exams.
- Additional time to complete assignments.
- Peer tutoring.
- Tape-recorded textbooks.
- Highlighted textbooks.

Teacher evaluations of student progress will show whether or not modifications are successful. Informal assessments may include daily assignments, tests, and observations. These assessments help "identify strengths and weaknesses that can subsequently become the basis of an individualized educational plan" (Rothstein, 2000, p. 93) should the child qualify for special education services. In most districts, school-wide screenings—such as routine vision and hearing tests—may alert educators to a possible disability and indicate that further assessment is in order (Yell, 1998). Bateman (1995) warns that prereferral interventions should not have the effect of delaying the referral of an eligible student.

Parental involvement is required by law once the decision is made to evaluate a child for special education but the parents should be informed of their child's difficulties much earlier. When alerted to a problem, teachers can share results of informal assessments, discuss observations, and solicit the parents' support. Cooperative efforts between home and school often resolve the problem and/or set the tone for a sound working relationship.

Referral to the Committee

When general classroom modifications are deemed ineffective, a referral can be made to the school's referral committee (sometimes termed the Student Support Team, Teacher Assistance Team, or MDT) usually by the teacher or the parent. Informal teacher assessments and information from parents provide the basis for this committee's decision. Yell (1998) describes the referral process:

> The referral is a formal request made to the MDT to have a student evaluated for the presence of a disability. Although school districts may have procedures regarding referrals, referrals are not subject to the federal special education laws. Following a student referral, the MDT determines if the student requires further assessment to determine eligibility for special education. (p. 225)

Not all student assistance committee decisions result in referral for a special education assessment. Services provided via bilingual education, gifted education, dyslexia programs, or other special programs might be more appropriate. If parents request an evaluation of their child for special education and the committee declines, the district must notify the parents in writing of the refusal. The notification must include the reasons for the refusal and inform the parents of their due process options (OSEP Policy Letter, 1994).

Figure 1

THE ADMISSION/REVIEW AND DISMISSAL PROCESS FOR SPECIAL EDUCATION

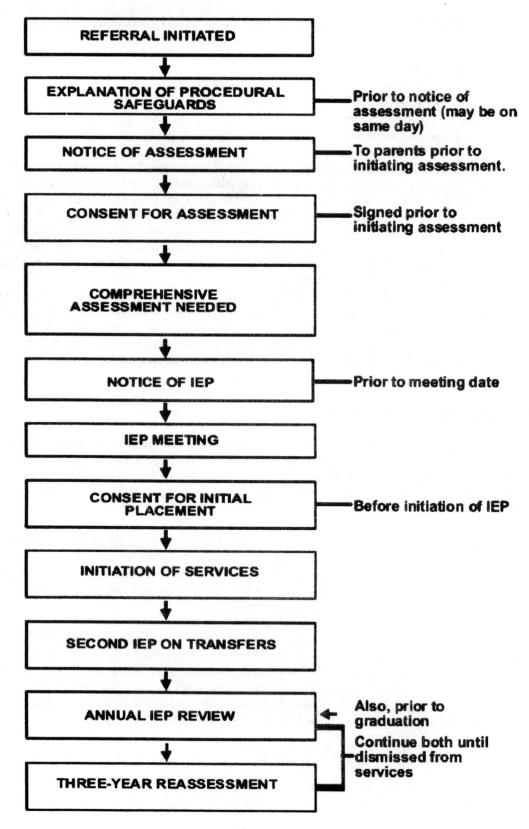

REFERRAL INITIATED

EXPLANATION OF PROCEDURAL SAFEGUARDS — Prior to notice of assessment (may be on same day)

NOTICE OF ASSESSMENT — To parents prior to initiating assessment.

CONSENT FOR ASSESSMENT — Signed prior to initiating assessment

COMPREHENSIVE ASSESSMENT NEEDED

NOTICE OF IEP — Prior to meeting date

IEP MEETING

CONSENT FOR INITIAL PLACEMENT — Before initiation of IEP

INITIATION OF SERVICES

SECOND IEP ON TRANSFERS

ANNUAL IEP REVIEW — Also, prior to graduation

Continue both until dismissed from services

THREE-YEAR REASSESSMENT

6

Referral to Special Education for Assessment

IDEA specifies the steps that precede the placement of a student in special education (see Figure 1). The 1997 reauthorization of IDEA specifies that the referral committee meet before an initial evaluation (if appropriate) or prior to any reevaluation (20 U.S.C. 1414 [c]) for the purpose of reviewing existing evaluation data and, on the basis of that review, determine the scope of the assessment. Once the decision is made about the appropriate assessments, IDEA requires that prior to the initiation of special education placement or services, a comprehensive and individualized evaluation of the child's educational needs be conducted. The evaluation must include all suspected areas of need, including, when appropriate, health, vision, hearing, social and emotional status, general intelligence, academic performance, communicative status, and motor abilities (IDEA Regulations 34 C.F.R. § 300.532[f])" (Yell, 1998, p. 226). These evaluations provide information necessary for a committee to determine whether or not a child is eligible for special education services.

Referral Documents. The contents of a referral packet are based on IDEA regulations, but what the packet looks like may differ slightly from state to state. The packet required in Texas serves as an example. Texas requires that the following be supplied before a formal assessment occurs:

- Demographic data, reasons for the referral, attendance records, and documentation of academic achievement.
- Samples of the student's work, ratings of the student's social and emotional behavior in the classroom, a brief assessment of language skills, and the child's academic characteristics, all provided by the classroom teacher. Additional information may be necessary if the student is being referred for speech services.
- Health information, including vision and hearing testing results, generally provided by the school nurse.
- Health history, family data, and home information provided by the parents or guardians. Recent changes in the family, discipline methods used with the child, and perceived causes of the problem help complete the data. If, for example, a child received a mild head injury early in life, the information would be useful in the overall assessment.
- Home Language Survey to determine the child's primary language and rule out language barriers as a basis for educational problems.

When these documents are completed and delivered to the appropriate special education personnel, the formal evaluation for special education begins.

Each state determines the number of days allowed to complete the referral process but once a child is identified, the IEP Team must conduct the evaluation in a timely manner (Yell, 1998). For example, Texas state law requires that after a referral is initiated the district has 90 days in which to process paperwork, conduct the assessment, write a report, and conduct a meeting to inform parents of the results.

Parent Consent. IDEA is very clear in its provision for parents' procedural safeguards. Parents must be aware of the procedural safeguards, receive, understand, and sign the explanation of those safeguards, be notified in a timely manner and in writing that an assessment of their child is going to take place, and give written consent for the assessment. These requirements guarantee parental involvement, a regulation under IDEA. Consent, according to the law, means that:

The parent has been fully informed of all information relevant to the activity for which [his/her consent] is sought, in his or her native language, or other mode of communication; the parent understands and agrees in writing to the carrying out of the activity for which his or her consent is sought, and the consent describes that activity and lists the records (if any) that will be released and to whom; and the parent understands that the granting of consent is voluntary on the part of the parent and may be revoked at anytime. (Section 300.500 of 34 CFR 300.1-300.765)

Consequently, the district is obligated to ensure that the parents fully understand and agree to the process that is about to begin. (The parents are not agreeing at this point to actual placement of their child in special education. The IEP Team uses the results of the assessments to determine the child's eligibility.) Assessment cannot begin until a parent is notified in writing of the district's intent to conduct an evaluation. Once parental consent is obtained, the district may proceed with the student assessment. "The notice must be understandable to the general public and must contain an explanation of the parents' due process rights as well as descriptions of what the school is proposing and the evaluation procedures to be used" (Yell, 1998, p. 227). If the parents refuse their consent to the assessment, the school district may use the hearing process established by IDEA to determine if the child should be evaluated (Ackenhalt, 1994). After all of the required information—including the parent's signatures—is received, the campus educational diagnostician or other appropriate professionals may begin to assess the student.

Assessments

The law requires that student assessment commence within a reasonable period of time following the receipt of parent consent (34 CFR §300.343). Results of the evaluation are used by an IEP Team to determine what services will be offered and who will deliver them. The IEP Team is often termed the multidisciplinary team, or the Admission, Review and Dismissal Committee. For clarity, the committee will be termed the IEP Team here. For initial evaluation the law states:

Each public agency shall ensure that a full and individual evaluation is conducted for each child being considered for special education and related services....to determine if the child is a "child with a disability" under Section 300.7; and to determine the educational needs of the child. (IDEA Regulations 34 CFR §300.320)

Yell (1998) summarized IDEA evaluation material and procedures requirements:

- Test and other evaluation materials must be provided and administered (a) in the student's native language or mode of communication unless not feasible to do so, (b) validated for the specific purpose for which they are used, and (c) administered by trained personnel in conformity with instructions.
- The evaluation must be tailored to assess specific areas of educational need.
- The evaluation must be designed to reflect the student's aptitude or achievement level rather than reflecting the student's disabilities, unless intended to do so. No single procedure is used as the sole criterion to determine eligibility.
- A multidisciplinary team, including one person knowledgeable in the area of suspected disability, makes the decisions. The student is assessed in all areas of suspected disability.

The selection of specific tests and materials for student assessment are left to each state. An exception is when a student with a suspected learning disability has a "severe discrepancy" between achievement and ability, although "severe discrepancy" is not defined by IDEA. Sometimes outside assessments (i.e., from a physician) may be accepted by the district. IDEA regulations (34 C.F.R. § 300.542-543) do specify that an observation of a student in the general education classroom must be conducted if a learning disability is suspected and a written report of the evaluation results must be provided to the IEP Team.

Children receiving special education services must receive a comprehensive reevaluation (similar to the original pre-placement evaluation) at least every three years (or more often if deemed necessary) to determine the child's continuing eligibility. The 1997 reauthorization of IDEA allows the IEP Team to waive assessment to determine eligibility for some students at this point (20 U.S.C. 1414 [c]). For example, repeated assessment of a student permanently without sight is unnecessary to determine that a visual impairment exists.

Individualized Education Program Development

The Individualized Education Program Team (IEP Team) is required to meet to review the available data. The IEP Team scrutinizes the results of the formal evaluation and also "draw[s] on information from a variety of sources, including aptitude and achievement tests, teacher recommendations, physical condition, social or cultural background, and adaptive behavior" (Yell, 1998, p. 232). This information provides the basis for the Team's decision to qualify the child for services under IDEA.

If the child is determined to be eligible, the Team must decide if the student requires special education services. If so, placement options are considered and the placement decision is made in accordance with Least Restrictive Environment (LRE) requirements of the law. Unfortunately, there is no simple rule for determining the LRE for each child. At one end of the spectrum the LRE may include a full-day placement in the child's regular classroom with only minor instructional or behavioral modifications. At the other end the courts have determined that restrictive placements (e.g., residential and institutional placements) were the appropriate LRE (Tucker, 1998).

In the court case of *Roncker v. Walter*, the courts established the portability test. Under the portability test, "If the particular services that make a more restrictive setting more appropriate can be transported to a less restrictive setting, such a modification is required by the LRE mandate" (Tucker, 1998, p. 389).

In any event, the IEP Committee must make timely decisions. "A meeting to develop an IEP for the child must be conducted within 30-days of a determination that the child needs special education and related services" (IDEA Regulations 34 C.F.R. 300.343). Furthermore, an eligible student cannot receive services until the IEP is developed (IDEA Regulations, 34 C.F.R. § 300.342 [b]). The signatures from all in attendance at the IEP Team meeting, including the parents or guardian, signify (a) knowledge of, and (b) agreement to the services planned for the student.

IDEA specifies the persons who are to be included on the IEP Team. These include:

- A representative of the educational agency (e.g., principal).
- The student's special education teacher and the student's general education teacher. One of these teachers must be the student's teacher, the other one can be any teacher that fits the category (Yell, 1998).
- The student's parents or guardians.
- A person who can interpret the instructional implications of the evaluation results (i.e., the educational diagnostician).
- The child, when appropriate but required for transition IEP meetings.
- Related services personnel.
- For a transition IEP, a representative of any other agency that is likely to provide or pay for the transition services (e.g., state rehabilitation agency, state MHMR representative).
- Other persons at the discretion of parents or the educational agency.

The Individual Education Program (IEP) controls all aspects of the student's special education program. Outlined in the IEP are the measurable annual goals and short-term objectives
for the student's education, the basis for placement in special education, the length of the school year, evaluation and measurement criteria, and the related services a student might need. This document is not only the management tool of the program but also the basis for the school's legal responsibilities. Additionally, the document enables parents to accurately follow their child's progress.

The student's parents must be invited (and every effort made to include them) to participate in all the decisions pertaining to their child. IDEA specifies that parents are to be partners in the development of the IEP and specific procedures are outlined to ensure that the parents fully participate in formulating the IEP (34 C.F.R. § 300.345). Parents are given advance notice of the meeting to ensure their participation. The meeting must be scheduled at a mutually agreed time and place. The notice must indicate the purpose, time, location of the meeting, and inform parents of persons attending. If a parent cannot attend, the agency must use other methods to ensure their participation. Finally, the parents shall be given a copy of the completed IEP. If the parent is unable to attend the IEP meeting, the school must maintain records of attempts to arrange a meeting conducive to the parents' schedule.

Following the IEP Team meeting the school has a duty to inform the teacher(s) of the contents of the IEP. Failure to implement the IEP and the classroom modifications listed within the IEP may result in lawsuits that are time consuming and costly to districts (e.g., *Doe v. Withers*, *1993*).

In most instances, the principal is imbued with the authority to designate resources to educational programs on the campus. Because of this authority, the principal may chair the IEP Team meetings. Since procedural requirements are well documented in IDEA, it is incumbent upon the chair to have an agenda to follow when leading an IEP Team meeting. Meeting requirements may vary from state to state, so principals are encouraged to learn the procedures applicable in their state. A sample agenda is found in Figure 2.

Annual Reviews. IDEA specifies that the IEP will be reviewed annually. If any changes to the IEP are proposed before the yearly review, parents are notified and invited to attend an IEP Team meeting where modifications to the IEP are considered. IDEA regulations state that "As long as the school provides adequate notice and conducts meetings in accordance with procedures set forth in IDEA, parental consent is not required for review and revision of the IEP. If parents reject revisions, they have the option of calling a due process hearing" (Yell, 1998, p. 189).

Related Services

Related services are additional aids or services that a student may need to more fully benefit from the special education program. These services are specified by the IEP Team and written into the student's plan. IDEA defines related services as "services that may be required to assist the child with a disability to benefit from special education" (IDEA, 20 U.S.C. § 1401 [a][17]). IDEA provides a lengthy list of related services that qualify but the more frequently prescribed include:

• Transportation services	• Counseling	• Assistive technology
• Occupational therapy	• Physical therapy	• Transition services
• Speech pathology	• Psychological services	• Mobility services

Even with the definition provided by IDEA, the terms of related and medical services "have been proven difficult to apply" (Barkoff, 1998, p. 136). Considerable litigation has helped define the nature of a related service (Essex, 1999). Through the cases of *Board of Education of*

Figure 2

Individualized Education Program Team Meeting Agenda*

I.   Introductions: Unless all parties are familiar with other members of the team, each member should introduce himself or herself and state his or her role in the meeting. This process serves two purposes. First, the person assigned to take minutes of the meeting will be able to record the names accurately. Second, attorneys who are present will be identified.

II. Statement of purpose of the meeting.

III. Review of appropriate assessment data.

IV. Development or review of Individualized Education Plan (IEP):

        A. Review previous IEP objectives.

        B. Discuss competencies.

        C. Summarize needs.

        D. Write or approve new objectives.

        E. Discuss modifications.

        F. Discuss service alternatives: Identify the general and special education alternatives and supplementary aids and services provided, tried, or considered.

        G. Consider the least restrictive environment.

        H. Consider any necessary related services.

        I. Consider special transportation needs.

        J. Consider graduation requirements.

V.   Determine student placement.

VI. Review the minutes of the meeting.

VII. Obtain signatures from all attending the meeting.

*All steps may not apply to every IEP Team Meeting.

Hendrick Hudson Central School District v. Rowley, Irving Independent School Distrit, Tatro, and *Cedar Rapids School District v. Garret F.,* the courts have clarified the differences between a related service, which must be offered by the district, and a medical service.

In *Rowley* the court was presented with a student who had minimal residual hearing and was an excellent lip-reader. Based on the student's success in class and the testimony of the student's sign language interpreter, the Supreme Court decided that the school district was not required to provide an individual sign language interpreter for the student in order to maximize her educational opportunities. According to the Court, disabled children do not need to be provided with all services but only those that provide a meaningful educational benefit.

In *Tatro* the Supreme Court was presented with a case where an eight year-old student with spina bifida required clean intermittent catheterization (CIC). Since non-medical personnel with minimal training could perform CIC, the Court ruled that CIC was a related service. In the *Garret F.* case a student involved in a motorcycle accident at an early age was left paralyzed and required constant medical attention. The Supreme Court reviewed the services required of Garret F. and found that although they might be more costly, the services were no more medical than those required of Tatro (Bartlett, 2000).

Using guidance from the courts, the following guidelines will assist districts in determining related services:

- The district must provide a related service only if the student requires special education services (Imber & van Geel, 2000).
- When considering transportation services, each case must be considered on its own merits. If the transportation is necessary for the child to receive the benefit of special education services, then the transportation must be provided at no cost to the parents (Imber & van Geel, 2000).
- Medical services that must be performed by a physician or hospital likely do not fall within the parameters of a related service (Rawson, 2000).
- Services that require a physician's prescription or order are related services but the physician need not be present (Imber & van Geel, 2000).

Related services can be costly and often raise legal questions, especially regarding the more expensive services such as transportation, occupational and physical therapy, psychological and health related services (Yell, 1998). While medical services can be expensive, they are excluded as related services except for diagnostic or evaluative purposes.

Although some services might appeal to a parent or committee member, the school is required to provide only those services that assist students with disabilities to benefit from special education. The services that an IEP Team determines necessary must be provided for the student. For example, if the IEP directs that counseling will be provided twice a week for 30 minutes, the district is bound to that commitment.

Transition Services. The welfare of students beyond their secondary education was a concern when IDEA was rewritten in 1990. Written into IDEA at that time was the purpose of requiring transition services which is to infuse a longer-range perspective into the IEP process so that students have a better opportunity to reach their potential as adults (Tucker & Goldstein, 1992). Individualized transition plans for students with disabilities must be included in the student's IEP by the time they are 16. IDEA Amendments of 1997 added the mandate that certain transition services begin at age 14. Transition services are

...a coordinated set of activities for a student, designed within an outcome-oriented process, that promotes movement from school to post-school activities, including post-secondary education, vocational training, integrated employment (including supported employment), continuing and adult education, adult services, independent living, or community participation. (20 U.S.C. § 1401 [A] [19])

As transition services are based on the student's needs and preferences, the student must be invited to attend the IEP meeting at which transition services are planned. A representative of the agency likely to provide or pay for the service must attend as well.

IEP Meetings. The initial placement IEP meeting is critical as this is when services to be provided for the child are outlined for the first time. The yearly review and the three-year reevaluation IEP Team meetings are equally important as they provide ongoing evaluation of the student's progress. The IEP Team, though, is required to meet at other times as well. The IEP Team may convene if any alteration in the IEP is made or if a change in placement is deemed appropriate. For example, a student may progress more rapidly through the curriculum than expected, calling for new goals and objectives (an alteration in the IEP), or s/he needs to spend time in a more restricted environment for a short period of time (a change in placement). When a student transfers from one school district to another the committee must meet even to provide services on a temporary basis until the receiving school receives records. If a parent, teacher, administrator, or other interested party requests a meeting, the IEP Team must conduct a meeting.

Student Discipline

Possibly the most controversial aspect of all special education legislation and litigation is that of student discipline. The controversy stems from the perceived inability to discipline two students, one with a disability and one without, in the same manner for the same misbehavior. Essex (2000) notes that "It has long been held that children with disabilities may not be punished for conduct that is a *manifestation* of their disability"(p. 80), and the courts have consistently ruled that handicapped students must be given special consideration (Alexander & Alexander, 1998). For educators there is seldom a bright line between behavior that results from a disability and behavior that is not a result of a disability. Essex (2000) states that students with disabilities "may be disciplined by school authorities for any behavior that is not associated with their disability, using regular disciplinary procedures, as reflected in school policies" (p. 80). There are instances where a certain situation warrants specific disciplinary actions, however, and "an effort must be made to ensure that the punishment does not *materially* and *substantially* interrupt the child's education" (p. 80).

The types of discipline that materially and substantially interrupt the child's education consist of student transfers, suspensions, and expulsions. Discipline actions of this nature result in a change in placement for students. A change in placement triggers due process protections afforded by IDEA (see 20 U.S.C.S. § 1415).

What constitutes a change of placement? A change in placement occurs if the child is removed from his or her educational setting for more than ten consecutive days, or if the child is subjected to a series of removals of more than ten days in a year where the removals reveal a pattern because of their proximity to each other. Unfortunately, IDEA provides no guidelines for determining what reveals a pattern and the Office of Special Education Programs (OSEP) has provided little assistance. Moran (2000) indicates that factors likely to be considered include (a) the length of each removal, (b) total amount of time the child is removed, and (c) the proximity of the removals to one another. Prior to any change in placement, a meeting of the multidisciplinary team must be held (Rawson, 2000).

When parents reject the change in placement and request a due process hearing, the "stay put" provision of IDEA becomes effective. The "stay put" provision stems from IDEA's requirement that "during the pendency of any proceedings...the child shall remain in the then-current education placement" (20 U.S.C.S. § 1415 [I]). School officials who believe that the child's current educational placement poses a danger to the child or to others may seek relief from the courts from the "stay put" provision; however, before a court order is successful, school officials must show that they have "made reasonable efforts to accommodate the student's disabilities" (Moran, 2000, p. 124-125).

If, however, there is a minor change in placement, "the only limitation set upon a school district is that it treat a child with a disability in the same way that it would treat a non-disabled child" (Tucker, 1998, p. 485).

Procedures

Once misbehavior occurs, the school officials must first determine if the student is a disabled student who falls under IDEA guidelines. If the student is covered by IDEA and the removal results in a change of placement, the multidisciplinary team must determine if the behavior was a manifestation of the student's disability. If the team does not determine that there is a nexus between the disability and the behavior, then school officials may discipline the student as they would any non-disabled child.

Manifestation Determination. Moran (2000) notes that, within 10 days of the decision by the school officials to change the student's placement, the IEP team "must consider in terms of the behavior subject to disciplinary action, all relevant information including: evaluation and diagnostic results including the results or other relevant information supplied by the parents; observations of the child; and the child's IEP and placement" (p. 129). After consideration, the IEP team can determine that the behavior was not a result of the handicapping condition if:

- The child's IEP and placement were appropriate,
- The special education services were consistent with the IEP and placement, and
- The child's handicapping condition did not impair the child's judgment and ability to control his/her behavior.

If the student is subjected to a series of disciplinary removals that cumulate to 10 days in a school year, the IEP Team must meet and complete a functional behavioral analysis and develop a behavior intervention plan (BIP). The BIP describes the modifications necessary for a student to continue to receive FAPE without his or her behavior impeding his or her education. If a BIP is already in place, the IEP Team must review the BIP and make appropriate adjustments.

When a child continues to engage in misbehavior or has been removed from his or her educational placement for more than ten school days, the multidisciplinary team must conduct a functional behavior assessment (FBA) and then, if necessary, modify the student's BIP or educational placement (Moran, 2000). The FBA requires that school officials "use a variety of assessment tools and strategies to gather relevant functional…information, including information provided by the parent" (20 U.S.C.S. § 1414 [2]).

Drugs or Weapons. Due to the high profile nature of school violence as evidenced in Littleton, Colorado, Jonesboro, Arkansas and other schools across the country, Congress specifically addressed the use of drugs and weapons when revising IDEA. "Special provisions exist if a student (1) carries a weapon to school or to a school function or (2) if a student knowingly possesses or uses illegal drugs or sells or solicits the sale of a controlled substance" (Moran, 2000, p. 134). Under those circumstances a student may be removed to an alternative educational placement for up to 45 days without the agreement of the parent even if the IEP Team determines the behavior is a manifestation of the child's disability. (During the alternative educational placement the child's progress in the general curriculum must continue that will enable the child to move without interruption toward the goals of his or her IEP.)

Reports to Law Enforcement Authorities. School officials are required to report crimes committed by children with disabilities. School officials are also required to transmit educational and disciplinary records to the authorities subject to limitations imposed by the Family Educational Rights and Privacy Act (Rawson, 2000).

Section 504 of The Rehabilitation Act of 1973

In 1973 Congress passed the Rehabilitation Act which significantly impacts America's schools. Legislation leading to this Act was enacted to address needs of disabled war veterans, but The Rehabilitation Act of 1973 expanded the education, transportation, housing, and health care rights of those with severe handicaps. More recently, however, Section 504 of this Act was carefully scrutinized and interpreted as having implications for public schools. Section 504 states:

> No otherwise qualified handicapped individual in the United States, as defined
> In section 706(7) of this title, shall, solely by reason of his handicap, be excluded
> from participation in, be denied the benefits of, or be subjected to discrimination
> under any program or activity receiving Federal financial assistance or under any
> program or activity conducted by any Executive agency or by the United States
> Postal Service.... (29 U.S.C. § 794, 1973)

As public schools receive a portion of their funding from the federal government, Section 504 applies and protects from discrimination students with a disability, whether the condition is covered by special education eligibility guidelines or not. Thus schools are obligated to ensure that students with a disability receive the same benefits and services provided to other students. They must have the rights, privileges, advantage, or opportunity enjoyed by others receiving an aid, benefit, or service and must be allowed equality of participation and benefit (22 CFR §217.4[ii]).

IDEA provides a defining list of conditions under which students are eligible for special education services. The 504 Section definition of persons with handicaps is broader, including:

- Those who have a physical or mental impairment which substantially limits one or more major life activity,
- Those who have a record of such an impairment, or
- Those who are regarded as having such an impairment (22 CFR §217.3[i]).

Thus, students who qualify for Section 504 consideration might have heart disease, obesity, dyslexia, communicable or life-threatening diseases, short-term illnesses, asthma, AIDS, or be drug- or alcohol-addicted. Figure 3 provides a visual delineation between qualifying conditions under IDEA and Section 504.

The duty of the school is to first identify students who fall under the broad umbrella of Section 504 and then make appropriate accommodations for them. For example, a student on crutches might be identified as handicapped under Section 504 and be allowed to leave classes early to make transitions to other classes (a modification). This student does not meet any of IDEA's criteria for special education services but does fulfill Section 504's definition of a student who has a physical impairment that limits the major life activity of attending school. On the other hand, a student who is blind has an impairment that severely limits their major life activities and would classify as handicapped under Section 504 but would also meet the special education eligibility of sight impairment. In other words, "According to Section 504, an evaluation or reevaluation that is in compliance with the procedural requirements of IDEA will also be in compliance with the requirements of Section 504" (Yell, 1998, p. 225).

The school district must identify students who qualify for accommodations under Section 504 and parents must be notified of that decision. Parental consent is not required for the children to receive modifications at school but a periodic review and evaluation of these students by a district Section 504 committee is required.

The difference between Section 504 and special education is sometimes confusing. While both address concerns of students with disabilities, those who qualify for special education do so if the disability is seen to adversely affect the child's educational performance. Section 504, on

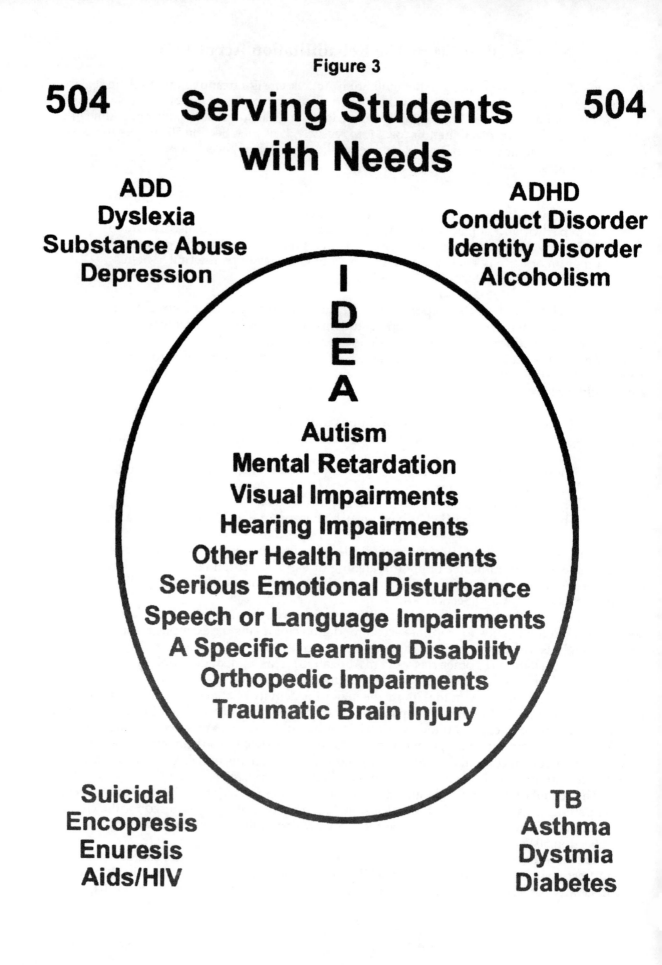

Figure 3

Serving Students with Needs

504   504

ADD
Dyslexia
Substance Abuse
Depression

ADHD
Conduct Disorder
Identity Disorder
Alcoholism

I
D
E
A

Autism
Mental Retardation
Visual Impairments
Hearing Impairments
Other Health Impairments
Serious Emotional Disturbance
Speech or Language Impairments
A Specific Learning Disability
Orthopedic Impairments
Traumatic Brain Injury

Suicidal
Encopresis
Enuresis
Aids/HIV

TB
Asthma
Dystmia
Diabetes

the other hand, focuses on the question of whether or not the handicapping condition limits one or more major life activities and raises the issue of discrimination. Where IDEA asks if a student's education is reasonably designed to confer benefits, Section 504 is concerned with the protection of civil rights and asks if the child's education is comparable to that received by those who are not disabled.

School Leaders' Role in Special Education

Administration of special education services for students with disabilities is becoming more difficult and complex (Pazey, 1993). Supervision of special education requires that the building principal make arrangements for appropriate facilities, juggle schedules, ensure paperwork is completed correctly and on time, supervise and evaluate teachers, discipline students, and attend IEP meetings. Additionally, as instructional leader for the entire campus, the principal ensures that special education students receive appropriate instruction. The principal also plays an active role in maintaining healthy working relationships among parents, teachers, and central office staff whose connections with educating special education students are highly varied. Creating a climate of care and concern for students is woven throughout all of the principal's duties so that students with disabilities—and all students for that matter—can thrive. Yet, transcending all must be the principal's concern for remaining within the letter of the law due to the litigious nature of special education.

Teacher leaders also play a key role in the delivery of special education services. As role models for the entire staff, teacher leaders set the tone of the school regarding how special needs students are treated and how their instruction is approached. These teachers influence whether or not students with disabilities are welcome in regular education classes and greatly determine the relationship between regular staff members and special education staff. In meetings, these leaders model a nonadversarial position, facilitating the staff's ability to meet the needs of students.

Management. Careful attention to management tasks is not only a legal requirement but provides an opportunity for school leaders to build an effective working relationship with special education staff and administrators. For example, making certain that referrals, requests, and other paperwork are correct "the first time" and are completed in a timely fashion indicates that the leaders view such tasks as cooperative endeavors. On the other hand, those who place on others the majority of the responsibility for identifying eligible students, attending meetings, completing paperwork correctly, and responding to requests probably views special education as an isolated program, unrelated to regular education. This stance is neither conducive to collaborative working relationships with the special education staff nor is it in the best interests of students.

Leadership. The school's leaders are the building's instructional leaders. For special education this means making certain that students are challenged, assessed, and appropriately placed. During the prereferral process they make certain that a student has an educational need before allowing the process to proceed. Prompting can result in locating resources, adapting instruction, or making other modifications that enable a student to experience success without the services of special education. For example, Grossman (1995) talks of the misrepresentation of students of poverty and of ethnic minority backgrounds, particularly males, in special education. Putting an end to such misrepresentations is ultimately the principal's responsibility but is facilitated by teachers who are concerned about the equitable treatment of students.

During the referral process leadership means being attuned to whether or not legal guidelines are followed. Later, to guarantee that modifications outlined by the IEP Committee are understood and followed, leaders provide the staff with training in alternate teaching techniques.

In IEP Team meetings, the Team Chairperson ensures that:

- Sufficient time is allowed for team members to prepare for the meeting.
- Sufficient time is allowed for all members to actively participate in the meeting.
- An agenda is available.
- Team members adhere to the agenda.
- The meeting begins on time and members do not feel rushed.
- All appropriate personnel are present.
- Every effort has been made to include the parents.
- The development of the IEP is a collaborative project, including parents.
- Personnel are assigned necessary roles during the meeting (e.g., someone takes minutes).
- All discussions during the meeting focus on the best interest of the student.

After the meeting, the principal is responsible for monitoring teachers to make certain that the IEP is implemented.

School leaders also demonstrate their interest in the welfare of students with disabilities by supervising the instruction of special education students although, for these students, teaching and learning may vastly differ from that of other students. When evaluating teachers, the principal's knowledge of these instructional and learning differences results in fair assessments.

Legalities. Staying current and maintaining the letter of special education law is essential for both administrators and teachers.

> By virtue of the close association that special education has with legislation and litigation it is of considerable importance that a principal be familiar with the requirements of legal tenets to ensure their appropriate implementation. Moreover, because of the continually evolving legal framework upon which special education is based, the principal must keep current with legal issues and trends related to the field. (Quigney, 1996, p. 223)

Yet, many principals lack the appropriate training to supervise special education programs. Valesky and Hirth (1992) found that many states do not mandate knowledge of special education in principal preparation programs. Sage and Burrello (1994) found that most principals are not evaluated on their management of special education programs, a situation that does not provide incentives for furthering knowledge of special education laws and issues. Even with training, the daily demands of administration combined with the constant changes in rules and regulations make it difficult for any administrator to remain current on laws, regulations, and local procedures. In order to maintain a working knowledge of special education law a principal communicates frequently with the special education staff and attends workshops that address legal issues. New information then must be conveyed to the entire staff.

Relationships. Principals and teachers are constantly called upon to deal with parents, teachers, students, central office staff, and community members who are connected to special education in one form or another. Fostering cooperation and understanding with and among these parties is in the best interest of the students.

Rifts develop between special and general education teachers, for example. General education teachers sometimes resent the privileges that appear to be granted to special needs students and their teachers and begrudge the extra work associated with classroom modifications and individualized instruction. Special education teachers, on the other hand, sometimes become frustrated when general education teachers fail to understand or implement modifications outlined in the IEP. Misunderstandings between the two factions can fester and even reach the point of open conflict if not given appropriate attention. The differences can sometimes be resolved using conflict resolution techniques or by bringing in an outside facilitator.

School leaders should take time to establish working relationships with parents of special needs students. The gulf between parents of special education students and the principal and teachers can widen for other than the usual reasons. First, while most parents appreciate the school staff's efforts on behalf of their child, concern for litigation may cloud interactions with the parents. Second, educators may not understand what living with a child with a disability entails. Consequently, empathy and patience are required when parents exhibit anger, frustration, or have unusual expectations.

School leaders alone cannot ensure positive relationships between the various parties connected with special education but can deliberately model desired behavior and actively discourage negative attitudes on the part of staff and students. After all, school leaders are the ones who establishes the tone, the climate for learning, the level of professionalism, and the morale of the teachers (Stewart, Laghari, and Gett, 1983). The staff, students, and parents take note when leaders take a personal interest in students in conversations, in classrooms and the lunchroom, and in the hallways.

Climate of Care. Pazey (1993) labels the ethic of care the missing link for successful special education programs. She also recognizes the need for justice and argues that "the competence of caring and intuition has just as much importance as that of justice, and needs to be assimilated into leadership…"(p. 8). She quotes Desjardins:

> There is a kind of dearth for society in general when the care perspective is not recognized as an essential to bringing wholeness to the justice perspective. Everyone loses when the care perspective is not part of the place, part of institutions, part of both personal and professional relationships, and part of the efforts toward world understanding and peace. (p. 140)

How are care and concern for legal justice combined with regard to special education? The two are entwined when the letter of the law is carried out but the spirit of care and concern is also apparent. The two are evident when meetings with parents follow protocol but school personnel make certain parents clearly understand what is said, tests are interpreted, and actions explained. Care and justice are evident, for example, when the principal stops to make sure a student in a wheelchair can navigate the cafeteria line and make food selections personally, when the principal makes a home visit to obtain a parent signature, when the principal arranges transportation for parents who have no means for attending a meeting regarding their child, and when the principal ensures that all contacts with parents and students are conducted with the utmost sensitivity. Pazey's concern for filling in that missing link—the ethic of care—is valid and must be addressed. One classroom teacher who learned the value of care said, "Special education is now me, and my classroom. Now we are all special and perhaps all irregular, too!" (Lamb, 1997, p. 6).

Applying Your Knowledge

Simon Petrie is an eight-year-old third grader at Smith Elementary School. He was referred and assessed for special education services based on his difficulty with learning to read. Simon was found to qualify for special education services due to an assessed learning disability. Consequently, an IEP Meeting is in session and the committee is discussing Simon's placement. Simon's mother and two teachers are in open disagreement over the choice between continuing Simon's current placement in a general education reading class and reassigning him to a resource class with a special education teacher.

At Smith Elementary School the third graders are ability grouped for reading and math. Simon currently attends Mrs. Hicks' class for reading and is in Mr. Miller's homeroom the rest of the day. Mrs. Hicks vehemently opposes continuing Simon's placement in her reading class as she does not feel qualified to address his learning disability. Additionally, she states that that particular reading class is very large and she will not have time to work individually with Simon. Mr. Miller argues that the modifications the committee is requiring of teachers are not extensive and can easily be carried out in a regular classroom. Mrs. Petrie, Simon's mother, voices her concern that Simon will be viewed as "different" by the other children if he goes to a special education class instead of his regular class during reading. She says, "He is already teased by the other students because he can't read. Sending him to a resource class might cause him to be picked on even more." Mrs. Jones, the principal, listens to their concerns. Mrs. Hick's position surprises the principal and she wishes the disagreement had been discussed before the meeting without the parent present. She sits quietly, uncertain about her next step.

Questions:

1. What are the major issues in this case, legal and otherwise?
2. Are other placement choices available for Simon? *Inclusion! Tutorials. Good use of home*
3. Should the diagnostician have talked to the teachers and the principal before the meeting and resolved the disagreement privately? *Yes, Consider alternatives on a professional level....*
4. Does Mrs. Hicks have a valid point? Since Mr. Miller will not be teaching Simon reading should Mr. Miller have remained silent?
5. How should Mrs. Jones, the principal, handle this situation now that she is aware of the differing opinions? *Reschedule + revisit Subject + Solution. Not a time for arguin*
6. What options do each of the committee members have at this point?
7. What weight does the parent's opinion have in the final decision? *Much!*
8. What can be done about the treatment Simon is receiving from other students?
While Simon is out of room, have discussion w/ class on disability impact on self esteem. Walk in that student's shoes.

Questions for Thought
"Help, not hinder one's success" play an active role to assist.

1. Differences of opinions often occur between general education and special education teachers. What can a building administrator do to facilitate cooperation between the two groups?
2. Can teachers and administrators truly exhibit care and concern for students with disabilities and simultaneously stay within the numerous legal guidelines?
3. Special education law is complicated and continually changing. Can general education teachers and building principals be expected to be knowledgeable of the changes? If so, how can this be accomplished?
4. Attending special education formal and informal meetings and being mindful of legalities can take considerable time for a principal who already has a substantial number of duties. Should the law allow for assigning additional administrators to a campus for the sole purpose of meeting special education guidelines?
5. How can students with disabilities be integrated into regular classrooms? What resources are needed? What training does the general education staff need?
6. Conduct a classroom debate on the merits and drawbacks of fully including students with disabilities in general education classes.
7. How does IDEA differ from Section 504 of Rehabilitation Act of 1973?
8. What can a principal do to demonstrate instructional leadership for a special education program?

For Further Information Online

A Researcher's guide to the U.S. Department of Education
     http://192.239.34.2/pubs/ResearchersGuide/Programs.html
Special Education Learning Disabilities Resources http://www.iser.com
Disabilities Sites of Interest http://www.merrywing.com/newsites.htm
Disability-Related Resources on the Web http://TheArc.org/misc/dislinkin.html
Internet Resources for Special Children http://www.irsc.org/
Also contact your state's education department

References

Ackenhalt, Letter to, 22 IDELR 252 (OCR 1994).

Alexander, K., & Alexander, M. D. (1998). *American Public School Law.* (4th Ed.). Boston: MA: West/Wadsworth.

Assistance to States for the Education of Children with Disabilities (1995), 34 CFR 300.

Barkoff, A. N. (1998). Comment: Revisiting de jure educational segregation: Legal barriers to school attendance for children with special health care needs. *Cornell Journal of Law and Public Policy, 8,* 135.

Bartlett, L. (2000). Medical services: The disputed related service. *Journal of Special Education, 33,* 215-223.

Bateman, B. D. (1995). *Better IEPs: How to develop legally correct and educationally useful programs.* Longmont, CO: Sopris West.

Essex, N. L. (1999). *School law and the public schools.* Boston: Allyn and Bacon.

Grossman, H. (1995). *Teaching in a diverse society.* Boston: Allyn and Bacon.

Imber, M., & van Geel, T. (2000). *Education law* (2nd ed.). Mahwah, NJ: Lawrence Erlbaum Associates.

Kemerer, F., & Walsh, J. (2000). *The educator's guide to Texas school law.* (5th ed.). Austin: University of Texas Press.

Lakin, K. C., & Reynolds, M. C. (1983). Curricular implications of Public Law 94-142 for teacher education. *Journal of Teacher Education, XXXIV*(2), 13-16.

Lamb, A. M. (1997). The room down the hall. Special education as viewed by a regular education classroom teacher. *Catalyst for Change, 27,* (1), 5-6.

McEllistrem, S., Roth, J., & Cox, G. (1998). *Students with disabilities and special education.* Rosemount, MN: Data Research, Inc.

Moran, M. (2000). Discipline following the IDEA '97 final regulations. In Redfield, S. (Ed.), *Seventh Annual Education Law Institute: Special Education* (121-143). Concord, NH: Franklin Pierce Law Center.

Osborne, A. G., Jr. (1996). *Legal issues in special education.* Boston: Allyn and Bacon.

OSEP Policy Letter, 21 IDELR 998 (OSEP 1994).

Pazey, B. (1993, October). *The missing link for the administration of special education: The ethic o care.* Paper presented at the Conference of the University Council of Educational Administration, Houston, TX.

Quigney, T. A. (1996). Revisiting the role of the building principal in the supervision of special education. *Planning and Changing, 27*(3/4), 209-228.

Rawson, M. J. (2000). *A manual of special education law.* Naples, FL: Morgan Publishing Co.

Rothstein, F. (2000). *Special education law.* (3rd ed.). New York: Longman.

Sage, D. D., & Burrello, L. C. (1994). *Leadership in educational reform: An administrator's guide to changes in special education.* Baltimore, MD: Brookes Publishing Co.

Stewart, B. R., Laghari, L., & Gett, E. (1983). Administrators' perceptions of professional education competencies needed by teachers of vocational agriculture. *Journal of the American Association of Teacher Educators in Agriculture, 3,* 24.

Tucker, B. P. (1998). *Federal disability law in a nutshell.* St. Paul, MN: West Group.

Tucker, B. P., & Goldstein, B. A. (1992). *Legal rights of persons with disabilities: An analysis of public law.* Horsham, PA: LRP Publications.

Underwood, J. K., & Mead, J. F. (1995). *Legal aspects of special education and pupil services.* Boston: Allyn and Bacon.

Valesky, T., & Hirth, M. (1992). Survey of the states: Special education knowledge requirements for school administrators. *Exceptional Children, 58*(5), 399-405.

Walsh, J., & Gallegoes, E. (1997, September). *Washington has a brand new IDEA! What does it mean for Texas.* Paper presented at the Region X and XI Education Service Centers Conference for Educators on Changes in Special Education Law, Grapevine, TX.

Yell, M. L. (1998). *The law and special education.* Upper Saddle River, NJ: Prentice Hall.

Court Cases

Board of Education of Hendrick Hudson Central School District v. Rowley, 458 U.S. 176(1982).

Brown v. Board of Education of Topeka, 347 U.S. 483 (1954).

Cedar Rapids School District v. Garret F., 526 U.S. 66 (1999).

Irving Independent School District v. Tatro, 469 U.S. 809 (1984).

Mills v. Board of Education 348 F. Supp. 866 (D.D.C. 1972).

Pennsylvania Association for Retarded Children (PARC) v. Commonwealth, 343 F. Supp. 279 (E.D.Pa. 1971).

Roncker v. Walker, 700 F. 2d. 1058 (6th Circuit, 1983).

Chapter 2

Title I Programs

Mark Littleton

> *The primary purpose of the program has not changed since the time when it first became law—to ensure equal educational opportunity for all children regardless of socioeconomic background and to close the achievement gap between poor and affluent children, by providing additional resources for schools serving disadvantaged students.*
> U.S. Department of Education,
> Planning and Evaluation Service.

Objectives:
- Understand the history and purpose of programs for the educationally disadvantaged.
- Explain current fiscal and procedural guidelines of Title I programs at the campus level.
- Describe how current issues related to Title I and other compensatory programs affect the operation of those programs at the campus level.
- Provide supervisors with an understanding of effective program design and instructional practices related to Title I programs.

The U.S. Constitution makes no provision for public education. However, the constitutions of each of the 50 states make provisions for public schools (Alexander & Alexander, 2001). As a consequence, it would be logical to believe that federal involvement is minimal, at best. Yet, the federal government has been engaged in subsidizing various aspects of public education since the 19th century, and the federal government's role in public education was substantially shaped in the mid-1960's by the Elementary and Secondary Education Act (ESEA) (Finn, 1995). Part of the 1965 EASA, Title I was enacted to assist in America's war on poverty by directing federal funds to assist students from low-income families. Now authorized under Improving America's Schools Act (IASA), Title I provides over $8 billion in federal funds (Robelen, 2000). These funds target schools whose student population is "disproportionately poor" (Puma & Drury, 2000, p. 2).

Although it is more of a federal subsidy than a "program" in the strictest sense (Puma and Drury, 2000, p. 6), the success of Title I is open to debate (Puma & Drury, 2000; Le Tendre, 1999; Fashola & Slavin, 1998; Ravitch, 1997; Jendryka, 1993). Proponents argue that the federal subsidy has provided assistance to millions of children in approximately 13, 000 districts across the United States (Le Tendre, 1999). Detractors argue that standardized test scores for targeted students show no improvement and Title I schools deliver a curriculum that is not challenging (Puma & Drury, 2000). Regardless, Title I funds affect over 46,0000 schools (Le Tendre, 1999), and remain a substantial portion of the budget for many of these campuses. It would be prudent of school leaders to understand the mechanism for funding Title I programs and to know what practices enhance the success of those programs at the campus level.

History

If only in a political sense, the federal government has been reluctant to become directly involved in public education. Congress specifically prohibits intrusion into public education in U.S.C.S. 1232 (a), which states

> No provision of any applicable program shall be construed to authorize any department, agency, officer, or employee of the United States to exercise any direction, supervision, or control over the curriculum, program of instruction, administration, or personnel of any educational institution, school, or school system.

However, the federal government has been very interested in education. At the onset, the federal government took an indirect role in public education choosing to affect policy with subsidy. This indirect control was performed in two ways. First, grants were offered to states with the stated intent of supporting the common good for the general public. (Please refer to Table 1 for a brief explanation of federal aid to education.) Second, grants with conditions (or strings) were offered to help subsidize special programs. Until the mid-1960s, federal funding focused on issues of national interests such as land grants and national defense projects (Alexander & Alexander, 2001). More recently, federal funds have been directed toward specific educational programs. The passage of ESEA was a significant policy statement showing the federal government's interest in education.

Table 1
Federal Legislation Assisting Education

Morrill Act of 1862 – provided land grants for colleges specializing in the agricultural and mechanical arts.

Smith-Hughes Act of 1917 – provided federal aid for vocational programs in public schools below the college level.

Lanham Act of 1940 – provided federal aid to local governments for the construction of facilities, including schools.

National Defense Education Act (NDEA) of 1958 – provided federal funds to promote scholarship in the sciences.

Economic Opportunity Act of 1964 – provided federal funds for the War on Poverty, including Head Start.

Congress and the Nation, 1969, p. 711

It was a stroke of political genius that President Johnson directly addressed religious squabbles and concerns of educational lobbyists with a single piece of legislation. Proponents of federal aid to education wanted to pass a general aid to education bill, but ESEA, with its more narrow focus of alleviating economic imbalances, survived the legislative process (Roeber, 1999). The Act focused on providing aid to children of poor families instead of general aid to public and private schools (Spring, 1998).

Of the eight titles in ESEA (see Table 2), the most significant piece is Title I, a section of law designed to assist educationally and economically deprived children. It is interesting to note the clarity of purpose of Title I as stated in Section 201 of ESEA.

[Congress recognizes] the special educational needs of low-income families and the impact that concentration of low-income families has on the ability of local educational agencies to support...and improve their educational programs.

Table 2

Elementary and Secondary Education Act of 1965

Title I	Educationally deprived children
Title II	Libraries and textbooks
Title III	Supplementary education
Title IV	Cooperative research
Title V	State education departments
Title VI	Handicapped children
Title VII	Bilingual education
Title VIII	Dropout prevention & adult education

Title I quickly became a popular federal subsidy with near-unanimous approval upon each reauthorization (Jendryka, 1993). As often happens with federal subsidy programs, federal controls increased with each reauthorization (Fowler, 2000). Elmore and McLaughlin (1982) note that these increasing compliance requirements were to increase the federal government's presence in defining "certain specific responses at the local level" (p. 165). Sometimes called "a skillfully constructed package of compliance and assistance measures," procedural requirements and fiscal accountability increased dramatically during the first 15 years of Title I's existence (Elmore & McLaughlin, 1982). Federal regulations designed to assist with reading and mathematics instruction required that Title I funds be used to supplement, not supplant, state and local funds (Puma & Drury, 2000).

According to First (1992), ESEA provided the framework for the federal compensatory programs:

Responsibilities of the federal government included establishing the rules under which the program is to operate.... The responsibilities of the state government included explaining requirements to local school districts.... [And] the responsibilities of the local government included designing programs and providing services. (p. 51)

Yudof, Kirp, and Levin (1992) note that ESEA "exhibited the difficulties as well as the potential of federal involvement in education" (p. 698). Congress commissioned a study of ESEA in the 1974 reauthorization. Because of the perceived intrusion into public education by the federal government, program evaluation was a critical component of Title I (Fowler, 2000). In an extensive review, the National Institute of Education was very critical of the implementation of Title I at the federal and state levels. Apparently, the "federal preoccupation with compliance objectives" had occupied so much of state administrators' time that little attention was given to assistance (Elmore and McLaughlin, 1982, p. 168).

The increased emphasis on fiscal accountability led schools to focus on a particular curriculum option called "pull out." (Program design options will be discussed in more detail later in the chapter.) Puma & Drury (2000) note that "pull outs came under increasing fire for their lack of coordination with regular classroom instruction and, in 1978, the 'schoolwide' option was introduced" (p. 3).

The size of Title I along with its complex set of regulations, "made it a prime target for the Reagan administration, which hoped to eliminate the program entirely" (Yudof, et al., 1992, p. 698). Congress resisted the temptation to eliminate Title I but then provided for fewer federal restrictions in the 1981 Education and Improvement Act (ECIA). In the ECIA, Title I was renamed Chapter 1, a name that remained until the 1994 reauthorization (*National Research Council*, 1999; Goldberg, 1987).

The Hawkins-Stafford Consolidation amendment to the ESEA in 1988 required that federally funded programs be measured by "opportunity to learn" measures. These measures were designed to describe the educational process. Each district receiving Chapter 1 (now Title I) funds was to use the indicators to assess the quality of the program. The Hawkins-Stafford amendment signaled the return of administrative guidance as well as the beginning of parental involvement (Schwartz, 1995).

The 1994 reauthorization of the Title I in the Improving America's Schools Act (IASA) represented a significant shift in the compensatory program. Although the most significant change from Chapter 1 to Title I was the increase in parental involvement (Yudof, Kirp, & Levin, 1992) IASA required states to establish challenging standards and benchmarks that are the same for Title I and non-Title I students (*National Research Council*, 1999). Congress recognized that

> Although the achievement gap between disadvantaged children and other children has been reduced … the most urgent need for educational improvement is in schools with high concentration of children from low-income families and achieving the National Education Goals will not be possible without substantial improvement … [and] educational needs are particularly great for low-achieving children in our Nation's highest-poverty schools…. (20 U.S.C.S. 6301[1-3])

IASA attempted to align federal policies with state and local policies (Wirt & Kirst, 1997). According to Puma & Drury (2000), three programmatic themes emerged during this alignment. Under the umbrella of a standards-based reform theme, IASA required states to develop "challenging standards of performance and assessments that measure student performance against the standards" (*National Research Council*, 1999, p. 9). Upon identifying the struggling schools, states were then to provide additional assistance to the schools.

The second programmatic theme signaled a significant operational shift. Prior to 1978, Title I provided for targeted assistance programs that addressed the needs of individually identified students. In 1978 an additional program design was offered (Wang, Wong, & Kim, 1999). Schools were allowed the option of the school wide design; provided that the district match federal funds with their own funds. Few schools opted for the school wide design due to the matching funds requirement until the passage of the 1988 Hawkins-Stafford amendment eliminated the matching funds requirement. Schools in which at least 75% of the student population were identified as low-income qualified for the school wide design. This design lets the school co-mingle federal, state, and local funds to provide a comprehensive, coherent program of instruction. Under the IASA, the poverty-rate for the funding of school wide programs was adjusted from 75% to 50%, allowing a considerably larger number of schools the freedom to combine funding sources (Puma & Drury, 2000).

Finally, IASA provided for more program management flexibility than previous reauthorizations of ESEA. In the Education Flexibility Partnership Act of 1999 (Ed Flex) federal and state officials were given authority to waive some federal requirements if those requirements were viewed as inhibiting school improvement (USDOE, 2001; Puma & Drury, 2000). Prior to IASA, a large number of public schools received Title I (or Chapter 1) funds – approximately 70% of elementary schools. Although IASA, through its funding provisions, reduced the percentage of schools receiving aid, there was "a precipitous increase in the percentage of high-poverty secondary schools receiving funding" —61 % to 93% (Puma & Drury, 2000, p. 6).

Even in the post-IASA era when the federal guidelines have been relaxed, many states continue to experience difficulty in achieving the requirements of IASA (Olson, 2001). The primary reasons for states' failure to achieve the requirements rests with their inability to design challenging standards and then to create assessments to measure students' progress against those standards (USDOE, 2001; National Research Council, 1999).

Federal Compensatory Guidelines

As has already been mentioned, federal guidelines for Title I are complex. Covering the minutia of program guidelines is beyond the scope of this book. However, an understanding of some of the broad fiscal and procedural guidelines may assist in effective program implementation and supervision.

Fiscal Guidelines

In the $ 8 billion Title I program, federal funds are distributed to the state education agencies (SEA). The SEAs then distribute the funds to the qualifying local districts. According to Puma and Drury (1999), "Title I funds are distributed to counties, districts, and schools—generally in proportion to the number of poor school-age children in those jurisdictions" (p. 5).

In targeted assistance programs, Title I funds may be used only to supplement state and local resources. These funds "cannot be used to provide services that are required by law to be provided to children with disabilities, migrant children, limited English proficient children" (Texas Education Agency [TEA], 2001, paragraph B).

Funds for school wide programs may be used in combination with other federal, state, and local funds. The funds must be used to support activities identified by a comprehensive school reform plan, which is developed with the involvement of community and school personnel. Although the Title I funds may be co-mingled, schools are admonished to maintain an accurate record of how Title I funds are distributed. TEA (2001) guidelines for school wide programs highlight that the funds used for a school wide program lose their program identity, but not their fiscal identity.

Procedural Guidelines

Although the fiscal structure of the distribution of Title I funds varies from state to state and the federal guidelines often are complex, the goal of Title I remains the same. In a 2001 report published by the U.S. Department of Education, the Planning and Evaluation Service noted that

> The primary purpose of the program has not changed since the time when it first became law—to ensure equal educational opportunity for all children regardless of socioeconomic background and to close the achievement gap between poor and affluent children, by providing additional resources for schools serving disadvantaged students. (p. 2)

Approximately 12.5 million students receive Title I services. The vast majority of these students are at the elementary level. Figure 1 shows that 67% of the students receiving Title I assistance are elementary students, 12% are pre-elementary students, 15% are in grades 7, 8, & 9, and 5% are in high school. Figure 2 illustrates the percentage of high poverty schools that receive Title I funds. Almost one-half (46%) of the schools which receive Title I funds are considered high poverty schools, while only 18% of the low poverty schools receive Title I funds (U.S. Department of Education [USDOE], 2001).

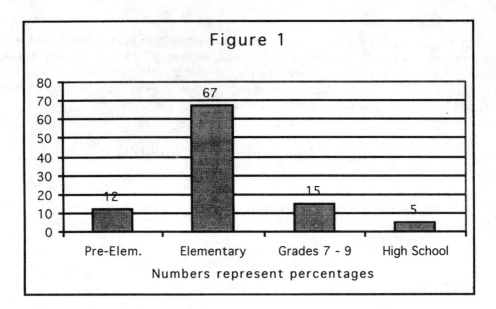

Figure 1

Numbers represent percentages

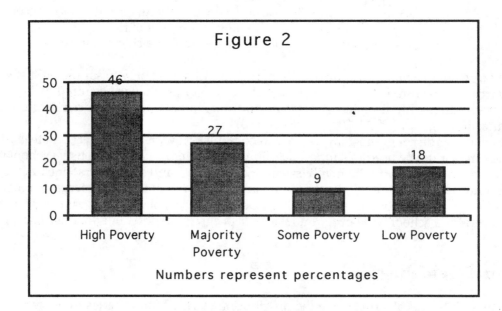

Figure 2

Numbers represent percentages

High-Poverty – 75% or more of the students are at the poverty level
Majority Poverty – 50% - 74% of the students are at the poverty level
Some Poverty – 35% - 49% of the students are at the poverty level
Low-Poverty – Less than 35% of the students are at the poverty level

Source: U.S. Department of Education, Planning and Evaluation Service. (2001). *High standards for all students: A report from the national assessment of Title I on progress and challenges since the 1994 reauthorization.* Washington, DC: 2001. Doc. No. 2001-16.

Since the 1994 reauthorization, Title I requires states to develop challenging content standards; develop performance standards indicating student progress; develop assessments aligned with the content and performance standards in mathematics and reading or language arts; and develop an accountability system to determine yearly progress. The state must use a common assessment instrument to measure the assessment of all students in the state. Furthermore, the assessment system must achieve the following:

1. Include multiple measures of student performance.
2. Be administered in grades 3–5, 6–9, and 10–12.
3. Be valid and reliable.
4. Include all students.
5. Report results in a form disaggregated by gender, racial and ethnic group, English proficiency, migrant status, disability, and socioeconomic status.
6. Provide individual student reports to parents and teachers (U.S. Department of Education [USDOE], 2000).

Developing a comprehensive system of this nature was foreign to most states. Consequently, it has been difficult for some states to meet the assessment system requirements in a timely manner.

Parental Involvement

Parental involvement is key to an effective Title I program. However, quality parental involvement has not been achieved in most Title I schools (Wang, Wong, & Kim, 1999). This lack of parental involvement is particularly noticeable from poor families (USDOE, 2001). IASA strengthened Title I's "emphasis on school/family community partnerships by: (1) specifying partnerships ... linked to student learning; (2) asking schools to develop ... a 'compact'...; and (3) allowing funds to be commingled to create unified programs that serve all parents" (Puma & Drury, 1999, p. 27).

IASA encourages strong parent-school partnerships to develop a broad-based support for the inculcation of high standards for all students. In an attempt to address a lack of parental involvement, Funkhouser, Stief, and Allen, (1998) propose that compacts be made between the school and the parents. These compacts "spell out goals, expectations, and shared responsibilities of schools and parents as partners" (p. 1). Schools that receive Title I funds must

1. Convene a meeting with parents to explain Title I.
2. Meet with parents so the parents may participate in decisions about their child.
3. Give parents information about the program (Center for Law and Education, n.d.).

Contemporary Issues

Current and on-going issues surround the funding of the largest federal education subsidy program. There are those who propose that the federal government cease the funding of Title I programs (Jendryka, 1993) and those who continue to show their support (Council of Chief State School Officers, 1999). The determination of whether targeted assistance programs or school wide programs are the most effective is still being debated (Puma & Drury, 1999). Locating qualified teachers and developing effective staff development programs remain major concerns for many school districts.

School-Based Reform

Through its flexibility, IASA allowed Title I schools to engage in systemic school-based reform. The USDOE (2001) lists nine "key components" to school-based reform that assists low-performing schools in raising student achievement (p. 33). Those components include:

1. Utilizing research-based, innovative, and proven methods for teaching and learning.
2. Implementing a comprehensive design including "instruction, assessment, classroom management, professional development, parental involvement, and school management" (p. 33).
3. Setting measurable performance goals.
4. Designing high -quality staff development.
5. Obtaining buy-in from all school personnel.
6. Developing meaningful partnerships with families and the community.
7. Seeking high -quality external support.
8. Utilizing an evaluation plan that focuses on student achievement.
9. Combining resources to sustain the reform effort.

There is a paucity of research on the effectiveness of Title I programs since 1994. However, there is some indication that Title I programs are bringing academic success to disadvantaged children in high-poverty schools. There is strong evidence that smaller class size (facilitated by Title I programs) is effective in increasing student achievement (Puma & Drury, 1999).

Program Design

Targeted Assistance. Implementation of Title I programs takes one of two different designs. The predominant design has been the targeted assistance design which are "pull-out programs that deliver supplementary instruction to low-achieving students during the time they would have spent in their regular classes" (Puma & Drury, 1999, p. 7). In-class instruction is another aspect of the targeted assistance design. The in-class model allows for segregated groups within the academic classroom. Often the in-class model was little more than the pull-out model located within the academic classroom. As mentioned earlier, the targeted assistance design was the exclusive design until 1978. As an example, in Texas the Texas Education Agency (TEA) (2001) directs districts to develop targeted assistance programs that:

1. Help students meet the state's performance standards.
2. Are based on improving student achievement.
3. Incorporate a plan considering the needs of the students served.
4. Utilize effective instructional strategies.
5. Support the regular instructional program.
6. Provide for a well qualified staff, supported by professional development.
7. Increase parental involvement.

Targeted assistance programs have proven to be a "target" for many Title I critics. Anstrom (1995) warns that "curricular fragmentation resulting from Chapter 1 [now Title I] students missing out on core academic instruction while attending remedial reading and math classes has been a frequently occurring side effect" (p. 3).

School Wide. Prior to the 1994 reauthorization, school wide programs required that 75% of the student population qualify as low-income. Wang, Wong, and Kim (1999) note that "although Title I legislation has permitted school wide programs since 1978, these programs were rarely implemented prior to the passage of the IASA, partly due to the requirement that school districts match federal grants with their own funds (p. 5). IASA further encouraged the school wide program by reducing the low-income student population requirement to 50%. As a result the number of schools moving to the school wide design increased.

There are eight components required of all school wide programs including:

1. A needs assessment of the entire school based upon the performance of students against established performance standards.
2. Reform strategies designed to help students meet the state's performance standards, and addressing the needs of all students.
3. A qualified instructional staff.
4. Professional development for school personnel.
5. Strategies for parental involvement.
6. Strategies for assisting preschool children.
7. A means to include teachers in the decision making process.
8. Activities designed to assist students who need additional assistance with meeting the performance standards (TEA, 2001).

Qualified Teachers

Our nation is in the throes of a teacher shortage (Fetler, 1997). LeTendre (1999) reported that there are almost as many teachers' aides teaching Title I classes as there are certified teachers. Ravitch (1999) reported that approximately one-half of the teachers in Title I programs are teaching out of their field. Combined with the research indicating that teachers with extensive training in the content areas of math and science are most effective in raising student achievement, the dearth of qualified teachers is particularly disturbing. (See Brewer & Goldhaber, 1996). Additionally, the teachers of Title I classes need quality staff development to "upgrade and maintain the skills" (Puma & Drury, 1999, p. 14). Too often, targeted, high-quality staff development is not available.

Private School Participation

As it was originally passed, the Elementary and Secondary Education Act of 1965 was designed to benefit children from low-income families. It was designed to improve instruction for *all* children. In all reauthorizations, as with the original bill, private school children are included under the provision of helping all children. However, the federal government does not send federal funds directly to private schools. As the funds are granted to the local educational agencies (school districts), the agencies become responsible for serving eligible students within the boundaries of their district. Often, private school administrators and public school officials work closely to generate requests for federal funds. After consultation with private school administrators, public school officials must provide for equitable participation in the Title I program for eligible private school students (*Chapter 2*, 2001).

There has been considerable discussion and some litigation regarding the use of public funds to assist private schools. However, the courts have determined that Title I funds can be used to assist eligible students in private schools. An ambitious student interested in further discussion is encouraged to investigate the cases of *Agostini v. Felton* (1997) and *Mitchell v. Helms* (2000).

Vouchers

Rosenthal (1999) points out that the current Republican leadership wants to provide greater flexibility in the Title I program. Combining the large IASA monies (of which Title I is the largest portion) into block grants is one way to do this. Under the voucher concept, the federal government would provide parents of Title I eligible students with vouchers. These vouchers would be taken to the school of parental choice (private or public). The school, in turn, would send the voucher to the state for reimbursement for educating the child. However, such a move makes it difficult to ensure that low-income students benefit from Title I funds. The use of vouchers in the Title I program is sure to prompt political debates and possibly court challenges.

School Leaders' Role in Title 1 Programs

As with many federal programs, Title I is reauthorized periodically. As a result, rules and policies change regularly. Fowler (2000) notes that "these are important policy issues for ... districts, and should be followed closely" (p. 220). An astute supervisor will follow the changes closely to ensure that his or her school is not in danger of losing funds.
Supervisors also need to know what works. Fortunately, Title I programs have been thoroughly researched, and there is ample information concerning indicators of a successful program. Wang, Wong and Kim (1999) suggest that school wide programs are more effective than targeted assistance schools. Also, USDOE (2001) research suggests that when teaching reading, teachers should:

- Give children access to a variety of reading and writing materials.
- Present explicit instruction for reading and writing, both in the context of authentic and isolated practice.
- Create multiple opportunities for sustained reading practice in a variety of settings.
- Carefully choose instructional-level text from a variety of materials.
- Adjust the grouping and explicitness of instruction to meet the needs of individual students (p. 35)

The same study (USDOE, 2001) suggests that effective teaching of mathematics include:

- Focusing on problem solving. Students need conceptual understanding to deal with novel problems and settings and to become autonomous learners. Instruction should encourage multiple solutions to problems.
- Defining basic skills to involve more than computation.
- Emphasizing reasoning and thinking skills, concept development, communicating mathematically, and applying mathematics. Students must learn mathematics with understanding, building new knowledge from experience and prior knowledge.
- Presenting content in a logical progression with an increasing emphasis on higher-order thinking skills, such as problem-solving and mathematical reasoning, and mathematical communication.
- Integrating topics of numeration, patterns and relations, geometry, measurement, probability and statistics, algebra, and algorithmic thinking. Instruction should broaden the range of mathematical content studied, an aspect of teaching in which low-income children are often short-changed.
- Taking advantage of calculators and computers to extend students' mathematical reach. (p. 36)

Understanding the research regarding effective reading and mathematics instruction is not sufficient. The instructional staff (teachers, teacher's aides, etc.) need continual staff development and training to hone their instructional skills and to stay abreast of current effective instructional methodology (USDOE, 2001; Puma & Drury, 1999). Teachers are, after all, the most effective resource in improving student achievement (Darling-Hammond, 2000; Greenwald, Hedges, and Laine, 1996). Quality professional development programs for Title I teachers will be strong in content, be distributed over an extended period of time in which teachers are actively engaged, utilize study groups and mentoring, and be aligned with the standards and assessment instruments used to measure student progress (USDOE, 2001).

Summary

Federal funding of Title I programs represents the largest single investment in public education by the federal government. Beginning with President Johnson's War on Poverty in 1965, Title I has reached millions of students in thousands of classrooms across the nation. Title I is a powerful tool, raising standards for all children.

However, the best of tools will not work if they are not used properly. There is evidence to suggest that Title I programs operate best on a school wide basis, particularly when class sizes are reduced. All children, those receiving Title I services included, should be held to high standards of performance and taught by a qualified staff who engage in appropriate professional development activities. Teachers should utilize instructional strategies known to be effective and focus on improving student performance. Last, but certainly not least, parents need to be involved in every phase of the process. Parental involvement is often the key to student engagement and, consequently, student learning.

The shrewd supervisor is not only knowledgeable of effective programs and instructional practices, but she or he is cognizant of the rules and regulations associated with implementing a Title I program. As a result, professional development is important for the supervisor as well as the teacher. Only when supervisors are aware of effective program design, instructional practices, and program requirements and limitations can they ensure that the Title I program supports the entire instructional program of the school.

Applying Your Knowledge

A bedroom community is located in a suburb of a large metropolitan area. The district is located conveniently near to the headquarters of several large corporations, but it is rapidly becoming an industrial center. The elementary school (grades 1 – 6) where you are employed has a student population of 610. The demographics of the school are quite interesting. Approximately 15% of the students live in homes where the household income exceeds $150,000. These students live in a neighborhood that is stable, where the parents drive to manage major divisions of large corporations. Your research has found that students from high-income households are the top students and have instructional needs addressed through gifted/talented and other special programs. Interestingly, during the previous school year 48% of the students in your school were from low-income households. However, due to the rapid immigration of low-income families to the industrial region, the projected low-income population is expected to reach 53%. Student scores are declining as the number of students from low-income households increase.

Questions:

1. What would be the best Title I program design for your campus? Why?
2. If the district faces financial trouble while your campus is placing a greater emphasis on federal assistance programs (like Title I), how might the parents in the high-income households react? How could you ameliorate the situation?

Questions for Thought

1. What is the purpose of the Title I program? Has the purpose changed since its beginning in 1965?
2. What are the major differences between targeted assistance programs and school wide programs? Which do you think would be most effective?
3. What can school leaders do to enhance the effectiveness of Title I programs?
4. Do you view the use of vouchers from federal funds as deleterious to the public school system? Why or why not?
5. How can schools involve parents (of students in Title I programs) in a significant way?

For Further Information Online

U.S. Department of Education **http://www.ed.gov**
Texas Education Agency **http://www.tea.state.tx.us**
Also contact your state's education agency

References

Agostini v. Felton, 521 U.S. 203; 117 S.Ct. 1997 (1997).

Alexander, K., & Alexander, M. D. (2001). *American public school law*. Fifth edition. Belmont, CA: West/Thomson Learning.

Anstrom, K. (1995). New directions for Chapter 1/Title I. [Online]. *Directions in Language and Education, 1*. National Clearinghouse for Bilingual Education. <http://128.164.90.197/ncbepubs/directions> [2000, Sept. 23].

Brewer, D. J., & Goldhaber, D. D. (1996). Educational achievement and teacher qualifications: New evidence from microlevel data. In B. Cooper and S. Speakman (Eds.), *Advances in Educational Productivity* (243-264). Greenwich, CT: CAI Press.

Center for Law and Education. (No date). Title I as a tool for parent involvement. [Online]. *CLE Issue/Project Areas*. from<http://www.cleweb.org/issue/titleI> [2000, Sept. 18].

Chapter 2 ... U.S. Department of Education Programs Serving Private School Students. (2001). [Online]. U.S. Department of Education. <http://www.ed.gov/pubs> [2001, Feb. 7].

Congress and the nation, Volume II, 1965-1968. (1969). Washington, DC: Congressional Quarterly Service.

Council of Chief State School Officers. [Online]. *The Council of Chief State School Officers Join United Public-Private Support of Title I ESEA*. News Release. <http://www.ccsso.org/news> [1999, February 4].

Darling-Hammond, L. Teacher quality and student achievement: A review of state policy evidence. [On-line Serial] *Education Policy Analysis Archives*, 8. <http://olam.ed.asu.edu/epaa> [2000, January 1].

Elementary and Secondary Education Act. Public Law 89-10 (April 11, 1965).

Elmore, R. F. & McLaughlin, M. W. (1982). In A. Lieberman and M.W. McLaughlin (Eds.), *Policy Making in Education: Eighty-first Yearbook of the National Society for the Study of Education* (159-194). Chicago: The University of Chicago Press.

Fashola, O. S. & Slavin, R. E. (1998, January). Schoolwide reform models, *Phi Delta Kappan, 79*(5), 370-371.

Fetler, M. (1997, January 8). Where have all the teachers gone? [Online]. *Education Policy Analysis Archives*, 5. <http://olam.ed.asu.edu/epaa>

Finn, C. (1995). Towards excellence in education. *Public Interest, 120*, 41-54.

First, P. F. (1992). *Educational policy for school administrators*. Boston: Allyn and Bacon.

Fowler, F. C. (2000). *Policy studies for educational leaders*. Columbus, OH: Merrill.

Funkhouser, J. E., Stief, E. A., & Allen, S. E. (1998). *Title I school-parent compacts: Supporting partnerships to improve learning.* A report prepared for the U.S. Department of Education, Office of the Under Secretary Planning and Evaluation Service by Policy Studies Associates, Washington, DC.

Goldberg, K. Lawsuit challenges Chapter 1 and 2 aid to church schools. [Online]. *Education Week on the Web.* 1987, Dec. 9. <http://www.edweek.org>

Greenwald, R., Hedges, L., & Laine, R. (1996). The effect of school resources on student achievement, *Review of Educational Research, 66,* 361-396.

Jendryka, B. (1993). Failing grade for federal aid. *Policy Review, 66,* 77-81.

Le Tendre, M. J. (1999). *Title I must be #1 now!* [Online]. Speech presented at the National Association of State Title I Directors in New Orleans, LA. [Online]. <http://www.ed.gov/offices/OESE/CEP/neworlea2.html> [2000, Aug. 31].

Mitchell v. Helms, 530 U.S. 793; 120 S.Ct. 2530 (2000).

National Research Council (1999). *Testing, teaching, and learning: A guide for states and school districts.* Committee on Title I Testing and Assessment, R. F. Elmore & R. Rothman (Eds.). *Board on Testing and Assessment, Commission on Behavioral and Social Sciences and Education.* Washington, DC: National Academy Press.

Olson, L. States lagging behind on Title I rules, Ed. Dept. says. [Online]. *Education Week on the Web* <http://www.edweek.org> [2001, January 31].

Prohibition against Federal control of education. 20 U.S.C.S. § 1232(a) (2000).

Puma, M. J., and Drury, D. W. (2000). *Exploring new directions: Title I in the year 2000.* Alexandria, VA: National School Board Association.

Ravitch, D. (1999). Student performance: The national agenda in education. In M. Kanstoroom and C. E. Finn (Eds.), *New Directions: Federal Education Policy in the 21st Century* (12-16). Washington, D.C.: T. B. Fordham Foundation.

Ravitch, D. (1997, June 2). Success in Brookly, but not in D.C. *Forbes, 159,* 90.

Robelen, E. W. Budget agreement gives Ed. Department largest-ever increase. [Online]. *Education Week on the Web.* <http://www.edweek.org> [2000, Dec. 18].

Roeber, E. D. (1999). Standards initiatives and American educational reform, in G. J. Cizek (Ed.) *Handbook of Educational Policy* (151-181). Boston: Academic Press.

Rosenthal, I. (1999). ESEA debate heats up. *Technology and Learning, 20,* 43.

Schwartz, W. (1995). Opportunity to learn standards: Their impact on urban students. *ERIC Clearinghouse on Urban Education.* New York. (ERIC Document Reproduction No. ED 389 816)

Spring, J. (1998). *Conflicts of interests: The politics of American education.* Boston: McGraw-Hill.

Strengthening and Improvement of Elementary and Secondary Schools Helping Disadvantaged Children Meet High Standards, 20 U.S.C.S. § 6301 (2000).

Texas Education Agency. (2001). [Online]. Division of Student Support Programs. <http://www.tea.state.tx.us/support/titleia> [2001, Feb. 7].

U. S. Department of Education, Planning and Evaluation Service. (2001). *High standards for all students: A report from the national assessment of Title I on progress and challenges since the 1994 reauthorization.* Washington, DC: 2001. Doc. No. 2001-16.

U. S. Department of Education. [Online]. *Overview of Title I Assessment Fact Sheet.* <http://www.ed.gov/offices/OESE/saa> [2000, Feb. 7].

Wang, M. C., Wong, K. K., & Kim, J. R. (1999). *A national study of Title I school wide programs: A synopsis of interim findings.* A research report supported by the Office of Educational Research and Improvement, U.S. Department of Education, and the Laboratory for Student Success, Temple University Center for Research in Human Development and Education. (ERIC Document Reproduction Service No. 436 596)

Wirt, F. M., & Kirst, M. W. (1997). *The political dynamics of American education.* Berkely, CA: McCutchan Publishing Corp.

Yudof, M. G., Kirp, D. L., & Levin, B. (1992). *Educational policy and the law.* St. Paul, MN: West Publishing Company.

Chapter 3

Migrant Education

Judy T. Walker and Ana M. Decious

Key Maker

Some people see a closed door,
And turn away.
Others see a closed door,
And try the knob.
If it doesn't open,
They turn away.
Still others see a closed door,
And try the knob.
If it doesn't open,
They find a key.
If the key doesn't fit...
They turn away.
A rare few see a closed door,
And try the knob.
If it doesn't open,
They find a key.
If the key doesn't fit ...
They make one.

Anonymous

Objectives:
- Determine student eligibility for assistance with migrant education programs.
- Outline the historical development of migrant education programs.
- List the benefits of migrant education programs for eligible students.
- Explain how the seven areas of focus address the needs of migrant students.
- Explain how a school leader can enhance the success of a migrant education program.

The Office of Migrant Education (OME) in the U.S. Department of Education (U.S. Dept. of Education, 1999) works to improve teaching and learning for children—many of whom have lived a life-time of surviving from one day to the next—whose families migrate to find work in agricultural, fishing, and timber industries. Currently, OME administers programs and projects for migratory children in 49 states, the District of Columbia, and Puerto Rico. The goals are:

1. To improve coordination among all states to help improve educational outcomes for migrant children.
2. To foster partnerships between state directors, federal agencies, and other organizations in order to improve coordination of services to migrant families.

3. To ensure that migrant children have access to services that assist them in overcoming cultural and language barriers, health-related problems, and other challenges that place children at risk for completing their education (Office of Migrant Education: Harvest of Hope, 2000).

The OME directs that educational programs be based on the premise that migrant children, although affected by poverty and the migrant lifestyle, can and should have the opportunity to realize their full potential. Migrant Education Programs (MEP) support high-quality, comprehensive educational programs for migratory children by addressing disruptions in schooling and other problems that result from repeated moves. In addition to providing migrant students with enriched, extended activities that allow active engagement in challenging learning experiences, the migrant education programs and projects provide, to the extent possible:

- Advocacy and outreach activities for migrant children and families to help them gain access to other education, health, nutrition, and social services.
- Professional development programs—including mentoring—for teachers and other program personnel.
- Family literacy programs, including those developed under Even Start.
- The integration of information technology into educational and related programs.
- Programs to facilitate the transition of secondary school students to postsecondary education or employment (OME, 1999).

To meet the above objectives, Local Education Agencies (LEAs) are charged by legislative directive to: (a) implement programs that provide services to each migrant student comparable to services offered to other students, (b) implement programs that help migrant students achieve high academic standards, and (c) adopt policies and practices to ensure that migrant children and youth are involved in the regular school program.

For purposes of understanding this program, migrant students should not be confused with immigrant students. While an immigrant may be a migrant student, this is not always the case and misidentification of migrant students can lead to loss of funding. Under the law the term "immigrant children and youth" is defined as individuals age 3 through 21 who were not born in the United States and who have not been attending one or more schools in the United States for more than three full academic years. A migratory child, on the other hand, is defined as a child who:

- Is, or whose parent, spouse, or guardian is, a migratory agricultural worker—including a migratory dairy worker-or a migratory fisher—and
- In the preceding 36 months, in order to obtain (or accompany such parent, spouse, or guardian in order to obtain) temporary or seasonal employment in agricultural or fishing work, has either (a) moved from one school district to another, or (b) in a state that is comprised of a single school district, has moved from one administrative area to another within such district, or (c) resides in a school district of more than 15,000 square miles and migrates a distance of 20 miles or more to a temporary residence to engage in an agricultural or fishing activity. (20 USC §6399)

The majority of migrant students have special learning needs when it comes to schooling. Reading, writing, and speaking skills often suffer because of other priorities including lack of housing, inadequate food and clothing, inability to speak English, changing schools, and/or inconsistent schooling. Language barriers are experienced by the approximately 40% of migrant students who are in the process of learning English as a second language (National Commission on Migrant Education, 1992). Multiple moves within a year require children to adjust to new friends, different cultural and academic expectations, and varying graduation requirements. Approximately 25% of migrant students enroll in school more than 30 days after school begins and often leave prior to the end of the spring semester (Research Triangle Institute, 1992). Frequent relocations and language differences seriously hinder access to community services (Coballes-Vega, & Salend, 1988). The cumulative effects of these factors often lead to poor academic performance and low self-esteem of migrant students (Whittaker, Salend, & Gutierrez, 1997). Data released by the Office of Educational Research and Improvement at the U.S. Department of Education revealed that migratory Hispanic children born outside the 50 states have a 43% dropout rate (Perritt, 1997).

Historical Background

On November 20, 1960, Edward R. Morrow, a TV investigative reporter, produced and broadcasted an exposé on the wretched living conditions and treatment of migrant workers in a documentary called *Harvest of Shame* (Murrow, 1960). Nutritional concerns, living conditions, parental goals for their children, the hardships of traveling from work site to work site, child labor and labor laws, schooling for migrant students, the impact of the weather, and the lack of services available for migrant workers and their families were depicted in this fifty-two minute documentary. The reaction from the public was so swift and the demands for reform so vocal that Congress and the President quickly put into law reforms for the treatment of migrants (The Office of Migrant Education: Harvest of Hope, 2000).

Legislation leading to the development of programs to improve the comprehensive learning of migrant children and their families originated with the passage of the Elementary and Secondary Education Act (ESEA) of 1965, our government's single largest investment in elementary and secondary education. This legislation targets resources to help ensure that disadvantaged students have access to quality public education and is reauthorized every five years. Overcoming the poverty, mobility, and limited English proficiency characteristic of migrant children requires a high degree of program flexibility and attention to educational and support services far beyond those traditionally funded by state and local governments. For this reason, Congress authorized the Migrant Education Program (MEP)—Title I, Part C of the ESEA—to provide funding of programs aimed to support high-quality and comprehensive education for children of migrant agricultural workers and fishers. The programs differ from state to state, depending on the needs of each state's migrant children and the time of the year when they are present. When Congress first funded the migrant program, it had no idea how many workers with children would qualify—making a recruiting force necessary. MEP is the only federal education program with a recruiting provision. However, without continued recruitment, many migrant children would not be in school at all and, of those in school, very few would be served by MEP. The Pennsylvania Department of Education (1989) cited the following justification for formal recruitment:

1. Migrant families tend to be very self-sufficient and are not accustomed to looking outside of their own family for help.
2. Many do not speak English in their home, which, coupled with cultural differences between school and home, often places a barrier between home and the school.
3. Historically, there has been considerable turnover in the migrant population as migrants leave the migrant stream and enter various careers. Thus, as new families continue to enter the migrant workforce, the need to identify, inform, recruit, and educate migrant children does not diminish.
4. Migrant children are often invisible—quietly coming and going without attracting much attention.

When the MEP began fewer than 50% of the children of migrant farmworkers at the secondary level attended school (Johnson, Levy, Morales, Mores, & Prokopp, 1986). These youth were needed to assist in the fields or care for younger siblings. Despite the Federal Migrant

Education Program's goal to improve attendance, an estimated 200,000 to 800,000 children and adolescents continue to work in agriculture today (Commission on Security and Cooperation in Europe, 1993; Gabbard, Mines, & Boccalandro, 1994).

In 1992, the National Association of State Directors of Migrant Education noted, "The education of too many migrant students is characterized by low expectations, inferior resources, and differential treatment" (The Office of Migrant Education: Grant Information, 2000, p. 1). They challenged educators of migrant students to "Mobilize students, staff, and parents around a vision of a school in which all students can achieve. Migrant students not only can and do graduate from high schools, but graduate with honors" (p. 1).

The challenge led Congress, in the Reauthorization Act of 1994, to pass legislative reform bills that marked a change in the direction of education for children who are failing or at risk of failing. The 1994 legislation included the Goals 2000: Educate America Act, the School-to-Work Opportunities Act, and the Improving America's Schools Act (IASA) which reauthorized the Elementary and Secondary Education Act of 1965. Influenced by years of research, Congress recognized that a categorical approach to identifying children according to various needs or risk factors was counter-productive to the goal of improving education for all children. The language of the 1994 reauthorization of the ESEA reflected this change in thinking, stating, "All children can master challenging content and complex problem-solving skills. Research clearly shows that children, including low-achieving children, can succeed when expectations are high and all children are given the opportunity to learn challenging material" (20 U.S.C. 6301).

The Improving America's Schools Act focused resources on the following key elements of educational improvement efforts:

1. High standards for all students.
2. Focus on teaching and learning.
3. Flexibility to stimulate local school-based reform coupled with accountability for student performance.
4. Close partnerships among families, communities, and schools.
5. Resources targeted to where needs are greatest. This legislation required ESEA programs to be integrated into a state's overall school improvement effort and to focus around a core of challenging state standards. ESEA programs, including the Education of Migratory Children (Title I, Part C), now promote the alignment of all education components—curriculum and instruction, professional development, school leadership, accountability, and school improvement—to ensure that all children can attain challenging standards.

High Standards for All Students

The reauthorized Title I aims to improve the fundamental quality of curriculum and instruction for students served through the program by requiring that schools:

- Use effective strategies to improve children's achievement in basic skills and core academic areas by increasing the amount and quality of learning time and emphasizing instruction by highly qualified professional staff.
- Provide students who have trouble mastering established standards with additional assistance that is timely and effective (Focus on Teaching and Learning, 1996).

By requiring that Title I schools hold all students served by the program to the high achievement standards approved by their state, the law presumes that Title I resources will help these students to acquire the full range of knowledge and skills expected of all students. As of

1994, Title I is no longer intended to operate solely as a remedial program focused on low-level skills development; however, statutes require state MEPs to give priority for services to migrant children who:

- Are failing, or most at risk of failing, to meet the state's content and performance standards.
- Have had their education interrupted during the regular school year (Priority for Serving Migrant Students, 2000).

A Focus on Teaching and Learning

Migrant educators have long recognized that attention to academics alone will not ensure that children will achieve high standards, especially when other issues such as health and social needs are not met. The MEP supports the leveraging of all resources to support effective teaching and learning for migrant children. Migrant Professional Development includes training programs for school personnel to enhance their ability to understand and appropriately respond to the needs of migrant children. Migrant educators, like others in the education community, have eliminated most "pull out" programs, offering instead opportunities for migrant students to actively engage in challenging learning experiences through enriched, extended-time activities.

Flexibility to Stimulate Local Reform
Coupled with Accountability for Results

Federal funding granted by the MEP is awarded to State Education Agencies (SEAs) who are responsible for subgranting to Local Education Agencies (LEAs). Among other possible factors, the level of funding to the LEAs is determined by the following:

- Number of students and extent of the need of students selected for participation.
- Number of students whose education has been interrupted during the regular school year.
- Personnel required (both numbers and type).
- Extent to which the LEA will coordinate services with other state and local agencies serving migrant children and youth.
- How the proposed use of funds will facilitate the enrollment, attendance, and success in school of migrant children.
- Availability of MEP funds, and availability of instructional and other services from other funding sources.
- Facility and equipment needs.

LEAs receiving subgrants have considerable flexibility in determining how funds will be used to help migrant children succeed in school. However, under the Improving America's Schools Act, the MEP is integral to, not separate from, other state and local education reforms that center on high expectations for all children. Each state must develop or adopt annual assessments that:

- Are the same assessments used to measure the performance of all children.
- Are aligned with the state's content and performance standards.
- Provide student attainment of such standards.

- Include limited English proficient students, assessed to the extent possible in their primary language.
- Enable results to be disaggregated in a variety of ways, including by migrant program eligibility.

Performance is defined by how effectively the agency enables all children served under Title I to meet the state's challenging content standards in the grade levels to be tested.

Close Partnerships Between Families, Communities, and Schools

Section 1304(3) of Title I, Part C requires that state and local migrant education programs and projects be carried out, to the extent feasible, in a manner consistent with the parental involvement requirements of Section 1118 of Title I, Part A. Therefore, state and local education agencies providing services through the Migrant Education Program must make every reasonable effort to comply with parental involvement requirements in operating their programs and projects. These components are emphasized under Section 1118:

1. Policy involvement at the district and school levels, including parental involvement in developing school improvement plans.
2. Shared responsibility for high performance embodied in school-parent compacts.
3. Building capacity for parent involvement through such means as increased training and enhanced partnerships with community organizations and businesses.

Examples of parental involvement strategies that focus on the parents of migrant students with limited English proficiency include, but are not limited to:

- The use of bilingual and bicultural parent liaisons.
- Family literacy programs that bring parents into the school community to strengthen their role in improving the education of their children.
- Availability of staff proficient in multiple languages to translate any materials that go to the school community or parents and who serve as interpreters at school functions.
- Cultural awareness and language classes for teachers and other school staff working to build ties between home and school.
- Availability of translators for meetings.
- English as a Second Language (ESL) classes for interested parents of participating students.

In addition, the MEP requires "appropriate consultation" with state and local-level Parent Advisory Councils (PACs) in the planning and operation of state and local programs and projects of one school year in duration (Section 1304[c][3] of Title 1). While each state is permitted to determine what constitutes "appropriate consultation," the PACs should not be used as a substitute for meeting the parental involvement components under Section 1118.

Migrant families view education as their children's escape from the cycle of poverty and have a high respect for teachers' professional opinions (Diaz, Trotter, & Rivera, 1989). Parents are motivated by the opportunity to send their children to good schools; however, long working hours, childcare needs, and language and cultural differences may serve as barriers to establishing traditional parent-teacher communication. Additionally, economic survival is a high family priority and often limits school attendance by the students and participation in the school by the parents.

Local education agencies can facilitate the partnership between school and migrant parents by ensuring that rules are made available in the language of the parents, and that the purposes of applications, forms, and questionnaires are clearly explained to parents. Special attention should be given to school practices that may penalize students or parents, such as hidden costs or fines, confusing changes in bus schedules or school hours, or unclear visiting procedures. Also important are social and academic multicultural programs, dropout prevention efforts, college and career counseling, and "second-chance" opportunities for education and training through GED, accelerated and summer courses, and other such programs (Romo, 1996).

Program Description

The Migrant Education Program (MEP) is a basic state formula grant program that helps states offer services specifically for children of families who migrate to find work in agricultural, fishing, and timber industries. The funds provided to state education agencies are to be used to supplement, not supplant, education and support services for migrant children. For example, local funds for classroom supplies may not be reduced and replaced with migrant funds; however, migrant funds can instead be used to purchase additional supplies needed for serving migrant students.

Awards to each state are based on the number of eligible children identified within the state. The services offered differ from state to state and district to district, depending on the needs of each state's or district's migrant children and the time of year when they are present. Migrant funded districts are mandated to address the special needs of migrant children through the Migrant Education Program's Seven Areas of Focus.

The Seven Areas of Focus

Coordination of Migrant Services. Coordinated services can help address the problems children face outside the classroom that affect their performance in school by improving children's and parents' access to social, health, and education services. This focus is required at all grade levels and seeks to ensure that migrant students and their families have their needs met. It allows them to access all services for which they are eligible from entry in the MEP's Early Childhood Program for three-year-olds through graduation from high school or the obtaining of a General Education Diploma (GED) up to the age of twenty-two. Coordination activities are funded through monies reserved from the appropriation for the Basic State Formula Grant Program. Under the Improving America's Schools Act, up to $1.5 million of the funds reserved for coordination activities can be awarded each year as incentive grants to encourage states to work together and reduce administrative costs, thus increasing funds available for direct services to children. Discretionary grants are awarded to projects designed to improve inter- and intra-state coordination of migrant education activities.

Early Childhood Education. The Migrant Education Even Start Program (MEES) provides discretionary grants to programs specifically designed to improve the education opportunities of the nation's migrant children and adults by integrating early childhood education, adult literacy or adult basic education, and parent education into a unified family literacy program. MEES, authorized under Title I, Part B of the ESEA (20 U.S.C. 6362), provides funds for family-centered education projects to help parents gain the literacy and parenting skills they need to become full partners in the education of their young children (through age seven) and to assist those children in reaching their full potential as learners.

The early education program provides appropriate developmental activities that support migrant children's developmental growth in the cognitive, language, social, and affective domains. These programs must be high quality, research-based, aligned to the district curriculum, and conducted in the child's primary language. MEP funded districts are required to serve all identified migrant three- and four year-old children not being served by other community agencies such as Headstart or Even Start.

New Generation System (NGS) for Migrant Student Record Transfer. NGS is a multi-state consortium, constantly updated database used to record the most current demographic, health, and educational data on migrant students. This innovative data transfer system allows districts to access information throughout the United States and record the student's progress through the educational process. NGS permits the transferring of migrant student records, including enrollment, academic and health information, to educators and health professionals serving migrant students. This system holds promise for increasing awards of student credit across state boundaries; however, it is still in neophyte stages and many states have not realized, nor are utilizing, the NGS to its fullest potential.

State and Local Education Agencies have a requirement under the MEP to promote interstate and intrastate coordination of services, including the transfer of pertinent school records, for migratory children. In accordance with this MEP requirement, the nonconsensual disclosure of education records of migratory children, or personally identifiable information from these records, to authorized local and state education officials is permissible under FERPA (Family Educational Rights and Privacy Act of 1974). However, disclosures of such information to other than local and state education officials (i.e., health officials) may be necessary to carry out the coordination responsibilities. Such disclosures are permitted only after obtaining prior written consent from the parent or eligible student.

Parental Empowerment. Research and practice show that substantial, on-going family involvement in children's learning is a critical link to achieving a high-quality education and a safe, disciplined learning environment. Common strategies for increasing migrant parental involvement include:

1. Creating natural contexts for literacy development, often by providing direct services to parents and children at the same time.
2. Helping parents understand the demands of U.S. schools and providing them with skills to become their child's teacher and advocate.
3. Providing English language instruction and other services to parents to enable them to participate more actively in their communities.

A functional parental involvement program exhibits the following characteristics:

- The program is considered fundamental.
- The program is long term, carefully planned, and comprehensive.
- Administrators, teachers, and parents are involved in the entire scope of the program and share a common philosophy towards parental involvement.
- The program places priority on flexibility, accountability, shared expertise, open communication, mutual trust, and mutual respect.
- The program provides for continuity between home and school.
- The program moves activities into the community, whenever possible.
- The program provides parents and teachers with information and development opportunities.
- The program provides opportunities for parents to function in a variety of roles such as advisors, tutors, audience, school program supporters, co-learners, paid school staff, and advocates.

In addition to the parental involvement component, the district is required to establish a Parent Advisory Council (PAC) for the migrant program. The purpose of the Council is to advise the school district regarding the MEP's planning, operation, and evaluation.

Identification and Recruitment. Recruitment is defined as the identification and enrollment of eligible migratory children in the MEP. Recruitment needs to be continuous throughout the entire year and not confined to a particular time of year. The State Education

Agency is ultimately responsible for (a) implementing a statewide process that assures the reliability of eligibility determinations, and (b) for the quality of the information obtained. Figure 1 outlines the decision-making process for determining eligibility of students for migrant programs.

The State Education Agency, in conjunction with the Local Education Agency, must ensure that the local recruiter is knowledgeable about the statutory and regulatory requirements for eligibility and that quality control procedures are adequate to ensure that the student's eligibility cannot be questioned. The local recruiter, as an extension of the state education agency, identifies prospective migratory children and determines their eligibility for the MEP. The recruiter's primary responsibilities are to:

- Obtain and interpret information provided by parents, guardians, and others.
- Record, accurately and clearly, information that establishes a child to be a migrant under the statutory definition in Section 1309(2) and the regulatory definitions in 34 CFR 200.40.

Should a recruiter have questions about a child's eligibility for the MEP, the situation should be described in the comment section of the Certificate of Eligibility and referred to a higher-level official within the state (see Figure 2). Determining the number of migrant children residing within a state's boundaries is a difficult task since the children who have the most need for services may not attend school. Furthermore, language and cultural barriers may make families hesitant to advocate for services on behalf of their children, particularly if they are not accustomed to looking for assistance from their child's school. Also, the locations where migrant families reside may vary due to agriculture changes or in response to natural disasters affecting crop production. Therefore, it is important that states actively seek out migrant families and develop comprehensive recruitment plans that include both school- and community-based activities.

Graduation Enhancement. The MEP promotes the transition to postsecondary education through the promotion of student leadership academies, the development of college entrance exam programs, state performance improvement strategies, university correspondence courses, admissions counseling, and coordination of activities that ensure that all migrant students are prepared for postsecondary opportunities. The College Assistance Migrant Program (CAMP), a one-year federally funded scholarship for migrant students, is offered by 12 universities in six states and Puerto Rico.

Based on state and local needs assessments, districts are required to design programs for migrant students that will lead to higher graduation rates. In order to meet the same standards as other students, schools need to make systemic changes that address unique migrant needs. Fewer than 2% of migrant students graduate after the age of 19 (Duerr, 1986), making it critical that students are scheduled into classes that earn credit and teach concepts and skills necessary for graduation. Time, school climate, and cultural respect become crucial factors for migrant students. Most migrant students drop out of school due to their feelings about school, not because of grades or failures (Johnson, levy, Morales, & Prokopp, 1986).

Secondary Credit Exchange and Accrual. As secondary education students move from school to school, documentation of coursework becomes significant in their educational development. To reduce the educational disruption of migrant students, State and local education agencies adopt procedures for granting high-school migrant students with credits or partial credits and develop innovative methods that allow migrant students to complete required coursework in an expedited manner.

Figure 1

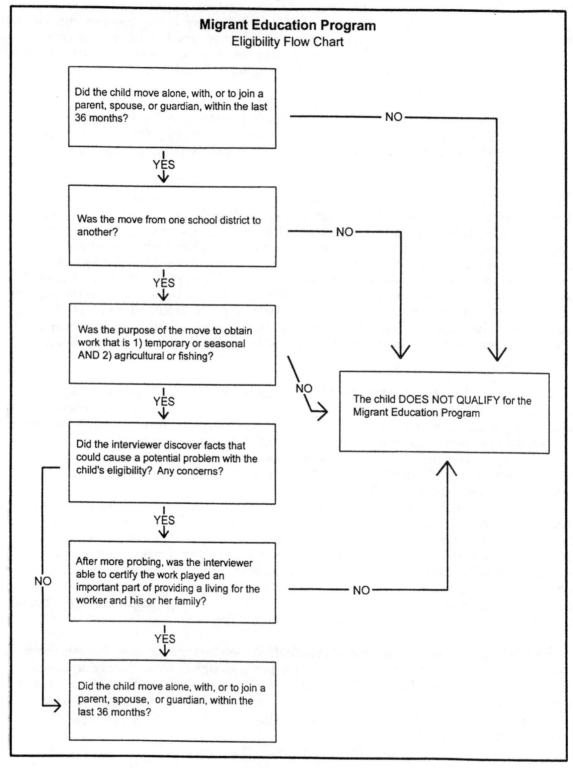

Migrant Education Program
Eligibility Flow Chart

Did the child move alone, with, or to join a parent, spouse, or guardian, within the last 36 months?

YES

Was the move from one school district to another?

YES

Was the purpose of the move to obtain work that is 1) temporary or seasonal AND 2) agricultural or fishing?

YES

Did the interviewer discover facts that could cause a potential problem with the child's eligibility? Any concerns?

YES

After more probing, was the interviewer able to certify the work played an important part of providing a living for the worker and his or her family?

YES

Did the child move alone, with, or to join a parent, spouse, or guardian, within the last 36 months?

NO

NO

NO

NO

NO

The child DOES NOT QUALIFY for the Migrant Education Program

Figure 2

Sample Certificate of Eligibility

Certificate of Eligibility

FAMILY DATA

Name and address of (1) person responsible for the child **OR** (2) self-eligible youth.	Name(s) of (1) the person from whom the information was obtained and (2) the person who was informed of the Family Educational Privacy Act and told that the child(ren)'s records may be sent to other schools where the child intends to enroll.
Legal Parent (if not named above):	

CHILD DATA

Name of Child/Youth	Sex	Birthdate
_____	____	_____
_____	____	_____
_____	____	_____
_____	____	_____
_____	____	_____
_____	____	_____

ELIGIBILITY DATA -- The children listed moved . . .

From (school, district/city, state, country)	To (street or school district)	Arriving (qualifying arrival date)
The child(ren) moved ( ) with, ( ) to join, OR ( ) on his/her own	( ) Parent, ( ) Guardian, ( ) Spouse, OR ( ) Self Name:	

To enable that person to obtain or seek ( ) Temporary, ( ) Seasonal, AND ( ) Agricultural OR ( ) Fishing employment **Qualifying Activity:**	Residency Date *States with stopover sites must record the departure date.*

Identify and describe other work (in addition to agricultural or sighing work), IF ANY, in which household members are engaged

Comments:

Based on the interview, the interviewer has determined that the qualifying work is an important part of providing a living for the worker and his/her family. Interviewer: Date:	Reviewer Initials: Date:

Some innovative methods that allow students to complete coursework are:

- University credits (correspondence, credit by exam, etc.).
- Project Smart (a technology-based summer program).
- Alternative school programs (local credit by exam, summer/night school).
- PASS (Portable Assisted Study Sequence) which allows students to not only move at an individual pace, but to take packets of work from the home-base school as they migrate to other locations for completion and submission for grading upon return to their home-base school.
- Out-of-state test administration of state standards assessments for graduation purposes.

Home-base schools—those from which migrant students plan to graduate—should consider adopting policies that ensure credits, full or partial, awarded in other schools are accepted. Districts having schoolwide programs are required to report secondary credit data to the state agency's system for migrant student record transfer in order to document courses taken and those recommended. Districts are also responsible for partial and complete credits awarded by schools for work completed during the enrollment period in each school. For coursework undertaken elsewhere, districts are required to consult with the respective schools or with the state's Migrant Interstate Program to clear up incomplete courses or grades.

School Leaders' Role in Migrant Education

School leaders play a key role in the success of education for migrant students. Frequently the degree to which curriculum, instructional strategies, and appropriate modifications are adopted are dependent on the principal's emphasis on migrant education. Principals, together with teachers, will:

- Focus on improving the quality of teaching through effective staff development programs aimed at addressing the needs of diverse students and providing modifications that recognize and overcome "learning gaps" created by attendance at numerous schools.
- Provide flexibility in course assignments and acquisition of credits.
- Ensure migrant students are assigned to appropriate classes and those of minimal size whenever possible.
- Make a concentrated effort to involve migrant parents in their children's activities.
- Offer parents a variety of services and activities in which to become involved.
- Offer classes and services that migrant parents need.
- Provide parents with childcare, food, and transportation to the school.
- Schedule activities in advance and at times convenient to parents.
- Develop programs of interest and need to migrant families.
- Ensure all written communication is in the family's native language and that a translator is present at all parent meetings.
- Create a campus environment where migrant parents feel comfortable.
- Understand all guidelines for expenditure of federal funds and ensure funding is used to the greatest benefit of the migrant students.
- Locate additional sources of funding and in-kind services to meet the needs of the students and their families.
- Ensure that communication between home and school is regular, two-way, and meaningful.
- Help teachers develop collaborative relationships with parents based on high expectations for student achievement and behavior.

- Actively seek feedback from parents, students, staff, and the community on the effectiveness of the program.
- Establish specific and measurable goals for the curriculum and for the parent involvement aspect of the program.
- Conduct frequent surveys and program evaluations to determine effectiveness in meeting program goals.
- Nurture a flexible, multicultural environment.

Because identification and recruitment must be conducted before any services can be provided, the principal must work closely with the recruiter. For example, times need to be scheduled throughout the year for the recruiter to locate, interview, and enroll all eligible migratory families in the area. The supervisor or principal must oversee this schedule and the completion of tasks by the recruiter. The principal and supervisor must be accessible to the recruiter at all times for purposes of answering questions regarding eligibility guidelines, policies, or procedures. Recruiters need to know that the principal values their work and understands it well enough to be of assistance when needed.

Contemporary Issues

All students face challenges as they pursue their education, but some individual students and some groups of students are faced with greater numbers and/or severity of challenges. Migrant students are among those who are burdened with a multitude of significant difficulties.

School enrollment for migrant children is lower than that of any other population group, and their high school dropout rate is twice the national average. Only 10% of migrant children complete the twelfth grade (Commission on Security, 1993). Economic necessity causes large numbers of migrant children to work. The average income for a farmworker family is less than $6,000 a year as compared to $28,000 for an average American family. Douglas Kruse, Rutgers University labor consultant, found that 290,200 children were employed unlawfully in 1996; that among them 59,000 were under the age of 14; that 123,000 of those children worked in the nation's fields, orchards, and sheds from California to the Midwest to Delaware; and of that number, 61,000 of the 14 to 17 year olds lived apart from their parents (Krebs, 2000). Women and children around the age of 14 comprise 38% of farmworkers. They labor at jobs involving long hours and dangerous working conditions. An estimated 27,000 children, age 19 and under, who both live and work on farms suffer work-related injuries, and an additional 300 die from work-related accidents with children accounting for 20% of all farm fatalities (Wilk, 1993).

Even young children may be in the fields because day care is not available to them—private day care is too costly and inaccessible to migrant workers. Migrant Head Start (funded by MEP) served 34,000 infants and children in 1994, but lacks sufficient funding to serve all that need it. In one labor camp a 4-year-old boy was found with a rope tied to his hand on one end and to a bed on the other—the length of the rope enabled him to reach the food left for him and the bathroom, but kept him inside. This was the only day care available to him (Commission on Security and Cooperation in Europe, 1993). Other documentation continues to surface revealing a "Harvest of Shame" still exists today that condemns thousands of hardworking men, women, and children to lives of pain, poverty, and despair. Rod Minott of KCTS in Seattle, reporting on the problems faced by migrants in the U.S. in 1998, began his broadcast with this description:

...The family of six has followed harvests from California to Washington State. Like many other workers, they've been unable to find housing here, so they pitched a tent on some public land just footsteps from the Colombia River. As Maria Gomez makes dinner, her four-month-old son lies nearby in a tent filled with flies. Gomez says homelessness has been especially harsh on the infant, who is ill with asthma. (Minott, 1998, p. 1)

Migrant children's chances for academic success are greatly hindered by their parents' occupation and the dismal living conditions they must often endure. Often, migrant children enter school with limited foundations in early literacy skills, minimal language skills, and frequently with multiple health issues resulting from years of exposure to extreme elements, poor nutrition, and farm chemicals. Many enter school at an older age and drop out before they can graduate from high school. Most migrant children attend at least two different schools each year and many attend as many as six different schools that vary in the content, sequence, and delivery of the curriculum. Migrant children may have to adjust to new friends, a second language, different cultural and academic expectations, and varying graduation requirements several times a year.

In the book *Migrant Children Balance Studies and Labor*, editor Erica Bellamy features 14-year-old Hugo who migrates each year with his parents, two sisters, and a brother across the nation following seasonal employment. Hugo begins the first semester of school each fall in Wisconsin where his family ends their yearly travels with employment at a Del Monte cannery. In mid-October when the harvest season is over, Hugo and his family will return to Texas. "I get one or two credits here and then I lose them and I gotta take them over again in Texas," says Hugo, whose credits from the previous year did not appear on his Texas transcript (Bellamy, 1999, p. 1).

The Improving America's Schools Act requires the Secretary of Education to assist the states in the development of a more effective means of transferring student records. The phasing out of the existing Migrant Student Records Transfer System resulted in many districts relying on mail, telephone, and fax to transfer records for migrant students. As of 1999, 19 states had some type of electronic system in place with many of these systems being used for maintaining rather than transferring, student records (U.S. Department of Education, 1999).

In the United States in 1996-1997 approximately 580,000 MEP participants, including 475,000 served in the regular term and 285,000 in the summer term. Most migratory students are concentrated in California (210,000) and Texas (115,000). Five other states—Florida, Washington, Oregon, Kansas, and Kentucky—each reported more than 20,000 students eligible for funding (Henderson, Daft, & Fong, 1998). Over the last decade, summer projects have grown faster than regular programs. Summer projects increased from serving approximately 100,000 students in 1984-1985 to 285,000 in 1996-1997 and now serve approximately 60% of the number of students served during the regular term (Henderson, Daft & Fong, 1998). The increased numbers are probably due to a combination of increasing overall numbers of migrant workers along with more effective recruiting by the state and local education agencies.

Funding for migrant programs is based on a formula that relies on data that are burdensome to collect. Statutory references to "estimates" and "full-time equivalents (FTE)" are ambiguous. Final allotments of money can be based on the number of residency days for each migrant child in each state or the use of increasingly dated FTE adjustment facts calculated with 1994 data. Because migrant programs are operated and administered by states, states that receive small program allocations have difficulty in both establishing adequate MEP programs for migrant children and paying the costs of needed state administration. These difficulties are intensified by the annual fluctuations in some states' need for agricultural workers (e.g., due to droughts, floods, employer closings, and relocations) which sometimes result in abrupt drops in certain states' funding allocations. Even states that have maintained stable numbers of migrant children from one year to the next have seen allocations fall as other states identify additional migrant children and require more of the overall MEP allocation.

While the instability of state funding levels reflects the dynamic reality of a mobile population, it also severely impairs the ability of states with relatively few migrant children to maintain an effective migrant education program. At times, a state's federal funding drops while the number of migrant children remains stable or increases. When this occurs, both recruiting efforts and services provided to migrant children are curtailed resulting in reports that reflect lowered numbers of migrant youth being served. The result is a downward spiral in both the quality and availability of services.

Summary

The Migrant Education Program (MEP) was authorized as Title 1, Part C of the Elementary and Secondary Education Act of 1965 in an effort to counter the discontinuity of migrant life. Initially, the MEP made funds available for supplemental instruction and support services in health and nutrition only for the school-aged children of migratory farm workers. Later, the program was extended to include children of migratory fishers and forestry workers and to serve children ages 3–21 in recognition of the importance of early childhood programs and the need for continued services beyond the nominal age of high school graduation.

MEP is based on the premise that poverty, mobility, and school achievement are related, and that children who are both poor and migratory are more likely to have difficulty in school. Just as a migrant's way of life is itinerant, so is the education of migrant children. Accordingly, extra help is likely to be needed to compensate for the effects a mobile lifestyle has on student learning. The purposes of MEP are to:

- Provide for states some support for educational programs for migratory children.
- Help reduce the educational disruptions and other problems that result from repeated moves.
- Ensure that students are provided with appropriate educational services.
- Grant migrant students the same challenging state required academic content and student performance standards that all children are expected to meet.

Local education agencies, based on state and local needs assessments, are required to design programs that will lead to higher graduation rates. Finding and enrolling eligible migrant children is a cornerstone of the MEP, and its importance cannot be overemphasized. Identification and recruitment of migrant children is critical because the children who are most in need of program services are often those who are the most difficult to find. Additionally, children cannot receive MEP services without a record of eligibility.

Since its inception in 1964, the Migrant Education Program has enabled states to help hundreds of thousands of migrant children. Innovative programs for providing services include:

- A summer program in North Dakota that uses the students' first language to improve learning and achievement.
- A summer institute in Florida that provides junior high students the opportunity to advance one grade level in a six-week residential program.
- A family program in Idaho that provides migrant parents with strategies for assisting their children in reading and other school assignments (A Focus on Teaching and Learning, 2000).
- A graduation enhancement for migrant students program in Texas with guidelines for counselors working with migrant students (Hatton, Gonzalez, Monteel, Cortez, Villarreal, Jackson, & Ochoa, 1997).

Through successful MEP programs, educators have built on the solid traditions of migrant families—strong family ties, cooperation among family members to benefit from the strong work ethics, and the assumption of important responsibilities at an early age. Despite the challenges of their migrant lifestyles, migrant students not only graduate from high school but also graduate as valedictorians, salutatorians, and honor students.

Applying Your Knowledge

You are the director of Migrant Education Program for your school district and are aware of all the options available to migrant students for completing graduation requirements. The high school eleventh grade counselor comes to you concerned about Pablo, an eleventh grade migrant student, who is worried about completing graduation requirements for next year. Pablo did not pass the math section of the state achievement test. He also did not complete the work for his tenth grade English class because last year he left school prior to the end of the semester in order to work in Minnesota. Consequently, Pablo received only a half credit in English. Pablo will be the first person in his family to finish school if he meets all the requirements. Pablo and his family migrate from Texas to Minnesota every year and his family is dependent on his income from working in the fields.

Questions:

1. What options does Pablo have?
2. What arrangements could the school district in Texas and Minnesota make to help Pablo complete his graduation requirements?
3. As a principal, would you talk to Pablo's parents about allowing him to stay and finish his eleventh grade year? If so, what arguments could you make to support your suggestion? Be sure to consider the strong family culture of most migrant families.
4. Would you talk to Pablo's tenth grade English teacher about the work Pablo needs to make up?
5. Should Pablo be treated differently than other students?

Questions for Thought

1. What alternative arrangements should be made for educating migrant students who have limited use of the English language?
2. If you were the District Supervisor of Migrant Programs, how would you allocate your attention between funding (identification and recruitment) and quality of academic programs for migrant students? Justify your decision.
3. Maintaining accurate academic records for students is critical for student success and for the accountability component of program evaluation required by the Federal Government. Could the current record keeping system be improved? If so, in what way?

For Further Information

Elementary and Secondary Act of 1994 **www.ed.gov/legislation/ESEA**
Migrant Education Program Formula Grants **www.ed.gov/pubs/Biennial/102.html**
Migrant Education: High School Equivalency Program **www.aspe.hhs.gov/cfda/p84141.html**
National Education Association: Legislative Action Center **www.nea.org/lac/esea**
Preliminary Guidance for Migrant Education, P. L. 103-382
    www.ed.gov/offices/OESE/MEP/PrelimGuide/pt3a.html
Secondary Education for Migrant Children **www.pass123.org**
The Office of Migrant Education **www.ed.gov/offices/OESE/MEP**
Also contact your state education agency

References

A focus on teaching and learning. (November 12, 2000). Preliminary Guidance for Migrant education Program, Title I, Part C Public Law 103-382 [Online]. <http://www.ed.gov/offices/OESE/MEP/PrelimGuide/pt3a.html> [2000, Dec.].

Bellamy, E. (1999). Migrant children balance studies and labor. *The Children's Express* [Online]. <http://www.ypress.org/migrants/amigrant.html> [2000, Dec.]

Coballes-Vega, C., & Salend, S. J. (1988). Guidelines for assessing migrant handicapped students. *Diagnostique, 13*, 64-75.

Commission on Security and Cooperation in Europe. (1993). *Migrant farmworkers in the United States. Implementation of the Helsinki Accords.* Briefings of the Commission on Security and Cooperation in Europe (July 20, 1992; October 9, 1992; February 19, 1993; March 1, 1993; April 8, 1993). Washington, DC: U.S. Government Printing Office. (ERIC Document Reproduction Service No. ED 393 631)

Diaz, J., Trotter, R., & Rivera, V. (1989). *The effects of migration on children: An ethnographic study.* Harrisburg, PA: Pennsylvania Department of Education, Division on Migrant Education.

Duerr, M. (1986). *A report on dropout and graduation rates for the high school class of 1985 in region II migrant child education.* (ERIC Document Reproduction Service No. ED 284 708)

Focus on teaching and learning: Title I support for enriching curriculum and instruction. (1996). Mapping Out the National Assessment of Title I: Interim Report-1996 [Online]. <http://wwwgov/pubs/NatAssess/sec3.html> [2000, Dec.].

Gabbard, S., Mines, R., & Boccalandro, B. (1994). *Migrant farmworkers: Pursuing security in an unstable labor market.* Washington, DC: U.S. Department of Labor, Office of the Assistant Secretary for Policy.

Hatton, S. R., Gonzalez, E. M., Montecel, M. R., Cortez, A., Villarreal, A., Jackson, L., & Ochoa, N. (1997). *Graduation enhancement for migrant students: GEMS.* San Antonio, TX: Authors.

Henderson, A., Daft, J., & Fong, P. (1998). *State Title I migrant participation information: 1996-1997.* Washington, DC: U.S. Department of Education, 1-20.

Johnson, F., Levy, R., Morales, J., Morse, S., & Prokopp, M. (1986). *Migrant students at the secondary level: Issues and opportunities for change.* Las Cruces, NM: ERIC Clearinghouse on Rural Education and Small Schools. (ERIC Document Reproduction Service No. ED 270 242)

Krebs, A. V. (November 24, 2000). *After all these years, a harvest of shame is still borne on the backs of children* [Online]. <http://www.populist.com/98.2fields.html> [2000, Dec.].

Minott, R. (1998, December 25). *On the road? A news hour with Jim Lehrer transcript* [Online NewsHour]. <http://www.pbs.org/hewshour/bb/international/july-dec98/housing_12-25.html> [2000, Dec.].

Murrow, E. R. (1960). *Harvest of shame.* New York: McGraw Hill Farms.

National Commission on Migrant Education. (1992). Invisible children: A portrait of migrant education in the United States. *Exceptional Children, 20,* 5-8. Washington, DC: U.S. Government Printing Office.

The Office of Migrant Education: Harvest of Hope (2000). [Online]. <http://www.ed.gov/offices/OESE/MEP> [2000, Dec.].

Pennsylvania Department of Education, Migrant Education Program. (1989). *National identification and recruitment: Administrator's guide, recruiter's guide, and trainer's guide.* Harrisburg, PA: Author.

Perritt, D. C. (1997, March). Can technology increase course opportunities for migrant students? *NASSP Bulletin, 81*(587), 15-18.

Priority for Serving Migrant Students. (November 12, 2000). Preliminary Guidance for Migrant Education Program, Title I, Part C Public Law 103-382 [Online]. <http://www.ed.gov/offices/OESE/MEP/PrelimGuide/pt2a.html> [2000, Dec.].

Research Triangle Institute. (1992). *Descriptive study of Chapter 1 migrant education program.* Research Triangle Park, NC: Author.

Romo, H. (1996). The newest "outsiders": Educating Mexican migrant and immigrant youth. In J. L. Flores (Ed.), *Children of la frontera: Binational efforts to serve Mexican migrant and immigrant students* (pp. 61-91). Charleston, WV: ERIC Clearinghouse on Rural Education and Small Schools. (ERIC Document Reproduction Service No. ED 393 635)

The Office of Migrant Education: Grant Information. [Online]. <http://www.ed.gov/offices/OESE/MEP/grants.html> [2000, Nov. 21].

The Office of Migrant Education: Harvest of Hope. [Online]. <http://www.ed.gov/offices/OESE/MEP> [2000, Nov. 24].

U.S. Department of Education. (1999). *Promising results, continuing challenges: The final report of the national assessment of Title I.* Washington, DC: Author.

Whittaker, C. R., Salend, S. J., & Gutierrez, M. B. (1997, March). Voices from the fields: Including migrant farmworkers in the curriculum. *Reading Teacher, 50*(6), 482 - 493.

Wilk, V. (1993). Health hazards to children in agriculture. *American Journal of Industrial Medicine, 24,* 283-290.

Chapter 4

Upward Bound
and Other TRIO Programs

Gwen Schroth

These programs require an educator who can look beyond race,
poverty, and gender to search for students whose eyes light up at the
prospect of a college education.

Gwen Schroth

Objectives:
- **Provide the historical background that led to the creation of TRIO Programs.**
- **Discuss the basic components of the TRIO Programs.**
- **Outline the differences between the various programs.**
- **Show how the school staff can contribute to the success of the programs.**

Of the billions of taxpayer dollars expended to ensure equality of educational opportunity for America's children, the TRIO Programs are unique—they focus on encouraging students to prepare for, enter, and graduate from college. For school administrators, counselors, and teachers, knowledge of these programs is critical, as they are the ones who identify and recruit students who will profit the most from TRIO services. Basic information about the three programs—hence termed TRIO—is provided here so that educators can make those choices wisely.

The TRIO Programs are collectively designed to seek out and help low-income, first-generation (neither parent has completed college) students, and persons with disabilities succeed at a postsecondary education such as college or vocational training. A low-income student is an "individual whose family's taxable income did not exceed 150% of the poverty level amount in the calendar year preceding the year in which the individual initially participated in the project" (Talent Search, 1999, p. 261). TRIO comprises three major programs. Talent Search is the program that provides resources to identify students with exceptional potential for success at postsecondary education. Upward Bound furnishes support for middle and high school students, and Student Support Services maintains that aid during college.

Large gaps in academic performance and disparity in college enrollment rates between students from economically disadvantaged and economically advantaged families evidence the need for these programs. Mortenson (1995) found a 30 percentage point differential between high school graduates from low-income families enrolling in college and high-income students who go to college. Rosenbaum (1992) argues that middle-class and college-educated families take for granted the availability and advantages of a college education, but the disadvantaged assume they cannot afford additional education.

Those providing TRIO services help students (a) obtain information about and apply for financial assistance for postsecondary education through such sources as grants, scholarships, and loans; and (b) overcome class, social, and cultural barriers to obtaining a postsecondary education. Continuous support is available to students beginning as early as elementary school and continues through college graduation. The programs target first-generation students from low-income families and those with disabilities. Although older than the targeted middle and high school students, first-generation military veterans preparing to enter postsecondary education may also avail themselves of TRIO Program services.

The preparation of school administrators, counselors, and teachers to work cooperatively with TRIO providers is essential to the success of the programs. Therefore, the following are discussed in this chapter: (a) the historical backgrounds of the programs, (b) descriptions of the programs, (c) how they are funded, (d) their success, and (e) the responsibility of the target school's leaders. Of all the TRIO Programs, Upward Bound will receive the most attention here because it is the most intense of the secondary school programs, receives the most government funds, and has the strongest links to school administrators, counselors, and teachers.

Historical Background

In 1954, the Supreme Court's ruling in *Brown v. the Board of Education* recognized the urgency for equitable educational opportunities for all students. For disadvantaged students a college education remained unattainable because of academic, economic, cultural, and social barriers (Moore, 1997). By the early 1960s Congress realized that the nation's commitment to providing educational opportunities for all Americans, regardless of race, ethnic background, or economic circumstance extended beyond high school. In support of this commitment, Congress established a series of programs to help low-income Americans enter college, graduate, and move on to participate more fully in America's economic and social life (Upward Bound, 1999).

Johnson's War on Poverty spurred the passing of the Economic Opportunity Act of 1964, legislation that increased attention to the country's large disadvantaged population and raised an awareness of the social and economic advantages of educating all children. Johnson's legislation provided funds for a number of programs among which was the first TRIO Program—Upward Bound. This program gave aid to disadvantaged students for the pursuit of postsecondary degrees. Initially under the administration of the Office of Economic Opportunity, Upward Bound was transferred to Higher Education Programs within the Department of Education in 1968.

The success of Upward Bound and an awareness of its limitations contributed to the decision to allot additional funds for a related program, Talent Search. Established through Title IV of the Higher Education Act of 1965, Talent Search:

> Was created to enhance identification of candidates for Upward Bound and provide academic, career, and financial counseling to its participants and encourage them to graduate from high school and continue on to the postsecondary school of their choice. Talent Search also serves high school dropouts by encouraging them to reenter the educational system and complete their education. (Talent Search, 2000, p. 2)

In 1968 the Special Services for Disadvantaged Students Program was created and later termed Student Support Services (SSS). Authorized by the Higher Education Amendments, SSS became the third in the series of educational opportunity programs. SSS Programs provide disadvantaged college students with academic and motivational support to enable them to complete their postsecondary education and pursue graduate studies.

The three major endeavors, Upward Bound, Talent Search, and Student Support Services became known as the TRIO Programs. During the years following the formation of the first three, some smaller but related programs were attached although the term TRIO Programs remained (Federal TRIO Programs, 2000). The Veterans Upward Bound Program was formed to provide intensive basic skills development for military veterans; the Educational Opportunity Centers were opened to help students select a college and obtain suitable financial aid. In 1986 the Ronald E. McNair Post Baccalaureate Achievement Program was developed to aid disadvantaged students prepare for and succeed in doctoral studies. The Upward Bound Math and Science Program was added in 1990 to increase students' math and science skills. The TRIO Dissemination Partnership Program was funded when the Higher Education Act was amended in 1998. This Partnership Program allows host institutions to work with other institutions and community-based organizations that do not have TRIO grants but are serving low-income and first-generation college students. The Training Program for Federal TRIO Programs provides funding to develop the expertise of those who lead and direct the TRIO Programs.

In 2000, over 1,900 TRIO Programs served nearly 700,000 low-income Americans between the ages of 11 and 27 (Federal TRIO Programs, 2000). Since their inception, the programs have formed an extensive cadre of experienced professionals to serve the students. Over time, these professionals "have gained political sophistication and experience that has enabled them to become a nationwide network of people able to protect and expand TRIO, as well as speak to and work for the broader agenda of equal opportunity" (Federal TRIO Programs, 2000).

Program Descriptions

TRIO programs are organized at host sites—most often two- or four-year colleges and universities—and programs are designed around the needs of the participating students. In a study by Fasciano and Jacobson (1997), TRIO Program project directors who worked with disadvantaged students reported that the major obstacles to entering college were inadequate financial resources and academic deficiencies, in particular writing and study skills. Once in a TRIO program, the primary reason for participants' failure to complete college was found to be lack of family support, difficulties living away from home, and adjustment problems. Consequently, interventions target academic deficiencies, personal support, and help in finding financial assistance.

The number of students in TRIO Programs is growing but many deserving individuals do not receive services. Since its first year of full funding in 1966, Upward Bound alone more than doubled in size (Myers & Schirm, 1997). Despite this growth, far more students are eligible and seek participation than are served (Moore, 1997). In a study of Upward Bound students, Waldman, Myers, Jacobson & Moore (1997) estimated that less than one percent of all youth who are of an age that reflects enrollment in grades 8-12 and who are income-eligible are actually served.

The host institutions must apply to the federal government for funds and then seek student participants from nearby targeted schools (or within the host college or university in the case of SSS). Government records that combine all TRIO Programs show that about 39% of the students served are White, 36% are African-American, 16% are Hispanic, 5% are Native American, and 4% are Asian-American. Roughly 16,000 TRIO participants are students with disabilities and nearly 20% of all African-American and Hispanic freshmen that entered college in the early 1980s received assistance through these government programs (Federal TRIO Programs, 2000).

Regardless of the program, services must help students (a) complete high school or college, (b) improve their academic skills, and (c) refine their personal development skills.

The Upward Bound Program

Upward Bound represents the largest federal intervention aimed at helping students attain a postsecondary education (Myers & Schirm, 1997).

In 1966, the first year that funds were appropriated, 42 projects serving 50,000 clients were supported at a cost of $2 million. In academic year 1989-90, the Education Department awarded $426.1 million for 177 projects, designed to serve more than 200,000 clients. (Hexter, 1990, p. 50)

In 1996 there were more than 500 Upward Bound Projects and each served an average of 90 students (Myers & Schirm, 1997). By the year 2000, 772 Projects were in operation (Upward Bound, 2000). The average per-pupil cost was about $4,000. About 68% of the projects were hosted by four-year colleges, 28% by two-year colleges, and 4% by community-based organizations and high schools. Investigating a sample of Upward Bound Programs, Waldman, Myers, Jacobson, and Moore (1997) found four of five target schools were high schools; the rest were middle or junior high schools. Six out of ten programs targeted urban schools.

Eligibility. Students may apply for Upward Bound if they are between the ages of 13 and 19 (except veterans who may enroll at any age). Additionally, "two-thirds of the Upward Bound participants in each project must be potential first-generation college students whose families have incomes at or below 150 percent of the poverty threshold, the remainder must meet either the low-income or the first generation requirement" (Myers & Schirm, 1997, p. 2). The Code of Federal Regulations, (Upward Bound, 1999) also specifies that participants must:

- Be a citizen or national of the United States.
- Be a permanent resident of the United States.
- Have a need for academic support.
- Have completed the eighth grade but not have entered the 12th grade.

(Exceptions to these rules are made for some students such as those intending to become citizens and residents of Guam and other territories.) Additionally, Upward Bound participants must reside in the target area (about a fifty-mile radius of the host institution), be determined by the project director to be committed to the project, and free to take part in the services offered (Upward Bound, 1999). Institutions receiving funds may attach further restrictions for applicants. For example, the Metropolitan Center for Urban Education at New York University requires students to reside on Staten Island and gives preference to students with disabilities (NYU Upward Bound, 2000).

Selection of students is most often made upon the recommendation of the students' building principal and/or teachers, but social workers, clergy, or other interested parties may refer students as well (Upward Bound, 2000). Once identified as eligible for Upward Bound, interested students must complete a needs assessment so that the institution to which they are applying can determine eligibility. The following questions from one university's application serve as an example:

- What are your educational plans?
- What are your plans for after high school (vocational training, junior college, four-year college, work, or military)?
- Do you know what type of career you would like to pursue?
- In which of the following areas do you need information: study skills, test-taking skills, self-awareness, decision making, financial aid, etc.?
- Are you satisfied with your grades? (UNT Upward Bound, 1998).

This university also requires that parents submit tax returns to determine financial status, sign that they understand the program, and indicate they agree to their child's participation. Students must indicate their agreement to remain in the program and seek a postsecondary education. The University of Georgia requires students to sign a contract in which they agree to sustain at least a 2.5 grade point average in their regular studies, maintain attendance, and participate in all activities (UGA Upward Bound, 2000). This university bases each student's stipend on participation at the tutorial/counseling sessions.

Services. The college or agency delivering the services applies for and delivers the type of academic program best suited for students in their area, but all Upward Bound projects must provide:

- Instruction in reading, writing, study skills, and other subjects necessary for success in education beyond high school.
- Academic, financial, or personal counseling.
- Exposure to academic programs and cultural events.
- Tutorial services for Upward Bound classes as well as those taken in the student's local school.
- Mentoring programs. Students are closely monitored so staff can intervene should the students experience problems.
- Information on postsecondary education opportunities.
- Assistance in completing college entrance and financial aid applications.
- Assistance in preparing for college entrance examinations.
- Work study positions to expose participants to careers requiring a postsecondary degree (Upward Bound, 2000).

Additionally, legislation permits the award of stipends to participants of approximately $60 a month during the summer and $40 a month during the school year (Hexter, 1990). These stipends help to offset income students lose from part-time employment due to their participation in Upward Bound. Some families who live in poverty depend upon financial help from their children. Therefore, providing stipends is critical to these students' decision to take part in the program.

Within the prescribed parameters, services provided to students may vary according to the interests of the institution. For example, the Metropolitan Center for Urban Education at New York University focuses its Upward Bound program primarily on students with disabilities and designs services around these students' unique needs (NYU Upward Bound, 2000). The University of Minnesota offers a fairly unique integrated course of study which has been particularly successful with their TRIO Program students (Hixson, 1981).

Academic Support. Upward Bound project directors consistently and increasingly emphasize academic improvement as a goal for participants (Fasciano & Jacobson, 1997). Supplemental to their regular studies and outside of regular school hours, students attend classes provided by Upward Bound. Students travel to the host institution for instruction and tutoring and/or receive it at their home school. Instructors coordinate their Upward Bound instruction with what students are receiving during the school day. For example, one Texas university requires students to attend five Upward Bound classes each week, alternating instructional delivery between the university and the student's home school. If a student is deficient in one particular area such as English or math, instruction is primarily focused on that subject (Brooks, 2000).

Each host site outlines the rules and regulations that students must follow to remain in the program. For example, the Upward Bound guidelines at Texas A&M University-Commerce state, "Any student who misses a class period or any other related scheduled activity without an excuse will appear before the Student Council and the Project Director for disciplinary action" (Brooks, 2000, p. 1). Similar rules are outlined for such contingencies as absences, tardies, late assignments, and misbehavior.

Winter and Summer Programs. Students are involved in weekly program activities during most of the regular school year. Participating on Saturdays and after school at either their own school or the program site, participants meet with counselors, receive instruction, and are tutored.

The summer program is more intense. The summer component is usually designed to simulate a college experience and often involves full-time residence on a college campus (Myers & Schirm, 1997). Therefore, students usually become residents at the college or university providing the Upward Bound services and live in dormitories alongside regular college students for six weeks during the summer. During this time students attend classes, are tutored, receive counseling, and attend cultural events. Projects offer a selection of about 14-20 courses during the summer and an average of 12 or fewer courses during the academic year (Myers & Schirm, 1997).

The Summer Bridge Component occurs during the summer following students' graduation from high school and is specifically designed to aid student's transition from high school to postsecondary environments. Along with classes and tutoring in basic academic areas, students may enroll in and receive credit for college courses. Training for taking the PSAT, SAT, and ACT is also made available. Interaction with guest speakers and taking field trips—including visits to other college campuses—also enhance the transition to college.

Cultural Exposure. One objective of Upward Bound is to provide opportunities for students to expand their cultural awareness. Students attend theatre productions, visit museums and art galleries, and travel to nearby historical sites. For some students these activities provide an initial exposure to cultural events and for some the first opportunity to travel beyond the bounds of their home town.

Counseling and Guidance. Most students receive psychological and social skills training while they are in the Upward Bound Program. While peer counseling is one method for dealing with students' personal problems, in some instances the institution's counseling department may conduct more formal assessments of students and even provide small group and individual counseling. Issues such as sex, pregnancy, and drugs are common topics in counseling sessions and, in summer, when students are removed from their ordinary circumstances, they are free to discuss more sensitive family issues and work to define what constitutes a healthy home environment (R. Brooks, personal communication, Aug. 23, 2000). Other topics of discussion include career opportunities, time management, problem solving, communication, and interpersonal relationships.

Summary. Upward Bound is a TRIO program that plays an important role in the lives of thousands of students, yet the project is limited to those who are fortunate enough to be included. Unfortunately, many students do not reside near to a college or university or to one that offers TRIO services. While new programs are added each year, many miss the opportunity to participate and, for them, significant barriers to receiving a college education remain.

Upward Bound Math and Science Programs

One branch program of Upward Bound is the Math and Science program that also targets students from low-income families for aid but more specifically helps participants recognize their potential to excel in math and science. Students are offered classes in computer technology, English, foreign language, and study skills along with math and science instruction. Entrance requirements mandate that applicants be eligible to participate in the Upward Bound program and have completed the ninth grade, although they do not have to be participating in a regular Upward Bound program (Upward Bound, 1999). Government records show that more than 124 programs served students throughout the country in 2000 (Upward Bound Math/Science, 2000). Each program serves about 50 students.

Talent Search

The Talent Search component of the TRIO Programs is an early intervention program that serves students in grades six through twelve. As with Upward Bound, those served must be both low-income and potential first-generation college students. A 1968 amendment to Title IV of the Higher Education Act of 1965 that created Talent Search stipulated that participants must have "exceptional potential" for postsecondary education (Hexter, 1990). By the year 2000, 323,541 Americans were enrolled in 361 Talent Search Programs (Talent Search, 2000). Approximately half of the Talent Search Programs are administered by postsecondary institutions and half by community agencies. A study of TRIO Programs by Waldman, Myers, Jacobson, and Moore (1997) showed that Talent Search more often targeted middle schools than high schools.

Rosenbaum (1992) summarized the three major goals of Talent Search:

1. Identifying youth of extreme financial and cultural need with an exceptional potential for postsecondary education and encouraging them to complete secondary school and undertake further education.
2. Publicizing existing forms of student financial aid, including aid furnished under the Higher Education Act.
3. Encouraging secondary school or college dropouts of demonstrated aptitude to reenter educational programs (p. 104).

The Code of Federal Regulations (Talent Search, 1999) specifies that those agencies receiving Talent Search dollars may provide the following services:

- Academic, financial, career, or personal counseling including advice on entry or re-entry to secondary or postsecondary programs.
- Career exploration and aptitude assessments.
- Tutorial services to help students achieve in their academic classes.
- Information on postsecondary education.
- Information on student financial assistance.
- Assistance in completing college admissions and financial aid applications.
- Assistance in preparing for college entrance exams.
- Mentoring programs to give students personal attention when problems arise.
- Special activities for sixth, seventh, and eighth graders.
- Workshops for the families of participants.

An advantage of this wide array of services is that they increase students' chances for entering and completing college, chances that improve if students subsequently take advantage of other TRIO Program services. One drawback is that Talent Search project directors sometimes attempt to provide interventions with a limited number of program staff (Hexter, 1990). "In a T S [Talent Search] program in the West, for example, five counselors each have caseloads of more than 200 students..." (p. 51).

Student Support Services

The Student Support Services Program (SSS) is a TRIO program that centers on helping students while they are in college or engaged in other postsecondary educational programs. The goals of SSS are to increase the college retention and graduation rates of its participants and facilitate the process of transition from one level of higher education to the next (Student Support

Services, 1999). For example, students who are obtaining an associate's degree are encouraged to continue on to a four-year program and bachelor degree students are urged to pursue graduate studies (U.S. Department of Education, 1994). The government requires that SSS provide students with:

- Instruction in basic study skills.
- Tutorial services.
- Academic, financial, or personal counseling.
- Assistance in securing admission and financial aid for enrollment in four-year institutions.
- Assistance in securing admission and financial aid for enrollment in graduation and professional programs.
- Information about career options.
- Mentoring.
- Special services for students with limited English proficiency.

Only institutions of higher education may sponsor SSS Programs and must insure that SSS participants are offered financial aid packages sufficient to meet their full financial needs. In 2000, 796 colleges and universities nationwide were host sites for SSS (U. S. Department of Education, 1994).

Educational Opportunity Centers

Educational Opportunity Centers (EOC) provide counseling and information on college admissions to qualified adults who wish to pursue a postsecondary education. A major goal is to counsel participants on how to obtain financial aid by informing them of the options and helping them fill out applications. As with other TRIO Programs, the intent is to increase enrollment in postsecondary institutions.

EOC projects may be conducted by institutions of higher education such as colleges and universities, but public and private not-for-profit agencies and organizations may receive funding as well. As with Upward Bound, eligibility for EOC services also requires participants to reside near to where services are provided. Additionally, participants must be at least 19 years old and two-thirds must be potential first-generation college students and low-income persons; those under 19 may be served only if services of a Talent Search Program are not available (Educational Opportunity Centers, 2000).

According to guidelines, Educational Opportunity Centers may conduct public campaigns to inform communities about opportunities for postsecondary education and training (Educational Opportunity Centers, 1999). They may also provide the following services:

- Academic advice and assistance in course selection.
- Assistance in completing college admission and financial aid applications.
- Assistance in preparing for college entrance examinations.
- Guidance on secondary school reentry or entry to a General Educational Development (GED) program or other alternative education program.
- Personal counseling.
- Tutorial services.
- Career workshops and counseling.
- Mentoring programs involving elementary or high school teachers or faculty members at institutions of higher education.

While these requirements are similar to Upward Bound and Talent Search in some respects, they focus more intensely on disseminating information and providing counseling about postsecondary education to disadvantaged students.

Funding

In 2000, Title IV made up 97% of the money appropriated under the Higher Education Act and made 42 billion dollars available to students. Government programs, through Title IV, provided aid to about seven million students through avenues such as grants, scholarships, and TRIO (Federal TRIO Programs, 2000).

Institutions of higher education, public or private not-for-profit agencies, a combination of institutions, agencies, and organizations, and in exceptional cases, secondary schools may apply for government TRIO grants. The amount of money granted to a particular institution depends upon the quality of the grant proposal, the funds available, and the number of youth eligible to participate from targeted schools. Funding is granted for a four-year period after which institutions must reapply.

Funding for TRIO Programs is steadily increasing. For example, in 1999, $220,500,637 was granted for Upward Bound services across the country serving about 52,960 students (Upward Bound, 2000). The average award to each of the 772 participating institutions was $285,623. The budget for 2000 increased to $228.7 million. Funds for other TRIO Programs are expanding as well. Upward Bound Math and Science and EOCs were funded at approximately $29 million in 1999 and $30 million in 2000.

Success of TRIO Programs

The graduates of TRIO reveal its success. "TRIO college graduates are working in business, industry, government, medicine, law, education, communications, sales, finance, politics, transportation, publishing, law enforcement, computer science and technology, engineering, and accounting" (Federal TRIO Programs, 2000). Of all the programs in TRIO, the success of Upward Bound and its graduates has been evaluated most extensively (Hexter, 1990). Long-term studies demonstrate positive effects on college participation. Students in Upward Bound are four times more likely to earn an undergraduate degree than those students from similar backgrounds who did not participate in TRIO (Federal TRIO Programs, 2000).

A study of Upward Bound by Myers and Schirm (1997) showed that, in comparison to a control group, (a) participants and their parents had higher educational expectations and higher parent involvement, (b) participants earned more academic credits during their high school years, particularly in English, social studies, and science, and (c) Hispanic students benefited most from the program. Moore (1997) found that the longer students remained in the program, the more likely they were to complete their college education. A study by Waldman et al. (1997) showed that students who stay in Upward Bound are more likely to attend college than other students, even those from high-income families. Myers and Schirm (1997), however, found that a troubling number of students—37%—drop out in the first year of Upward Bound, most often to take a job.

Similar to the results of studies on Upward Bound are the findings of an extensive examination of Student Support Services. Students who do attend college and join the SSS Program are more likely to remain in college than those from similar backgrounds who did not participate in the program (Chaney, Muraskin, Cahalan, & Goodwin, 1998). Those who took full advantage of the program were the most successful.

School Leaders' Role in TRIO Programs

Primary supervision of the TRIO Programs lies with the host institution receiving the funding, yet the role of the middle or high school leaders who recruit and screen students is crucial to the programs' success. These programs require an educator who can look beyond race, poverty, and gender to search for students whose eyes light up at the prospect of a college education. Needed here are principals, teachers, and counselors who recognize students with keen minds who are prevented by tradition and circumstances from expanding their horizons.

Upward Bound, in particular, requires the support of local school administrators and their staffs. Institutions of higher education contact neighboring schools for recommendations and depend upon the ability of educators to select students who can profit the most from the type of aid TRIO Programs offer. The challenge to building principals and their staffs is to take the time required to build close ties with project directors and teachers.

In regard to Upward Bound, some target schools have staffs who are supportive and involved in a broad range of activities (Waldman et al., 1997). In these schools, staff members are active in recruiting students, plan collaboratively with Upward Bound staff, and even work as instructors for the program. Parent support for their children while in Upward Bound further enhances student success and should be facilitated by the fact that parents of Upward Bound applicants tend to have higher levels of involvement in their children's schoolwork and in discussions about future education than the parents of similar students not in the program (Myers and Schirm, 1997).

Principals interested in accepting the challenge to help disadvantaged students break the barriers to a postsecondary education should make themselves aware of what the TRIO Programs have to offer and educate their staff accordingly. Principals and teachers can work to gain the confidence and trust of students who are highly capable of attending college but who are unaware of the available opportunities. Home visits may be necessary to persuade parents of the long-term merits of a postsecondary education for their child, especially when sacrifices will be required.

Finally, principals should develop a working relationship with the host institutions of the TRIO Programs so that trust is established and lines of communication remain open. Student success is far more likely when all interested parties care about students and are concerned enough to work together.

Summary

The information offered here is for school administrators and staff members whose duties include facilitating the success of a TRIO program but who are unaware of what the programs encompass. Educators who find themselves in this position are urged to make themselves aware of what nearby programs have to offer and then become personally involved in identifying and actively recruiting eligible students for these programs. Educators who have a strong sense of care and concern for students are advised to initiate collaboration between the host TRIO organization and the school so that the students are encouraged from all fronts to do what is necessary to prepare for and then complete a college education. The high drop out rate exhibited by Upward Bound students serves as an example of the type of opportunity for principals, counselors, and teachers to extend their concern. When teachers, counselors, and principals continuously seek out a potential dropout to offer personal support and provide the necessary guidance when problems appear insurmountable, the student is more likely to remain in school. Becoming advocates for students is, after all, educators' mission for all students.

TRIO Programs are not offered in all schools. Educators in these schools must themselves meet the challenge to encourage and support disadvantaged students to seek a postsecondary education. Educators can initiate such efforts by arranging for students to visit college campuses, informing students of financial aid possibilities, and displaying high scholastic expectations. Again, becoming advocates for students by showing care and concern is the key.

Applying Your Knowledge

You are the principal of a middle school and have been asked by a nearby university to identify some students for their Upward Bound program. You know the value of Upward Bound for disadvantaged students so you ask the teachers in your building for their cooperation in targeting students who would best be served by this program. Two teachers suggest that John, a bright, hard-working boy, would likely succeed in college given the opportunity and some encouragement. You make a visit to John's home to talk with his parents about Upward Bound and find that they would like him to have this opportunity but they cannot afford to pay his expenses. John listens to what you and his parents have to say. He looks thoughtful and responds, "I know that this is a good program but it requires that I spend most of my Saturdays and a part of my summer at the university. I want to join but feel I should not for two reasons. First, I have a weekend job which pays for my clothes, school expenses, and helps pay for groceries at home. I work full-time in summer, earning enough to help my younger brothers and sisters as well. My parents count on this income. Second, I enjoy playing football and would rather invest my time and energy there. The coach says I have a future in sports."

Questions:

1. How would you respond to John's arguments?
2. Is there anyone else you could ask for help in resolving John's dilemma?
3. Should you interfere with John's decision?
4. If you had too many qualified students for the university's limited number of openings, would your decision regarding John be affected?

Questions for Thought

1. What are the major advantages and disadvantages of each of the TRIO Programs?
2. The Upward Bound Program serves students within close proximity to a college or university. What, if anything, should be done for students who do not live near to a college or university?
3. Should the government be involved in programs that serve such small numbers of students and is the expense worth the outcome?
4. Should students who graduate from college with the aid of these programs be required to give something back in return for what was given them? If so, what would that be?

For Further Information Online

Educational Opportunity Centers **www.trioprograms.org**
Federal TRIO Programs **www.trioprograms.org**
Talent Search **www.trioprograms.org**
Upward Bound **www.trioprograms.org**
Also contact your local colleges and universities

References

Brooks, R. (2000). *Pressing toward the mark of high moral character, education, leadership liberation (Upward Bound Rules and Regulations)*. Commerce, TX: Texas A&M University-Commerce Press.

Chaney, B., Muraskin, L. D., Cahalan, M. W., & Goodwin, D. (1998). Helping the progress of disadvantaged students in higher education: The federal Student Support Services Program. *Educational Evaluation and Policy Analysis, 20*(3), 197-215.

Educational Opportunity Centers. 34 Code of Federal Regulations §644 (U.S. Government Printing Office 1999).

Educational Opportunity Centers (2000, February 25). [Online]. U.S. Department of Education. < http://www.trioprograms.org> [2000, August 28].

Fasciano, N. J., & Jacobson, J. E. (1997). *A grantee survey report. A 1990's view of Upward Bound: Programs offered, students served, and operational issues.* Washington, DC: U. S. Department of Education.

Federal TRIO Programs. (2000, August 23). [Online]. U.S. Department of Education. <http://www.trioprograms.org/ > [2000, September, 25].

Hexter, H. (1990). *A description of federal information and outreach programs and selected state, institutional and community models.* Background paper number three. Washington, DC: Advisory Committee on Student Financial Assistance (ERIC Document Reproduction Service No. ED 357 686).

Hixson, B. E. (1981, November). *The integrated course of student in the general college TRIO Program.* Paper presented at the Annual Conference of the Mid-American Association of Educational Opportunity Program Personnel, Fontana, WI.

Library of Congress, Congressional Research Service, U. S. Department of Education. *Major Program Trends, Fiscal Years 1980-1990.* (Washington, DC: CRS, 1989), unpublished.

Meyers, D. E., & Shirm, A. L. (1997). *The national evaluation of Upward Bound. The short-term impact of Upward Bound: An interim report.* Washington, DC: U.S. Department of Education.

Moore, M. T. (1997). *A 1990's view of Upward Bound: Programs offered, students served, and operational issues.* Washington, DC: U.S. Department of Education.

Mortenson, T. (1995, May.). Educational attainment. *Postsecondary Education Opportunity, 35,* 1-16.

NYU Upward Bound. (2000, May 12). [Online]. Metro Center for Urban Education at New York University. < http://www.nyu.edu/education/metrocenter/ >[2000, Sept. 25].

Rosenbaum, J. E. (1992). *Review of two studies of Talent Search.* U.S. Department of Education Office of Policy and Planning's Design Conference for the Evaluation of the Talent Search Program (pp. 103-132). Washington, DC: U.S. Government Printing Office.

Student Support Services. 34 Code of Federal Regulations §646 (U.S. Government Printing Office 1999).

Talent Search, 34 Code of Federal Regulations §643 (U.S. Government Printing Office 1999). Talent Search. (2000, May 26). U.S. Dept. of Education. <http://www.trioprograms.org/> [2000, Sept. 26].

UGA Upward Bound. (1999, July 15). [Online]. University of Georgia. <http://www.arches.uga.edu/Prolong.html> [2000, Sept. 25].

UNT Upward Bound. (1998, Oct. 23). [Online]. University of North Texas. <http://www.unt.edu/> [1998, Sept. 28].

Upward Bound. 34 Code of Federal Regulations §645 (U.S. Government Printing Office 1999). Upward Bound. (2000, July 27). [Online]. U.S. Dept. of Education. <http://www.trioprograms.org/ > [2000, Sept. 29].

Upward Bound Math/Science Program. (2000, Aug. 23). [Online]. U.S. Dept. of Education. < http://www.trioprograms.org/ > [2000, Sept. 26].

U.S. Dept. of Education, Division of Student Services. (1994). *Federal Trio Programs and the school, college, and university partnerships program.* Washington, DC: U.S. Government Printing Office.

Waldman, Z., Myers, D., Jacobson, J., Moore, M. T. (1997). *A report on Upward Bound target schools. A 1990's view of Upward Bound: Programs offered, students served, and operational issues.* Washington, DC: U.S. Department of Education.

Chapter 5

Vocational-Technical and Career Education

David Drueckhammer

Vocational-Technical education has a rich history of providing students with job skills, career awareness, leadership training, and applied academic training.

David Drueckhammer

Objectives:
- **Discuss the history of vocational education.**
- **Identify the types of vocational-technical and career education programs.**
- **Discuss the benefits of vocational-technical and career education programs.**
- **Identify student leadership opportunities available in vocational-technical and career education programs.**

The Carl D. Perkins Vocational and Applied Technology Education Act Amendment of 1990 defines vocational-technical education as organized educational programs offering sequences of courses directly related to preparing individuals for paid or unpaid employment in current emerging occupations requiring training other than a baccalaureate or advanced degree (Public Law 101-392 § 521[41]). Programs include competency-based applied learning which contributes to an individual's academic knowledge, higher-order reasoning, problem-solving skills, and occupational-specific skills necessary for economic independence as a productive and contributing member of society.

Vocational-technical education programs are focused on specific job skills. Programs are designed to provide career awareness and skills that will enable students to find employment after leaving school (Imel, 1993). Programs focus on the employment demands and needs of the region. Thus, school officials need to determine which programs are most vital for their geographic region and plan accordingly. Redirecting existing programs in a school is usually the approach taken to insure that programs meet the needs of the school system (Pucel, 1998). Generally, the changing of existing curriculum is more acceptable to a community than terminating present programs.

Vocational-technical education programs must focus on the intent of the program, have a well-organized curriculum, and provide substantial technical and academic depth so that students have numerous options upon completion of high school (Catri, 1998). The curriculum should increase the options available to students (Bottoms, 2000) and be of sufficient educational value to enable students to (a) find employment after program completion, (b) enter higher-level post-secondary technical training that is related to the secondary program, (c) or enter a traditional college or university degree program (Catri, 1998). Students well-trained in a technical area often find-higher paying employment both in terminal careers or as part-time workers pursuing additional education.

As students become interested in preparing for employment in a particular occupation, they discover subjects such as mathematics, science, communication skills, and social science are needed to be proficient in their technical field (Division of Vocational and Technical Education, 1991). The relevance of these topics increases as the learners experience real world problems and search for solutions (Prescott, Edling, & Loring, 1996). In this way vocational-technical education teaches academic knowledge using an applied approach and assists academic teachers in providing relevance to their instruction. Vocational and academic teachers may choose to coordinate instruction to maximize the positive influence of vocational-technical education on academic instruction. Administrators are often catalysts for activities within the school that lead to improved interaction between academic and vocational-technical teachers and programs.

Some view career education as education that helps students develop an awareness of career opportunities and prepares them for employment in careers of interest. The elementary school program helps students develop an awareness of career opportunities, the value of work, and a positive attitude about work. The middle school curriculum continues this educational process by providing exploratory experiences. The middle school student should become aware of educational preparation needed to be successful in careers. In high school the student further explores the world of work and aptitudes in relation to particular occupations. This may include specialized vocational-technical education.

The objectives of public school vocational-technical education programs vary somewhat depending upon the desires of school system and state guidelines. However, Wenrich, Wenrich, and Galloway (1988) state that the basic objectives of most vocational-technical education programs include:

1. Meeting the job training needs of students to fit the employee needs of business and industry.
2. Increasing the options available to students as they complete their high school education.
3. Serving as a motivating force for students in other areas of learning.

The History of Vocational-Technical Education

As outlined by Finch and McGough (1982) vocational-technical education has a rich and extensive history. This history was influenced by the changing needs of society, changes in employment, and federal legislation. The following summary of legislation includes only the major, most defining, acts that influenced vocational-technical education.

The Morrill Land Grant Act of 1862 established a public college in each state for the purpose of teaching agriculture and the mechanical arts. This act and the Hatch Act of 1887, which established state agricultural experimental stations, created a need for the education of the public in agriculture and related topics. As colleges and experimental stations discovered new technology that could improve the economic situation of agriculturists, legislators became aware of the need for educating non-college bound students. As a result, the Smith-Lever Act of 1914 established the agricultural extension service for the purpose of educating the general population, primarily in the areas of agriculture and home economics. Out of this educational movement the early vocational education programs were born.

Although some schools offered education in agriculture and home economics as a local option, most vocational programs did not begin until the passage of the Smith-Hughes Act of 1917. This act provided a continuing federal appropriation for vocational education in agriculture, trades and industry education, and homemaking. The George-Dean Act of 1936 increased funding for these programs and added funding for distributive or marketing education.

The George-Barden Act of 1946 increased federal funding, provided more flexibility, and permitted funds for equipment to be used for guidance and training of out-of-school youth. Funding was also provided for student organizations like the Future Farmers of America (FFA), the New Farmers of America (NFA), and the student organization for African-American students in segregated schools, thus expanding the role of the federal government in vocational-technical education. The Vocational Act of 1963 extended existing programs and developed new vocational education programs. It encouraged research and provided for work-study programs. Additionally, the act provided for training in agriculture skill areas. The act required 10% of home economics funds be used to train students for gainful employment (related jobs outside the home setting). Business and office occupation programs were funded for the first time under this appropriation.

The 1968 Amendments to the Vocational Act were intended to provide ready access to vocational training or retraining for persons of all ages in all communities. The training reflected actual or anticipated opportunities for gainful employment and was designed to meet the needs, interests, and abilities of the participants. The amendments provided funds for programs to train the disabled and disadvantaged and to develop post-secondary programs. This legislation greatly expanded the development of curriculum materials, encouraged research, and allowed for the purchase of equipment.

The Carl D. Perkins Act of 1984 (United States Department of Education, 2001, The Carl D. Perkins Vocational and Applied Technology Education Act, Public Law 101-392) replaced existing vocational educational legislation and marked a major change in funding from the federal government. This legislation did not provide funding for existing programs. Rather, the act provided for the improvement, innovation, and expansion of vocational-technical education programs. In addition, this legislation provided training for single parents and displaced homemakers. It worked to eliminate sex bias and stereotyping, and it encouraged research activities and vocational guidance and assistance for programs conducted by community-based organizations.

The Carl D. Perkins Vocational/Applied Technology Education Act of 1989 required states to become more accountable for the use of funds. It also established a formula for distribution of funds to local districts. The distribution stipulated that 70 % of the funding would be based on the district's number of students eligible for Chapter 1 services, 20% based on the number of students served by Rehabilitation Act Programs, and 10 % was to be based on enrollment in vocational programs.

Current Program Concentrations and Legislation

The Carl D. Perkins Vocational-Technical Education Act Amendments of 1998 provide the current federal funding for vocational-technical education. This legislation restructures and reforms programs previously authorized, establishing a new vision of vocational-technical education for the 21st century. The legislation establishes state performance accountability systems and provisions for nontraditional training and employment. Nontraditional training and employment includes careers in computer science, technology, and other emerging high skill occupations in which individuals from one gender comprise less than 25% of the individuals employed.

The vocational-technical education programs offered by states vary in curriculum content. However, most states offer programs with similar program areas. Most programs continue to be traditional; however local schools districts have the latitude to develop unique programs. A brief description of vocational-technical education program areas is provided.

Agricultural Science and Natural Resource Education

The purpose of this program is to improve human performance through education and training in food and environmental systems (Texas Education Agency, 2000, Agricultural Science and Natural Resources Education). The program is designed to prepare well-trained, entry-level employees for agricultural and natural resource business and industry. The program can be offered at both the middle school and high school levels. Most college and university agriculture students begin their agricultural education through this high school program

Business Education

Business education provides individuals with knowledge, skills, and abilities to meet needs for business employment and preparation for further instruction in higher education (Texas Education Agency, 2000, Business Education). Office and secretarial skills such as word processing and database management are stressed in this program. The curriculum trains students for a future in office-related occupations.

Health Science Technology

Health Science Technology provides an academic foundation with a healthcare emphasis through hands-on clinical experience and the knowledge and skills developed during the course of study (Texas Education Agency, 2000, Health Science Technology). The program provides entry-level job skills in the health occupation areas while providing students exposure to the field of health science.

Family and Consumer Sciences Education

Family and Consumer Sciences Education prepares students for personal and family life. It helps students address the challenges of living and working in a diverse, global society (Texas Education Agency, 2000, Family and Consumer Sciences Education). The program focuses on families and the business and industries related to well being. Areas of study include childcare, nutrition, clothing and fashions, and family finance.

Technology Education

Technology Education (TE) is a comprehensive experience-based educational program that allows students to investigate and experience the means by which humans meet their needs and wants, solve problems, and extend their capabilities (Texas Education Agency, 2000, Technology Education). Students gain knowledge and skills in the application, design, production and assessment of products, services, and systems. TE allows students to reinforce their academic knowledge and skills in a variety of activities and settings. It is generally organized into six content areas: (1) bio-related technology; (2) communication; (3) computer applications; (4) construction; (5) energy, power, and transportation; and (6) manufacturing.

Marketing Education

Marketing Education is the study of how the marketing process seeks to determine and satisfy the needs and wants of people who purchase goods and ideas (Texas Education Agency, 2000, Marketing Education). It includes businesses of all types and sizes (including not-for-profit organizations) using marketing in their local, regional, national, and global operations to direct the flow of products from the manufacturer to the ultimate consumer.

Trade and Industrial Education

Trade and Industrial Education covers a wide range of occupational skill areas. Typically these programs are highly specialized and provide training for specific employment areas (Texas Education Agency, 2000, Trade and Industrial Education). Examples include auto mechanics, cosmetology, and the building trades.

Student Organizations and Implementation of Programs

Student organizations are an integral part of vocational-technical education programs. The organizations provide students with the opportunity to develop the leadership skills needed to become leaders in government, community organizations, and the workplace. In addition, these organizations enhance the curriculum through educational activities, competitions, award programs, and scholarships for students. The activities are often motivational and encourage the development of interpersonal skills (Baldasard, 2001). Good vocational-technical education programs are often affiliated with specific state and national youth organizations. These youth organizations have undergone changes to keep them modern, current, and acceptable to students (Lasserre, 2001).

The youth organizations for each career area include:

- **Agricultural Science and Natural Resource Education** – The National FFA Organization   (formerly the Future Farmers of America).
- **Business Education** – Business Professionals of America and Future Business Leaders of America.
- **Health Science Technology** – Health Occupations Students of America.
- **Family and Consumer Science Education** – Family, Career and Community Leaders of America (formerly Future Homemakers of America).
- **Technology Education** – Technology Student Association.
- **Marketing Education** – DECA, An Association of Marketing Students (formerly Distributive Education Clubs of America).
- **Trade and Industrial Education** – Skills USA-VICA (formerly Vocational Industrial Clubs of America).

Information for each student organization is available through your state supervisor for the program area.

Each state has rules and guidelines for the implementation of vocational-technical education programs. Teachers and administrators should work closely with state officials to insure curriculum and program component compliance. State guidelines should fit within federal guidelines and requirements.

Contemporary Issues

Urban Programs

Large student numbers and significant economic resources often allow urban school districts the option of offering a wide range of vocational-technical programs. Programs are often specialized and connected with a local business (Hagen and Sherman, 2000). Some businesses and industries work with the local school district to support and develop programs to train workers. This has been a very effective way for businesses to promote a trained workforce and for school districts to utilize authentic settings to train students for employment.

Rural Programs

Rural school districts generally offer a smaller number of vocational-technical education programs and thus must serve a broader range of student interests within each program. Because they have traditionally been the major curricular offerings, Agricultural Science and Natural Resource Education and Family and Consumer Science Education are often the only vocational courses delivered at rural schools. These courses are particularly useful because they have a large degree of variety in the curriculum (Foster, Bell, and Erskin, 1995). As an example, an agriculture program may offer courses ranging from traditional plant and animal production to mechanical skills, computer applications, entrepreneurship, food processing, and natural resources. This variety gives the smaller school district the opportunity to be flexible in its offerings without having to make changes in teachers, facilities and equipment (Baldasard, 2001).

Tech Prep Programs

The Tech Prep philosophy of education has gained acceptance in many public school systems (Drueckhammer, 1994). Tech prep curricula are developed through the joint efforts of secondary schools, post-secondary institutions, business, and industry. The curriculum emphasizes academics using an applied approach to instruction as well as technical training. Students can generally earn post-secondary technical credit while enrolled in the secondary program. Careful coordination of the curriculum between the two levels allows for this credit.

Advisory Boards

The use of business and industry advisory boards can greatly enhance the quality and effectiveness of a vocational-technical program (Rainbolt, 1996). An advisory group has no administrative function and serves only to focus instructional programs on the needs of business and industry. The advisory group often provides advice on curricula, equipment, and facility issues. Careful consideration should be given to the selection of members for an advisory board. Members should be interested in the school's programs and be knowledgeable about vocational training.

Work-Based Programs

Cooperative work-based programs, or worked-based learning programs, have found wide-spread acceptance as a way for students to develop work place skills (Holderfield and McQueeny-Tankard, 2000). Students are generally given instruction during school time and are allowed to work in a pre-selected and supervised training station. The teacher, to insure the quality of the student's educational experience, should carefully establish training stations. Each student utilizes a training plan that includes the input from the student, teacher, employer, and parents. The teacher directing a work-based learning program must be knowledgeable in child labor laws and the requirements of the program. Most states require teachers to attend a certification workshop before directing a work-based learning program.

Teachers for Vocational-Technical Programs

As in any aspect of education, the most important factor to success of a vocational-technical program is the quality of the teacher. These teachers, however, are often in great demand (Guarino, Brewer, and Hove, 1999). The trade and industrial areas generally do not have teacher-training programs and must rely on people with industry experience as a source of teachers. School districts often find it difficult to be financially competitive and attract quality teachers in these areas. The highly knowledgeable auto mechanic or carpenter who has good interpersonal skills can generally locate a higher-paying job in the business sector than as a teacher.

School Leaders' Role in Vocational-Technical and Career Education

School leaders must understand the purposes and objectives of vocational-technical education programs if the programs are to be successful. School administrators, faculty and members of business and industry must work together to determine the educational needs of students and the employment needs of the area. Information from state workforce planning commissions and advisory committees can be of great value to a school leader. A wise leader will include vocational-technical teachers in the planning and development of the instructional program. Teacher ownership is a key ingredient in program development.

Effective school leaders encourage the development of strong youth organizations associated with the vocational-technical program areas. Through these organizations, students gain leadership skills and become involved with students who have similar career interests. These activities, along with awards and recognition provided through the youth organization, can positively affect student esteem. School leaders must recognize the student organization as an integral part of the instructional program. Teachers from a business or industry background may need assistance in organization and development of a student organization. The assignment of a mentor teacher to assist with student organization development should be considered.

Summary

Vocational-technical education has a rich history of providing students with job skills, career awareness, leadership training, and applied academic training. Programs should be of sufficient depth to provide students with up-to-date job skills and support for the academic programs of the school. A quality program includes an appropriate youth leadership organization and an advisory board to help keep the program current. A qualified teacher and administrative supervision and support are critical to maintaining quality instructional programs.

Applying Your Knowledge

You are the principal for a mid-sized suburban high school. The school's curriculum prepares students for college and includes no vocational-technical offerings. Most years about 50% of graduates enter post-secondary education programs. The school has had a low but consistent number of students who drop out before graduation. A growing number of students seem to be disinterested in the extracurricular activities of the school. The elected school board is made up of professional university-educated people and has focused on developing a college preparatory curriculum.

Questions:

1. How would the addition of vocational-technical education programs enhance your high school?
2. How would you determine student interest in vocational-technical education to insure adequate enrollment for program justification?

3. What approach would you take in determining which vocational-technical programs might be added to the school's offerings?
4. How will you secure school board and community support for the addition of vocational-technical education?

Questions for Thought

1. Should student interest or employment opportunities of the area be the major determining factor in deciding which vocational-technical programs should be offered?
2. Will the addition of vocational-technical education programs to the school reduce the drop out rate and increase student satisfaction for the non-college-bound student?
3. Should vocational programs serve only non-college-bound students?

For Further Information Online

Agricultural Science and Natural Resources **www.tea.state.us?Cate/agtech/index.html**
Family and Consumer Sciences Education **www.tea.state.tx.us/Cate/fcs-vso/index.htm**
Health Science Technology **www.tea.state.tx.us/Cate/healthsc/index.html**
Marketing Education **www.tea.state.tx.us/Cate/marketed/index.html**
Technology Education **www.tea.state.tx.us/Cate//teched/index.html**
Trade and Industrial Education **www.tea.state.tx.us/Cate/ti/index.html**

References

Baldasard, J. (2001, January). Small school, big opportunities. *FFA Advisors Making A Difference, 9*, 10.

Bottoms, G. (2000, November-December). Improving career/technical studies. *The Agricultural Education Magazine, 73*, 7.

Carl D. Perkins Vocational and Applied Technology Education Act (1990). Public Law 101-392.

Catri, D. B. (1998). Vocational education's image for the 21st Century. *ERIC Clearinghouse on Adult, Career, and Vocational Education,* Columbus, OH.

Division of Vocational and Technical Education (1991). *Incorporating applied learning techniques of basic skills into the secondary vocational education curriculum.* [Online].Arkansas State Department of Education. <http://www.texshare.edu/ovidweb/ovidweb.cgi> [2001, Jan.].

Drueckhammer, D. C. (1994). *A tech prep monograph for the agricultural sciences.* Texas Education Agency, Austin, TX.

Finch, C. R., & McGough, R. L. (1982). *Administering and supervising occupational education.* Englewood Cliffs, N.J.: Prentice-Hall.

Foster, R., Bell, L., & Erskin, N. (1995). The importance of selected instructional areas in the present and future secondary agricultural education curriculum as perceived by teachers, principals, and superintendents in Nebraska. *Journal of Agricultural Education, 36*, 1-7.

Guarino, C. M., Brewer, D. J., & Anders, W. (1999). Who's teaching and who will teach vocational education? Paper, *National Dissemination Center for Career and Technical Education,* Columbus, OH.

Hagen, L. R., & Sherman, M. J. (2000, November-December). Agriculture science and technology programs in urban markets: Adapt and thrive, stagnate and die. *The Agricultural Education Magazine, 73*, 12-13.

Holderfield, G., & McQueeny-Tankard, C. (2000, October). "It's the real world," partnership bridges gap between classroom and business. *The Technology Teacher, 60*, 19-21.

Imel, S. (1993). Vocational education's role in dropout prevention. *ERIC Clearinghouse on Adult, Career, and Vocational Education.* Columbus, OH.

Lasserre, M. (2001, January). A different kind of technology club. *Principal, 80,* 49-50.

Meyer, B. (2000, November/December). FFA Provides the Edge. *FFA Advisors Making A Difference, 9,* 3.

Prescott, C. A., Edling, W. H., & Loring, R. (1966, July). Education and work: Toward an integrated curriculum framework. A report on the Intergated System for Workforce Education Curricula Project. *Center for Occupational Research and Development, Inc.,* Waco, TX.

Pucel, D. J. (1998, December). The changing role of vocation education and the comprehensive high school. *ERIC Clearinghouse on Adult, Career, and Vocational Education.* Columbus, OH.

Rainbolt, B. (1996, November/December). Advisory committee key to success. *FFA Advisors Making a Difference, 1,* 4.

Texas Education Agency. (2000, November) *Agricultural Science and Natural Resources Education.* [Online]. <http://www.tea.state.us?Cate/agtech/index.html> [2001, Jan.].

Texas Education Agency. (2000, September) *Business Education.* [Online]. <http://www.tea.state.tx.us/Cate/bused/index.html> [2001, Jan.].

Texas Education Agency. (2000, September) *Family and Consumer Sciences Education.* [Online]. <http://www.tea.state.tx.us/Cate/fcs-vso/index.htm> [2001, Jan.].

Texas Education Agency. (2000, September) *Health Science Technology.* [Online]. <http://www.tea.state.tx.us/Cate/healthsc/index.html> [2001, Jan.].

Texas Education Agency. (2000, September) *Marketing Education* [Online]. <http://www.tea.state.tx.us/Cate/marketed/index.html> [2001, Jan.].

Texas Education Agency. (2000, September) *Technology Education.*[Online]. <http://www.tea.state.tx.us/Cate/teched/index.html> [2001, Jan.].

Texas Education Agency. (2000, September) *Trade and Industrial Education.* [Online]. <http://www.tea.state.tx.us/Cate/ti/index.html> [2001, Jan.].

Werich, R. C., Wenrich, J. W. & Galloway, J. D. (1988). *Administration of vocational education.* Homewood, Illinois: American Technical Publishers.

Chapter 6

Bilingual and English as a Second Language Programs

Rafael Lara-Alecio, Beverly J. Irby, and Doris J. Meyer

Language is enchanting, powerful, magical, useful, personal.
Language is our means of discovery of the world and our response
to the world. As teachers we serve as catalysts for our students
to make the best use of their two or more languages. Our
languages are the most powerful tools we have.

C. J. Olvando & V. P. Collier

Objectives:
1. Become aware of the historical perspective of bilingual and English as a Second Language (ESL) programs.
2. Become cognizant of legal issues affecting bilingual and ESL programs.
3. Describe various program delivery systems in bilingual ESL programs.
4. Be sensitive to contemporary issues in bilingual and ESL programs.
5. Consider the school leaders' roles in providing services and support to bilingual and ESL programs.

Historical Background

The increase in the Hispanic-language minority population and other language minority groups in the United States has provided public school districts' many opportunities to meet the educational needs of non-English speaking students. This section will review the history of bilingual education in American schools over the past 200 years and will also discuss the history of English as a Second Language (ESL) education programs in the United States.

Inception. Bilingual education programs are not new on the American educational scene. English was not always the language of instruction in public schools in the United States. From the mid-seventeenth century, classes were instructed in German in some mid-western states (Porter, 1998). While 600,000 elementary school children received instruction in German in rural areas and big cities, English survived (Kloss, 1977). In addition to German, bilingual programs in French and Scandinavian languages were implemented in American schools during the 18th and 19th centuries (Escamilla, 1989). Nineteenth-century laws authorized native language instruction in 12 states and territories, and children received instruction in languages as diverse as French, Norwegian, Czech, and Cherokee (Crawford, 1998). Waves of Italians, Poles, Germans, Russians, and Chinese also entered the American mainstream and made valuable contributions (Maceri, 1997) as English continued to survive. In several New England states, instruction was delivered in French in many parochial schools and in a few public schools; however, Greek was the language of instruction in Pittsburgh (Porter, 1998).

Wars and public sentiment influenced the decline of bilingual education programs. Cincinnati schools implemented English-German bilingual instruction in the late 19th and early 20th centuries to get their large population of German American students to abandon their private schools and attend public schools (Blanton, 1999). After World War I, public sentiment strongly opposed instruction in "any language but English—and especially not in German" (Porter, 1998, p. 2). Bilingual programs also waned under the influence of World War II (Escamilla, 1989). In fact, between the 1920s through the 1960s monolingualism flourished with English immersion or "sink or swim" policies dominating methods of instruction (ESC 19, 2001).

Longitudinal Review. The 1960s yielded two legislative actions that improved opportunities for English language learners:

- **Civil Rights Act: Title VI.** In 1964, Title VI prohibited discrimination on the basis of race, color, or national origin in the operation of federally funded programs.
- **The Bilingual Education Act, Title VII of the Elementary and Secondary Education Act of 1968.** This Act established federal policy for bilingual education for economically disadvantaged language minority students. It also allocated funds for innovative programs and recognized the unique educational disadvantages faced by non-English speaking students.

During the 1970s two major events influenced bilingual education. One was the lawsuit, *Lau v. Nichols* (1974), which was brought by Chinese parents in San Francisco and which resulted in a Supreme Court ruling that identical education did not constitute equal education under the Civil Rights Act. Congress also passed the Equal Educational Opportunity Act, which extended the *Lau v. Nichols* decision to all school districts. In 1978, Title VII was amended to emphasize transitional native language instruction and to expand the eligibility of services to students with limited English proficiency and permitted enrollment of English-speaking students in bilingual education programs.

In the late 1980s the Supreme Court issued a ruling in the lawsuit, *Phyler v. Doe* (1982), which denied the state's right to exclude children of illegal immigrants from public schools. In response to *Castañeda v. Pickard* (1983), in 1983 the Fifth Circuit Court of Appeals formulated three basic standards to determine school district compliance with the Equal Educational Opportunity Act:

- **Theory.** The school must pursue a program based on an educational theory recognized as sound.
- **Practice.** The school must actually implement the program with instructional practices, resources, and personnel to transfer theory to practice.
- **Results.** The school must not persist in a program that fails to produce results.

A second significant event occurred in 1983. Title VII was amended to allow for some native language maintenance, funding for English language learners with special needs, and support for family English literacy programs and teacher training. Once again in 1988, Title VII was amended to include increased funding for "special alternative" programs where only English was to be used, a three-year limit on Title VII participation, and fellowship programs for professional development.

The 1990s ushered in several comprehensive educational reforms in Title VII programming. Those reforms included the reinforcement of professional development programs, increased attention to language maintenance and foreign language instruction, improved research and evaluation at national, state, and local levels, additional funds for immigrant education, and participation of some private school students.

On December 20, 2000, Secretary Riley announced more changes to Title VII funded programs, which primarily focused on funding of dual language programs. Some 22 years had passed since Title VII had emphasized that English-speaking students be included in bilingual education. Earlier, in a comprehensive address on bilingual education on March 15, 2000, Richard Riley (2000), Secretary of Education, defended bilingual education and stressed the value of biliteracy. "For many, language is at the core of the Latino experience in this country, and it must be at the center of future opportunities for this community and for this nation. Parents and educators want all children to learn English because it is essential for success" (p. 2).

Historical Context for Bilingual Education for Hispanics. The ever-growing Hispanic student population has increased at five times the rate of the non-Hispanic population (Howe, 1994). This phenomenon has dramatically affected public school systems, especially those in urban areas (Howe, 1994). Hispanics accounted for 9% of the total United States population in 1990, and their numbers increased to over 11% of the total population by 1998 (Lester, 1999). Thirty-four million Hispanics currently live in the United States, an increase of more than 8,000,000 in only eight years (Gempel, 1999; Waldman, 2000a).

According to Waldman (2000), percentage-wise, Arkansas has had the largest Hispanic migration between 1990 to 1999 (up 170%), followed by Nevada (145%), North Carolina (129%), Georgia (120%), Nebraska (108%), Tennessee (105%), Oregon (89%), Iowa (89%), and South Carolina (78%). Other states showing over 50% increases are Utah, Idaho, New Hampshire, and Minnesota. The percentage of Hispanics who are very comfortable speaking both English and Spanish has doubled in the past four years while the percentages most comfortable speaking either language have declined. Since 1986, bilingualism has increased at work and in social situations (Waldman, 2000a).

Within the next five years Hispanics, the nation's fastest-growing minority group, are projected to be the largest, and likely the least educated, minority (Riley, 2000). Hispanic students are twice as likely as White students to experience poverty (U. S. Department of Education, 1994). Approximately 40% of them work below expected achievement levels by eighth grade, and only half of them graduate "on time" (Garcia, 1994). Hispanic expansion is permanent, and most Hispanics of all ages live in five states: California, Florida, Illinois, New York, and Texas (Gempel, 1999). Over 23% of the population of Houston, Texas alone are Hispanic (Waldman, 2000b).

History of ESL Education in the United States

The history of ESL education in the United States has been linked to the rich and poor alike. Foreign diplomats and university students were in need of ESL and around the same time in the early 1900s were the poor immigrant workforce (Crawford, 1999; Rosenblum, 1996). While schools and universities were involved in developing ESL programs for the elite, unions were organizing evening classes for factory workers to support the union and to be able to protect themselves in the workplace. Over the next six decades, ESL continued to be offered by the unions across the nation.

According to Crawford (1999), ESL was prescribed for language-minority children in schools in the 1950s. Although not widely used, "pull out" was the most common arrangement. Students were taken from regular classrooms between two and five times per week for a 45-minute period. By the 1960s it was determined that ESL students were learning English too slowly to keep up with their content subjects. Additionally, by the late 1970s and early 1980s so many of the language-minority students were being IQ tested in English that disproportionate numbers of them were placed in special education. During the 1990s, ESL gained popularity but continued to be a predominately "pull out" type program.

Program Descriptions

The following components should be considered when designing and implementing bilingual and ESL programs: (a) state guidelines, (b) student population to be served, and (c) district resources.

State Guidelines. Texas will be used as the example for state guidelines under this section. The statutory authority for services to English language learners (ELL) falls under Subchapter BB issued under the Texas Education Code §29.051-29.064, unless otherwise noted. The policy, §89.1201(a), indicates that every student in the state who has a home language other than English and who is identified as limited English proficient (LEP) shall be provided a full opportunity to participate in a bilingual education or English as a second language program. To ensure equal educational opportunity, as required in the Texas Education Code, §1.002(a), each school district shall:

1. Identify limited-English-proficient students based on criteria established by the state.
2. Provide bilingual education and English as a second language programs as integral parts of the regular program as described in the Texas Education Code, §4.002.
3. Seek certified teaching personnel to ensure that limited-English-proficient students are afforded full opportunity to master the essential skills and knowledge required by the state.
4. Assess achievement for essential skills and knowledge in accordance with the Texas Education Code, Chapter 39, to ensure accountability for limited-English-proficient students and the schools that serve them.

Furthermore, the Texas Education Code §89.1201(b) promotes the goal of bilingual education programs which is to enable limited English proficient students to become competent in the comprehension, speaking, reading, and composition of the English language through the development of literacy and academic skills in the primary language and English. Such programs are to emphasize the mastery of English language skills—as well as mathematics, science and social studies—as integral parts of the academic goals for all students to enable limited-English-proficient students to participate equitably in school.

The same policy, Texas Education Code §89.1201(c), addresses the goal of English as a second language program which is to enable limited-English-proficient students to become competent in the comprehension, speaking, reading, and composition of the English language through the integrated use of second language methods. Such programs shall emphasize the mastery of English language skills—as well as mathematics, science and social studies—as integral parts of the academic goals for all students to enable limited-English-proficient students to participate equitably in school.

The Texas Education Code §89.1201(d) states that bilingual education and English as a second language programs shall be integral parts of the total school program. Such programs shall use instructional approaches designed to meet the special needs of limited English proficient students. The basic curriculum content of the programs shall be based on the essential skills and knowledge required by the state.

The Texas Education Code §89.1205 requires the implementation of bilingual education and English as a second language programs. According to this section, a school district that has an enrollment of 20 or more limited-English-proficient students in any language classification in the same grade level district-wide shall offer a bilingual education program for all elementary grade levels, including prekindergarten through fifth, and sixth when it is clustered with elementary grade levels. Cooperative arrangements with other districts may be developed for the provision of services. For bilingual education programs, the Texas Education Code requires the provision of a dual-language program in prekindergarten through the elementary grades or an approved dual-language program which addresses the affective, linguistic, and cognitive needs of the limited-English-proficient students. In addition, school districts are authorized to establish a bilingual education program at grade levels in which the bilingual education program is not required. All LEP students for whom a district is not required to offer a bilingual education program shall be provided an English as a second language program. Implementation of this type of program takes place regardless of the student's grade level and home language and the number of such students.

Should a district not be able to establish a bilingual or English as a second language program, the district may request from the commissioner of education an exception to the programs and an approval to offer an alternative program. Waivers of certification requirements may be requested on an individual basis and are valid for only the school year for which they are negotiated.

The Texas Education Code §89.1210(b) indicates that the bilingual education program is to be a full-time program of instruction in which both the students' home language and English are used for instruction. The amount of instruction in each language should be commensurate with the students' level of proficiency in both languages and their level of academic achievement. The language proficiency assessment committee (LPAC) designates the students' level of language proficiency and academic achievement. According to the Texas Education Code §89.1210(d), instruction in an English as a second language program may vary from the amount of time accorded to instruction in English language arts in the regular program for non-limited English proficient students to total immersion in second language approaches. In Grades 6 or 7 through 12, instruction in English as a second language may vary from one-third of the instructional day to total immersion in second language approaches.

Student Population. Just as the law in Texas indicates that particular student language group populations should be considered when developing a program, all districts should determine the types of English language learners to be served. Many districts will find that their populations of language minority students are mobile, while others may be fairly stable. The language groups may be from a variety of language groups, educational levels, and cultural backgrounds. In Texas, most of the immigrants are of the Spanish-speaking language group from Mexico or Central America. The district must consider the numbers of students from the particular language group, the previous educational levels of the students, and the culture of the students when developing bilingual or English as a second language programs.

District Resources. Resources for provision of services to English language learners vary from district to district and state to state. For example, programs may be dependent upon geographic location, upsurges in immigrant settlements, district enrollment, physical space, availability of certified teachers, and/or the ability to attract certified teachers through stipends. These resources could influence significantly the type of services the district will provide.

Administrative Options for Bilingual and English as Second Language Programs

What follows is a brief description of potential administrative arrangements districts may choose in developing and implementing programs in (a) bilingual education and/or (b) English as a second language. When districts consider the type of program arrangement that best suits their population, the following should be taken into account:

- The program should meet the linguistic, academic, and affective needs of students.
- The program should provide students with the instruction necessary to allow them to progress through school at a rate commensurate with their native-English speaking peers.
- The program should make the best use of district and community resources (McKeon, 1987).

In Texas, for example, the Texas Education Agency recommends a framework for the implementation of the *Texas State Plan for Education of Limited English Proficient Students* (ESC 19, 2000). Districts must have in place the following:

- Policies related to language minority students.
- A program design.
- Student identification procedures.
- An identified Language Proficiency Assessment Committee.
- A means for student assessment.
- A formalized parent authority and responsibility policy, procedure, and plan.
- A plan for staffing and professional development.
- A summer school program.
- A plan for monitoring and evaluating programs.

All of the above items should be on file and have documented evidence of implementation for compliance monitoring by the Texas Education Agency and for public consideration.

Bilingual Education Program Models

Educators cannot agree on a single definition or model for bilingual education. Definitions and delivery models are so broad that they tell little about the teaching and learning processes that occur in the classroom or about their variety and patterns of occurrence (Escamilla, 1989; Strong, 1986). Ramirez (1992) found the following:

> In recognition that limited-English-proficient students typically enter school with English language and content skills lower than their native English-speaking peers in mainstream classrooms, the instructional goal of the Bilingual Education Act is to provide limited-English-proficient students with special instructional support that would allow them to 'catch up' with their native-English-speaking peers. (p. 2)

In 1997 Secretary of Education Richard W. Riley stated that bilingual education makes certain that children whose native language is other than English receive the necessary grounding in academics while transitioning to all-English classrooms (Supik, 1998). The goal of bilingual programs is the acquisition of English skills by language-minority children so they can succeed in mainstream, English-only classrooms (Ramirez, 1992). A variety of bilingual program models make use of students' primary language while developing English (Moran, 1993).

Transitional. Transitional bilingual programs have been described as those in which the students' first language and English are used in some combination for instruction, and where the first language serves as a temporary bridge to instruction in English (Baca & Cervantes, 1989, Birman & Ginsburg, 1983; Bruce, Lara-Alecio, Parker, Hasbrouck, Weaver, & Irby, 1994; Peregoy & Boyle, 1993; Trueba, 1979). However, there is no single method for helping LEP students catch up with their peers, and there is no single definition for transitional bilingual education programs. According to Bruce, et al. (1997), we must improve our understanding of bilingual education and provide descriptive accuracy. These descriptions should reflect actual instructional practices and be validated through reliable classroom observations.

Early-Exit. Early-exit programs provide some initial instruction, primarily for the introduction of reading, and instruction in the first language is phased out rapidly (Rennie, 1993). Ramirez (1992) described the early-exit program as one where children receive some instruction in their primary language, one-half hour to an hour per day, usually limited to the introduction of initial reading skills, with all other instruction in English. By the end of second grade, students participating in the early-exit model are expected to be exited from the program and mainstreamed into English-only classrooms (Ramirez, 1992).

The terms early-exit and transitional bilingual education (TBE) have been used interchangeably to define the model that uses more English instruction at an earlier time in an effort to move children into mainstream English classrooms quickly (Glossary, 1998). In a discussion of the Ramirez study, Thomas (1992) referred to the early-exit program as transitional bilingual education and declared it the most commonly funded type of bilingual program.

Late-Exit. Late-exit programs serve LEP students in grades kindergarten through six and students receive 40% of their instructional time in Spanish (Ramirez, 1992). Students in late-exit programs, in contrast to the amount of time spent in early-exit programs, receive a minimum of 40% of their instructional time in Spanish language arts, reading, and other content areas such as mathematics, social studies, and/or science (Ramirez, 1992).

Immersion. Ramirez (1992) describes the immersion strategy as one where instruction is almost exclusively in English and where teachers have specialized training to meet LEP students' needs and have strong skills in students' receptive language. In an immersion program, English, the target language, is taught in the content areas and a strong language development component is included in each content lesson. The child's home language is used primarily to clarify English and, on a case-to-case-basis, a LEP student who begins the program in kindergarten is expected to be mainstreamed in two or three years. According to Moran (1993), confusion sometimes occurs when the immersion model is misinterpreted, programs are set up, minority children are placed in English-only programs with native English speakers, and the immersion concept is misused on submersion models.

Dual Immersion. Dual immersion is a bilingual program in which non-English-speaking students and native English-speaking students learn together in the same class (Riley, 2000). In a comprehensive address on Hispanic education, Secretary of Education Richard Riley promoted dual-immersion programs as a way to help students learn two languages at the same time (Riley, 2000).

Submersion. The submersion approach, often described as the "sink or swim" approach, calls for placement of LEP students in classrooms where only English is spoken. The student's first language is not used for instruction, and no special attempt is made to help overcome language problems (Ovando & Collier, 1998).

Dual-Language. Moran (1993) described dual-language as an adaptation of the French Immersion Model from Canada, a program where native English-speaking students are immersed in the minority language, Spanish, alongside native Spanish-speaking students. Dual language programs are designed to help all participating students become fluent in both English and in a second language. English-speaking children are placed in classrooms with non-English speakers and all instruction is in both languages. As research has shown, the most successful programs begin in prekindergarten and continue through the 6th grade. According to Secretary Riley, students will develop high levels of proficiency in their first and second language. Academic performance will be at or above grade level in both languages and students will develop greater cross-cultural awareness and knowledge.

Two-Way. Two-way bilingual programs (known also as two-way immersion), developmental bilingual, bilingual immersion, and dual-language programs have taken root in schools across the country (Two-Way Bilingual Education, 1994). These programs integrate two groups of students, language minority and language-majority, and provide instruction through the minority students' target language and the majority students' language, English, with the goal of bilingualism for both groups (Christian, 1994).

English as a Second Language Program Models

English as a second language program models are generally classified as (a) specialized, pull-out English as a second language programs which focus on linguistics or (b) English plus programs in which the native language may be used in instruction of content areas. English instruction is longer or may represent the entire instructional program (McKeon, 1987).

Pull Out. (Generally used in an elementary setting.) In the most expensive of all program models (Crawford, 1997), yet the most common and least effective (Thomas & Collier, 1997), the student receives specialized instruction in a separate classroom from his/her regular classroom during the day. The student is taken from his/her regular classroom for this special instruction. The teacher may be stationary on a campus or may be itinerant (shared between several campuses). Students from different first-language backgrounds may be separated into groups for instruction. In Texas, the teacher must have an endorsement in English as a second language; however, in other states teachers may or may not be trained in this field (O'Malley & Waggoner, 1984). Most English as second language teachers are not bilingual.

Class Period. (Generally used in a middle or secondary school setting.) English as second language instruction is provided during a regular class period. Students generally receive credit for the course, just as they would other courses in a departmentalized setting. Students may be grouped according to their level of English proficiency.

Sheltered English or Content-Based Programs. (Used primarily to date with secondary school students.) In such programs, English language learners from different language groups are placed together in classes where teachers use English as the language of instruction in the content areas of science, social studies, and sometimes mathematics. The language is adapted to the proficiency level of the students. Teachers may use gestures and visual aids to help students understand. A teacher certified in English as a second language offers instruction in this effective program. (The program is effective due to accessibility to a broader curriculum; it is more cost-effective than the pull out model.) Sheltered English or content-based programs may parallel virtually all mainstream academic curricular offerings or may consist of only one or two subjects (Chamot & Stewner-Manzanares, 1985; Ovando & Collier, 1998).

Structured English Immersion. In the structured English immersion approach, instruction should be provided in the child's home language, but the second language, English, is not used at all until students have a mastery of the first language commensurate with their age and extent of formal schooling. This approach strictly focuses on providing sufficient oral, reading, and writing skills so LEP youngsters can eventually transition into mainstream programs (Pardo & Tinajero, 1993). Most students are mainstreamed after being in a structured immersion program for two or three years (Rennie, 1993); however, English-only proponents have misnamed this program model and have left out the native language and use English only. This program has become another type of English as a second language content instruction in a self-contained classroom. Structured has become equated with highly structured materials that carry students through a step-by-step learning process. An example of such a program is Distar Reading. Structured immersion models have not proved to be effective due to the fact that the materials did not fit the process of natural second language acquisition (Ovando & Collier, 1998).

High Intensity Language Training (HILT) Programs. (Used primarily at the secondary level.) According to McKeon (1987), in the HILT design students of various language backgrounds are grouped for a major part of the school day. Students receive intensive instruction in English as a second language, usually for three hours a day in the first year of instruction, less in succeeding years (Chamot & Stewner-Manzanares, 1985). McKeon (1987) indicated that mainstreaming students into regular classrooms is accomplished on a subject-by-subject basis and usually begins with less linguistically demanding classes such as music, physical education, and art. She indicated that some models may include content-based or sheltered English classes.

Contemporary Issues

In this section fears, fallacies, and myths that contribute to criticism and negative opinions of bilingual education are discussed. These mistaken notions are often based on misconceptions about goals and practices (Krashen, 1997). Crawford (1998) sought to clarify 11 of the myths and misconceptions that surround bilingual education in America.

Myth 1: Bilingual Education Is Losing Ground

Critics have claimed that bilingual education is losing ground to other languages in the United States (Crawford, 1998). Fear and suspicion still surround bilingual education, causing many Americans to advocate the use of English-only in the classroom. Research data suggests that both native-born and immigrant Hispanics do learn and speak English (Santiestevan, 1991). Veltman (1988) found that Hispanics want their children to speak English. Santiestevan (1991) concluded that the use of Spanish does not endanger the English language. Maceri (1997) related that fear of bilingualism colors critics' opinions of bilingual education as they see English threatened by other languages. Aceves (1997) asserted that advocates for bilingual education indicate members of the majority culture cast skepticism and fear upon bilingual programs because the programs have the potential to empower and liberate the subordinate language students. Immigrants can appear less threatening when they abandon their native languages and cultural beliefs and embrace American ways and English (Shannon & Escamilla, 1999). Puente and Kasindorf (1999) reported that nativists who fear the "browning of America" predict Hispanics will form islands of an alien culture, reject American citizenship, and continue to speak Spanish.

Hispanic leaders who are proponents of bilingual education have strongly resisted the efforts of those that speak out in favor of eliminating bilingual programs and insist that everyone in America speak only English. The advocacy of English-only by opponents of bilingual education united Latino[1] leaders and led Raul Yzaguirre to compare Hispanics' opinion of U. S. English to Blacks' opinion of the Ku Klux Klan (Crawford, 1992).

In 1998 and in 2000, voters in California and Arizona, respectively, passed Propositions 227 and 203 which eliminated the use of the child's first language for instructional purposes except in special occasions. According to Cummins (2000), California's Proposition 227 had considerable impact on bilingual education; however, most dual-language or two-way immersion programs have remained in tact. These programs are targeted to develop biliteracy, bicultural, and bilingual skills and practices among language minority and language majority students.

Myth 2: Newcomers Are Slow to Learn English

Another commonly held myth is that newcomers in the United States are learning English slower now than in previous generations, according to Crawford (1998). In actuality, after fifteen years in the United States, three out of four immigrants speak English on a daily basis (Veltman, 1998). Over a two-year period, students in bilingual education receive only about three additional months of learning compared to students in other programs (Greene, 1998).

---

[1] We have used Hispanic and Latino interchangeably.

Myth 3: Total Immersion is Best

Crawford (1998) identified as a fallacy the notion that the best way to learn a language is through total immersion. This total immersion belief has become a hot political issue. Addressing the Cobb County Chamber of Commerce about improving education, former House Speaker Newt Gingrich stated, "When we allow children to stay trapped in bilingual education, where you do not learn English, we are destroying their economic future" (Roman, 1998, p. A-1). Netkin (1997), an opponent of bilingual education, claimed that children learn best through immersion and stated that research indicates too many students end up not speaking either language well.

Contrary to the belief of many educators that the best way for non-English-speaking children to learn English is through total immersion, research indicates that increased exposure does not necessarily mean faster English acquisition (Myths and Misconceptions, 1992). Research has not supported the immersion theory—also known as the "sink or swim" theory—that the more children are exposed to English the more English they will learn. School failure among second-language learners has occurred as a result of such programs (Geneses, 1987). Krashen (1999) disputed studies that claimed successes of immersion programs because the studies did not compare children in those programs with similar children in bilingual education.

Myth 4: Children Are Retained Too Long in Bilingual Classrooms

Another fallacy, according to Crawford (1998), is that children learning English are retained too long in bilingual classrooms at the expense of English acquisition. Maceri (1997) answered critics' claims that students stay too long in bilingual classrooms and explained that, although children have an ability to learn a language without acquiring a foreign accent, learning a language is not an easy task, and children learn slowly. Crawford (1998) maintained that children should not be rushed into mainstream classrooms before they are adequately prepared to succeed.

Collier and Thomas (1989) indicated that although children readily learn the conversational English used on the playground, it takes several years to acquire the cognitively demanding language used in academic pursuits. Ramírez (1992) stated that data documents that learning a second language takes six or more years. De Avila (1997) discussed how long it takes for a student to become proficient in English and added that, despite present data that seem to suggest approximately five to seven years, the issue remains subject to debate. DeLucca (1998) made it clear that if bilingual programs are to be effective they cannot have specific timelines for transitioning students from their native language to oral proficiency in English. Rather, they must have established criteria for ascertaining both native language literacy and English proficiency. Hakuta, Butler, & Witt (2000) conducted a study that addressed the question of how long it takes English learners to attain proficiency and concluded that "oral proficiency takes 3 to 5 years to develop, and academic proficiency can take 4 to 7 years" (p. 13).

In contrast, English-only approaches to bilingual education can interrupt language growth at a crucial state and have negative effects on achievement (Cummins, 1992). In discussing the pedagogy used at several school sites, Aceves (1997) concluded that effective acquisition of critical skills are best attained through use of the student's most comprehensible language. A student who has not yet acquired proficiency in English will have difficulties in a school that emphasizes English over the student's native language.

Myth 5: Bilingual Education Is Provided in Numerous Languages in a School District

That bilingual instruction is provided in scores of native languages by school districts was another fallacy identified by Crawford (1998). Literature indicates school districts generally do not provide instruction in numerous languages except in areas where groups have strong political clout. For example, "The accommodationist position of school officials in cities like Baltimore, Cincinnati, and St. Louis could not have been affected without substantial political strength in the German community" (Blanton, 1999, p. 30). Unlike these German communities, immigrant groups such as Italians, Czechs, and Poles did not have the political power to bring about accommodation from local school districts (Blanton, 1999).

In large cities it was and is not unusual for people from numerous linguistic backgrounds to live in the same neighborhood. Frey (1998) denied the reality of a melting pot theory and described population shifts in the 1990s that showed continued concentration of minority groups in metro areas and specific regions. When children speak a number of different languages, there are rarely enough students in each language group to make bilingual instruction practical for all, and the shortage of teachers makes it impossible (Crawford, 1998). For example, in an urban school district in southeast Texas, families living within two miles of a single elementary school speak 28 different languages, according to Home Language Surveys filled out by students' parents (Cavazos, Irby, Lara-Alecio, Meyer, & Mixon, 2000). The district cannot finance bilingual education in 28 languages, so bilingual instruction is offered only in Spanish to meet the educational needs of 18% of the district's Hispanic students. Approximately 9,000 children are served in bilingual education classrooms on nineteen bilingual campuses, 30% of the district's 64 schools (Cavazos, et al., 2000).

Myth 6: Bilingual Education Equals Instruction Mainly in Native Language

Another myth is that bilingual education means instruction mainly in students' native languages with little instruction in English (Crawford, 1998). Transitional bilingual education was developed with federal funds provided mostly by Title VII of the Elementary and Secondary Education Act (ESEA). In transitional programs subject matter is taught in the home language until the student has sufficiently developed proficiency in English to allow successful participation in all-English classrooms.

A majority of the bilingual programs today deliver a substantial portion of the instruction in English (Crawford, 1998). In an observational study of the instructional use of Spanish and English in elementary transitional bilingual classrooms, Breunig (1998) found that English was the language most frequently used in third grade bilingual classrooms. Teachers in bilingual classrooms speak only Spanish at the beginning of the school year and gradually transition into English (Bruce, Lara-Alecio, Parker, Hasbrouck, Weaver, & Irby, 1997). As students gain fluency in English, teachers increase the amount of instruction in English until students have the proficiency to transition into mainstream classrooms (Lara-Alecio et al., 1994).

Glenn (1991), a supporter of bilingual education, noted that the best setting for educating LEP students—and one of the best for educating any pupil—is a school where two languages are spoken without apology and where proficiency in both languages is considered a significant cultural and intellectual achievement. Cummins (1998) stressed that any adequate bilingual program should strive to develop literacy in both the student's native language and in English.

Myth 7: Bilingual Education Costs More

Crawford (1998) classified as a fallacy the claim that bilingual education is far more costly than English language instruction. Netkin (1997), an opponent of bilingual education, suggested that money is perhaps the most powerful reason bilingual educators persist in their beliefs and that, "The size of budgets designated for bilingual education depends on how many students are enrolled in the program, giving educators at all levels a big incentive to sign up even more students for bilingual programs" (p. 2). Cardenas (1998) countered, "...the cost of bilingual education is trivial compared to the cost of the failure to provide an adequate education to a large segment of the school community" (p. 2). All programs serving limited-English-proficient students require additional teacher training, instructional materials, and administration, so they cost a little more than programs for native English speakers; however, the differential is modest in most cases (Crawford, 1998). Cummins (1993) stated that immersion strategy programs and bilingual programs are likely to be comparable in cost.

Myth 8: Dropout Rates Are Higher in Bilingual Education

Crawford (1998) also discussed the fallacy that disproportionate dropout rates for Hispanic students demonstrate the failure of bilingual education. There is no question that the dropout rates for Hispanic students are disproportionate to those of other groups (Krashen, 1999); however, Krashen (1999) indicated that this argument is circumstantial because Hispanic students are the largest client of bilingual education programs. In 1994, the percentage of high school dropouts among students 17 to 24 years old was 30% for Hispanics, 13% for African Americans, and 8% for Whites (Larsen & Rumberger, 1999). In 1998, the attrition rates for the Texas county in which this observational study was conducted was 60% for Hispanics, 32% for Whites, and 49% for African Americans (IDRA, 2000). In 1999, the attrition rates for the Texas school district in which this observational study was conducted was 60% for Hispanics, 32% for Whites, and 49% for African Americans (Cavazos, Irby, Lara-Alecio, Meyer, & Mixon, 2000).

High Hispanic dropout rates cannot be directly attributed to the failure of bilingual education. While this is frequently true, research indicates other factors that account for the large dropout rate of Hispanic students. Most Hispanic students do speak Spanish, but most Hispanic students do not enroll in bilingual education (Krashen, 1999). Lockwood (1996) identified low academic achievement and grade retention as reasons students do not finish school. Lockwood and DiCerbo (2000) cited the absence of personal attention by school staff regarding students' schooling, large classes, boring instruction that students cannot relate to the realities of their lives, and students' own limited vision of the future as factors that encourage students to drop out. Krashen (1999) cited several factors that contribute to the Hispanic dropout rates, including social class, time spent in the United States, the presence of print in the student's home, and other family circumstances.

Factors influencing dropout rates are not necessarily related to school. Outside factors such as students having to work to help support the family or having to care for younger siblings frequently have more weight than a school district's resources. Undocumented children in the United States face stress and challenges additional to those of other students and many leave school before graduation because they live under threat and suspicion (Hunter & Howley, 1990). After examining numerous studies to determine the reasons for the disproportionately high dropout rates of Hispanic students, Krashen (1999) concluded, "There is no evidence that bilingual education results in higher dropout rates" (p. 7).

Myth 9: Benefits of Bilingual Education Inconclusive

According to Crawford (1998), the argument that research is inconclusive on the benefits of bilingual education represents another fallacy. Several studies have proven bilingual education to be effective. Research shows that when bilingual programs are set up correctly, they work well (Krashen, 1996). DeLucca (1998) reported that studies have shown that students taught in their native language actually perform better than children instructed in English only. Well over 100 studies carried out over the past thirty years reflect a positive association between bilingualism and students' linguistic, cognitive, or academic growth (Cummins, 1998). Nearly 150 research studies report significant advantages for bilingual students on metalinguistic and cognitive tasks (Cummins, 1999). Gonzalez and Maez (1995) go so far as to assert that students who speak more than one language deserve to be regarded as linguistic resources and that it is important to nurture native language abilities.

Myth 10: Language-Minority Parents Are Not Supportive of Bilingual Education

Critics claim that language-minority parents do not support bilingual education because they feel it is more important for their children to learn English than to maintain the native language (Crawford, 1998). An Educational Testing Service (ETS) survey revealed that parents of language-minority children showed wide support for bilingual education (Baratz-Snowden, Rock, Pollack, & Wilder, 1988). When polled on the principles underlying bilingual education, the majority of parents indicated that they were strongly in favor of their children developing and maintaining their native language while also learning English (Krashen, 1996). Baratz-Snowden and others (1988) provided evidence that when it was made clear to parents that both students' home language and English were to be included in instruction, parents were supportive; when it was not done, parents reacted differently.

Aceves (1997) concluded that parental involvement in the schools reflects the level of parents' participation in society. The ethnically/linguistically diverse parents are more conspicuously absent than those of the dominant culture. Parents who lack cultural information about the schools need to know how the school system functions, and they need to know their parental rights as responsibilities (Delgado-Gaitán, 1991).

Cazden (1992) reported that parental involvement in a child's education is critical and that evidence strongly suggested that effective school and parent communication, combined with culturally-enriched, relevant curricula, would increase parental participation in the child's education. Once parents become involved in their children's education, they see the benefits of second language acquisition. Maceri (1997) pointed out that parents benefit from bilingual education as their children learn to function in the outside world and at the same time keep their links with the parents at home.

Myth 11: Bilingual Education Is a Panacea

Crawford (1998) identified another fallacy—that bilingual education is a panacea that will miraculously elevate student achievement levels. A shared language between students, teachers, and parents clearly facilitates communication (Cummins, 1998), but shared language alone will not increase student achievement. Maceri (1997) acknowledged that bilingual education is not a panacea, but admitted it does soften the cultural shock for immigrant students.

Putting Issues into Perspective

Crawford (1997) noted that "bilingual educators and researchers "seem to have no political agenda, hidden or otherwise, to advance outside the schools. Nor do they receive financial support from those who do.... By contrast, the academic critics seem to have few qualms about political activism or close ties to English-only lobbies" (p. 18). Clearly, widespread fears, fallacies, myths, and misconceptions regarding bilingual education abound, and research studies refute them; however, there is much upon which advocates and opponents can agree, Crawford (1998) attested. Both sides seem to agree that promotion of students' individual bilingualism is desirable. Research data indicate that promotion of students' home language will in no way impede development of English proficiency. Students who are bilingual deserve to be respected and regarded as linguistic resources, and it is important to nurture their language abilities (Gonzalez & Maez, 1995). Working together would be a good place to begin.

Olvando and Collier (1998) wrote of the value of incorporating multicultural literature into the curriculum, "Language is enchanting, powerful, magical, useful, personal. Language is our means of discovery of the world and our response to the world. As teachers we serve as catalysts for our students to make the best use of their two or more languages. Our languages are the most powerful tools we have" (p. 133).

School Leaders' Role in Bilingual and/or English as a Second Language Programs

Teachers, administrators, and supervisors of bilingual and/or English as a second language programs should take into consideration the following research and practical recommendations for developing and implementing programs:

- Develop supportive whole-school contexts that are inclusive of all curriculum programs (Lucas, Henz, & Donato, 1990; Tikunoff, Ward, Van Broekhuizen, Romero, Castaneda, Lucas, & Katz, 1991).
- Promote high expectations for language minority students, as evidenced by active learning environments that are academically challenging (Collier, 1992; Lucas, Henze, & Donato, 1990; Pease-Alvarez, Garcia, & Espinosa, 1991).
- Provide intensive staff development programs designed to assist ALL teachers (not just ESL or bilingual education teachers) in providing effective instruction to language minority students (Lucas, Henze, & Donato, 1990; Tikunoff et al., 1991).
- Employ expert instructional leaders and teachers (Lucas, Henze, and Donato, 1990; Pease-Alvarez, Garcia, & Espinosa, 1991; Tikunoff et al., 1991).
- Emphasize functional communication between teachers and students and among fellow students (Garcia, 1991).
- Organize instruction of basic skills and academic content around thematic units (Garcia, 1991).
- Promote frequent student interaction through the use of collaborative learning techniques (Garcia, 1991).
- Hire teachers with a high commitment to the educational success of all their students (Garcia, 1991).
- Place on bilingual campuses principals supportive of their instructional staff and of teacher autonomy while maintaining an awareness of district policies on curriculum and academic accountability (Garcia, 1991).
- Involve majority and minority parents in formal parent support activities (Garcia, 1991).
- Take pride in the bilingual program and find ways to demonstrate support (Carrasquillo & Rodriguez, 1998).

- Recognize the role of students' language in their social and academic development.
- Consider the students' culture and assist them in taking pride in it.
- Maintain good communication with the bilingual teachers and promote good communication between the bilingual teachers and the mainstream teachers and other special programs teachers.
- Learn about bilingual education and keep abreast of latest developments in research and policy.
- Evaluate the programs and revise accordingly with teacher input.
- Use the Bilingual Classroom Observation Protocol to assess and evaluate pedagogical practices in bilingual classroom settings (Lara-Alecio & Parker, 1994).

Summary

This chapter provided a brief overview of historical facts related to bilingual and English as a second language programs in the United States. Additionally, it furnished information regarding sample state policies and legal issues that school districts should consider when developing and implementing effective services to non-English speaking students. Misconceptions or controversial issues related to bilingual education were presented as well as research contrary to those misconceptions. Finally, recommendations for school leaders were outlined.

Administrators, supervisors, and teachers either at the central office level or on the campus level are urged to advocate the implementation of educational policies and effective biliterate/bicultural instructional practices. These should be based on current research and professional development in public education that ensure that *ALL LEARNERS* are equipped with the necessary skills to successfully compete in a linguistically diverse society.

Applying Your Knowledge

Eduardo Estrada, a recent immigrant from Mexico, is 7 years old. He attended public school kindergarten and half of first grade in his native city of Monterrey. Looking for the American dream, his parents moved to the United States. Jose, Eduardo's father, understands that without formal education and strong commitment he and his family will never reach their dream. Immediately upon arrival in the United States, Jose takes Eduardo to the nearby school. With the assistance of a translator, Jose is stating to the principal his desire for Eduardo which is to take advantage of any opportunity that the school can give him. The principal is aware that Eduardo makes the number of native Spanish-speaking students in first grade total 25. Jose is grateful for the opportunity for Eduardo, but is somewhat concerned when the principal tells him about the type program the school offers. In his mind, Jose questions whether Eduardo can handle the coursework in a language that is new to him and with a teacher who speaks no Spanish. Jose does not question the capacity of his son because he knows that he received excellent grades in school in Monterrey, where the teachers always stated how bright Eduardo is.

Questions:

1. A decision must be made as to the type of program to offer now that there are 25 students in the first grade whose native language is Spanish and who are recent immigrants. What are the steps the principal can take to determine the best program to serve the needs of the Spanish-speaking children in first grade in his school?
2. How can the principal be sure that Jose's desire for Eduardo is respected, and how can he communicate this to Jose?

3. How can the principal assist Jose and his wife in better providing academic support to Eduardo and providing support for Jose to move ahead in this new country?
4. How can the principal support the teachers in providing services to the second-language learners?
5. What options does Jose have in this situation?

Questions for Thought

1. To what extent do you think that the principal's knowledge about second-language learners' characteristics can help teachers assist students' performance in school?
2. To what extent does the principal's attitude toward immigrants make a difference in the accomplishments of the second-language learners in the school?
3. To what extent does the teachers' and administrators' attitudes toward bilingual or ESL education make a difference in the success of the program?
4. How can the school provide an enriched environment where the students' first language is respected?

For Further Information Online

English as 2nd Language (sample lessons) www. **esl.about.com/education/esl/**
English as 2nd Language (teacher and student resources) **www.esl.about./com/**
National Clearinghouse for bilingual Education **www.ncbe.gwu.edu**
Handbook for the implementation of bilingual/English as a second language education program **www.esc19.k12tx.us/handbook/Introduction.html**

References

Aceves, E. A. (1997). An analysis of a bilingual program continuum. (Doctoral Dissertation, San Diego State University, 1997). *Dissertation Abstracts Internatioinal.58-05A,* 1548.

Baca, L. M., & Cervantes, M. T. (1989). Background and rationale for bilingual special education. In L. M. Baca & H. T. Cervantes (Eds.). *The bilingual special education interface.* (2nd ed.) (pp.1-21). Columbus, OH: Merrill Publishing.

Baratz-Snowden, J., Rock, D., Pollack, J., & Wilder, G. (1988). *Parent Performance Study.* Princeton, NJ: Educational Testing Service.

Birman, B. F., & Ginsburg, A. L. (1983). Introduction: Addressing the needs of language-minority children. In K. A. Baker & A. A. deKanter (Eds.), *Bilingual education: A reappraisal of federal policy.* (pp. ix-xxi). Lexington, MA: LexingtonBooks.

Blanton, C. K. (1999). *The strange career of bilingual education: A history of the political and pedagogical debate over language instruction in American public education. 1890-1990.* (Doctoral Dissertation, Rice University, 1999). UMI Services, 9928507.

Breunig, N. (1998). Measuring the instructional use of Spanish and English in elementary transitional bilingual classrooms. (Doctoral Dissertation, Texas A&M University, 1998). *Dissertation Abstracts International, 59A,* 1046.

Bruce, K., Lara-Alecio, R., Parker, R., Hasbrouck, J. E., Weaver, L., & Irby, B. (1997). Inside Transitional bilingual classrooms: Accurately describing the language learning process. *Bilingual Research Journal, 21*(2&3), 123-145.

Cárdenas, J. A. (1998). The innovation of bilingual education. *IDRA Newsletter,* January 1998.

Carrasquillo, A. L., & Rodríguez, J. (1998, April). *Measurement success in Bilingual Education program: Case study of exemplary practices.* Paper presented at the annual meeting of the American Educational Research Association, San Diego, CA. (ERIC Document Reproduction Service No. ED 419 845)

Cavazos, G., Irby, B., Lara-Alecio, R., Meyer, D. J., & Mixon, D. (2000, February). *Components of the national bilingual research agenda for English language learners on high stakes assessment.* Poster session presented at the annual conference of the National Association of Bilingual Education. San Antonio, Texas.

Cazden, C. B. (1992). *Whole language plus: Essays on literacy in the United States and New Zealand.* New York: Teachers College Press.

Chamot, A. U., & Stewner-Manzaneres, G. (1985). *A summary of current literature on English as a second language. Part C.* Research agenda, Rosslyn, VA: InterAmerica Research Associates, 1985. (ERIC Document Reproduction Service No. ED 261 539)

Christian, D. (1994). *Two-way bilingual education: Students learning through two languages.* National Center for Research on Cultural Diversity and Second Language Learning.

Collier, V. P. (1992). A synthesis of studies examining long-term language minority student data on academic achievement. *Bilingual Research Journal, 16,* 187-212.

Collier, V. P., & Thomas, W. P. (1989). How quickly can immigrants become proficient in school English? *Journal of Educational Issues of Language Minority students, 5,* 26-38.

Crawford. J. (1999). *Bilingual education, History, politics, theory, and practice.* (4th ed.). Los Angeles, CA, Bilingual Education Services, Inc.

Crawford, J. (1998). *Ten common fallacies about bilingual education.* Washington, DC and McHenry, IL: ERIC Clearinghouse on Languages and Linguistics. (ERIC Document Reproduction Service No. ED 424 792)

Crawford. J. (1997). The campaign against proposition 227: A post mortem. *Bilingual Research Journal, 21*(1), 1-29.

Crawford, J. (1992). *Hold your tongue: Bilingualism and the politics of "English only".* Reading, MA: Addison-Wesley.

Cummins, J. (2000). Biliteracy, empowerment, and transformative pedagogy. In J. V. Tinajero & R. A. DeVillar (Eds.). *The Power of two Languages 2000. Effective Dual-Language Use Across the Curriculum* (9-19). New York: McGraw-Hill.

Cummins, J. (1999). *Research, ethics, and public discourse: The debate on bilingual education.* Washington, DC: National Conference of the American Association of Higher Education.

Cummins, J. (1998). *Negotiating identities: Education for empowerment in a diverse society.* Los Angeles: California Association for Bilingual Education.

Cummins, J. (1993). Empowerment through biliteracy. In J. Villareal & A. Ada (Eds.). *The Power of Two Languages* (9-24). New York: McMillan/McGraw-Hill.

Cummins, J. (1992). Bilingual education and English immersion: The Ramirez report in theoretical perspective. *Bilingual Research Journal,16,* 91-104.

De Avila, E. (1997). Setting expected gains for non and limited English proficient students. *NCBE Reference Collection Series. 9.* Washington, DC: National Clearinghouse for Bilingual Education.

Delgado-Gaitán, C. (1991). Involving parents in the schools: A process of empowerment. *American Journal of Education, 100*(1), 20-46.

DeLucca, T. R. (1998). *From Spanish to English: A case study of transitional bilingual students.* Unpublished master's thesis. California State University, Long Beach, California.

Escamilla, K. (1992). *A brief history of bilingual education in Spanish.* Charleston, WVA: Clearinghouse on Rural Education and Small Schools. (ERIC Document Reproduction Service No. ED 308 055).

Escamilla, K. (1989). *A brief history of bilingual education in Spanish.* Charleston, WVA: Clearinghouse on Rural Education and Small Schools. (ERIC Document Reporduction Service No. ED 308 055)

ESC 19. (2001). Handbook for the implementation of bilingual/English as a second language education program. [Online] <http://www/esc19.k12tx.us/handbook/Introduction.html> [2000, Nov.].

Frey, W. H. (1998). The diversity myth. *American Demographics. 20, 38.*

García, E. E. (1994). *Understanding and meeting the challenge of student cultural diversity.* Boston: Houghton Mifflin.

García, E. (1991). *Education of linguistically and culturally diverse students: Effective instructional practices. Educational practice report number 1.* Washington, DC: National Center for Research on Cultural Diversity and Second Language Learning (ERIC Document Reproduction Service No. ED 338 099)

Gempel, J. (1999, October 3). Hispanic growing in numbers, clout. *Washington Times,* p. C1.

Geneses, G. (1987). *Learning through two languages: Studies of immersion and bilingual language.* New York: Newbury House.

Glenn, C. L., & Lalyre, I. (1991). Integrated bilingual education in the USA. In K. Jaspaert & S. Kroon (Eds.), *Ethnic minority languages and education* (pp. 37-55). Amsterdam: Swets & Zeitlinger.

Glosarry: The language-learning lingo (April 21, 1998). *San José Mercury News* [Online] <http:www/7.mercurycenter. com/opinion/bilingual/glossary.htm> [1999, Sept. 17].

González, G., & Maez, L. F. (1995). Advances in research in bilingual education. *Directions in Language & Education. 5*(1). (ERIC Document Reproduction Service No. ED 394 302)

Greene, J. P. (1998). *A meta-analysis of the effectiveness of bilingual education.* Claremont, CA: Tomas Rivera Policy Institute.

Hakuta, K., Butler, Y. G., & Witt, D. (2000). *How long does it take English learners to attain proficiency?* (Policy Report No. 2000-1). Paper written for the University of California Linguistic Minority Research Institute.

Howe, C. K. (1994, October 9). Improving the achievement of Hispanic students. *Educational Leadership, 51*(8), 42-44.

Hunter, J., & Howley, C. B. (1990). *Undocumented children in the schools: Successful strategic and policies.* Charleston, WVA: Clearinghouse on Rural Education and Small Schools. (ERIC Document Reproduction Service No. ED 321-962)

IDRA Research Results (2000). Intercultural Development Research Association, San Antonio, TX.

Kloss, H. (1977). *The American Bilingual Tradition.* New York: Newbury House.

Krashen, S. (1999). *Bilingual Education: Arguments for and (bogus) arguments against.* Washington, DC: Georgetown University Roundtable on Languages and Linguistics.

Krashen, S. (1997). *Why bilingual education?* Charleston, WVA: Clearinghouse on Rural Education and Small Schools. (ERIC Document Reproduction Service No. ED 403-101)

Krashen, S. (1996). *Under attack: The case against bilingual education.* Culver City, CA: Language Education Associates.

Lara-Alecio, R., Parker, R. (1994). A pedagogical model for transitional English bilingual classrooms. *Bilingual Research Journal, 18*(3&4). 119-133.

Larson, K. A., & Rumberger, R. W. (1999). Dropout prevention for highest-risk Latino students. *The prevention Researcher, 3, 7.*

Lester, W. (1999, September 15). New census report illustrates nation's expanding diversity. *Houston Chronicle,* p. 2.

Lockwood, A. T., & Dicerbo, P. A. (2000). Transforming education for Hispanic youth: Recommendations for principals building-level decision makers. *Issue Brief 2.* Washington, DC: National Clearinghouse for Bilingual Education.

Lockwood, A. T. (1996). Caring, community and personalizations: Strategies to combat the Hispanic dropout problem. *Advances in Hispanic Education, 1.* Washington, DC: U.S. Department of Education.

Lucas, T., Henze, R., & Donato, R. (1990). Promoting the success of Latino language minority students: An exploratory study of six high schools. *Harvard Educational Review, 60*(1), 315-340.

Maceri, D. (1997). *Hispanic News Services* [Online].
   <http://www.latinolink.com/opinion97/1214hile.htm> [1999, Sept. 17].

McKeon, D. (1987). *Different types of ESL programs. ERIC Digest.* Washington, DC: ERIC
   Clearinghouse on Languages and Linguistics (ERIC Document Reproduction Service No.
   ED 289 360)

Moran, C. (1993). Content area instruction for students acquiring English. In J. Villareal & A. Ada
   (Eds). *The Power of Two Languages.* New York: MacMillan/McGraw-Hill.

Myths and misconceptions about second language learning. (1992). Washington, DC:
   Clearinghouse on Language and Linguistics. (ERIC Document Reproduction Service No.
   ED 350 885)

Netkin, H. (July 24, 1997). English not taught here. *Wall Street Journal,* p. A18.

O'Malley, J. M., & & D, Waggoner, (1984). Public school teacher preparation and the teaching of
   ESL. *TESOL Newsletter 18*(1), 18-22.

Ovando, C. J., & Collier, V. P. (1998). *Bilingual and ESL classrooms: Teaching in multicultural
   contexts* (2nd ed.). Boston: McGraw-Hill.

Pardo, E. B., & Tinajero, J. V. (1993). Literacy instruction through Spanish: Linguistic, Cultural,
   and Pedagogical Considerations. In J. Villareal & A. Ada (Eds.). *The Power of Two
   Languages* (26-34). New York: MacMillan/McGraw-Hill.

Pease-Alvarez, L., Garcia, E., & Espinosa, P. (1991). Effective instruction for language minority
   students: An early childhood case study. *Early Childhood Research Quarterly, 6,* 347-361.

Peregoy, S., & Boyle, O. (1993). *Reading, writing, and learning in ESL: A resource book for K-8
   teachers.* New York: Longman.

Porter, R. P. (1998). Twisted tongues: The failure of bilingual education. READ institute [Online].
   <http://www.gwu.edu/~pop biling.html> [2000, January 8].

Puente, M., & Kasindorf, M. (1999, September 7). The Hispanic experience: Unique, evolving.
   USA Today, p. 14A.

Ramírez, J. D. (1992). Executive Summary. *Bilingual Research Journal. 16*(1&2), 1-62.

Rennie, J. (1993). *ESL and bilingual program models.* Washington, DC: Clearinghouse on Language
   and Linguistics. (ERIC Document Reproduction Service No. ED 362- 072)

Riley, R. (2000). *Excelencia para todos—excellence for all—the progress of Hispanic education and the
   challenges of a new century.* Washington: Bell Multicultural High School.

Roman, N. E. (1998, January 6). House speaker Newt Gingrich calls for partial end of bilingual
   education. *The Washington Times,* p. A-1.

Rosenblum, S. (1996, February). *Union-sponsored work place ESL instruction.* (Project in adult
   immigrant education, Report No. EDO-LE-96-03). Center for Applied Linguistic. Bethesda,
   MD, Cosmos Corporation.

Santiestevan, S. (1991). *Use of Spanish language in the United States: Trends, challenges, and
   opportunities.* Charleston, WV: Clearinghouse on Rural Education and Small Schools.
   (ERIC Document Reproduction Service No. ED 335 176)

Shannon. S. M., & Escamilla, K. (1999). Mexican immigrants in U.S. schools: Targets of symbolic
   violence. *Educational Policy, 13.3,* 347-370.

Supik, J. D. (1998). Evaluating Title VII programs: An update of biennial evaluations. *Intercultural
   Development Research Association Newsletter,* p. 3.

Texas Educational Code §29.051-29.064. (1999, March). Chapter 89. Adaptations for Special
   population. Subchapter BB. Commissioner's rules concerning state plan for educating
   limited English proficient students.

Thomas, W. P. (1992). An analysis of the research methodology of the Ramirez study. *Bilingual
   Research Journal, 16*(1&2), 213-245.

Thomas, W. P., & Collier, V. (1997). *School effectiveness for language minority students.*
   Washington, DC: National Clearinghouse for Bilingual Education.

Tikunoff, W., Ward, B., Van Broekhuizen, D., Romero, M., Castañeda, L.V., Lucas, T., & Katz,
   A. (1991). *A descriptive study of significant features of exemplary special alternative instructional
   programs.* Washington: U.S. Department of Education, Office of Bilingual Education and
   Minority Languages Affairs.

Trueba, H. (1979). Bilingual education models: Types and designs. In H. Trueba & C. Barnett-Mizrahi (Eds.) *Bilingual multicultural education and the professional: From theory to practice* (54-73). Rowley, MA: Newbury House.

Two-Way Bilingual Education in Practice (1994). *A national and local perspective.* Washington, DC: Clearinghouse on Languages and Linguistics. (ERIC Document Reproduction Service No. ED 379-915)

U.S. Department of Education. (1994). *The condition of education, 1994.* Washington, D.C. Department of Education, National Center for Educational Statistics.

Veltman, C. (1998). *The Future of the Spanish Language in the United States.* Washington, DC: Hispanic Policy Development Project.

Waldman, A. (2000a, October 30). Eight Trends to Watch. *Multichannel News* [Online]. <http//www.findarticles.com/cf_1/m3535/44_21/67645400/print.jhtml> [2000, October 30].

Waldman, A. (2000b, October 30). The top 15 Hispanic markets. *Multichannel News* [Online]. <http//www.findarticles.com/cf_1/m3535/44_21/67645398/print.jhtml> [2000, October 30].

Chapter 7

Early Childhood Education

Holly Lamb

Human development research indicates that relatively stable, predictable sequences of growth and change occur in children during the first nine years of life. Predictable changes occur in all domains of development— physical, emotional, social, language, and cognitive—although the ways that these changes are manifest and the meaning attached to them may vary in different cultural contexts.

S. Bredekamp & C. Copple

Objectives:
1. **Explain developmentally appropriate practice for preschool children.**
2. **Describe the classroom components of an early childhood program.**
3. **Demonstrate how school leaders can support early childhood education programs.**

Historical Background

Prior to the 1900s, the early years of children's lives were not looked upon as unique. Rather, children were generally viewed as miniature adults. Nevertheless, several early philosophers did emphasize the importance of early childhood years for learning development. Locke (1632-1704), Rousseau (1712-1778) and Pestalozzi (1746-1827) maintained that children learn important life lessons and consequently require environments that provide concrete experiences for self-discovery (Eliason and Jenkins, 1994).

The "Father of Kindergarten," Friedrick Froebel of Germany (1782-1852), was one of the early pioneers of early childhood development and is considered responsible for the proliferation of kindergartens in the United States. He developed goals for educating kindergartners that are considered essential even today. Some examples of Froebel's contributions are activities directed at building fine muscle coordination and songs and fingerplays for children used to teach (a) concepts, (b) move children through transitions, and (c) help develop listening and speaking skills.

Montessori (1870-1952), the first female physician in Italy, established programs for children living in poverty. One of Montessori's deepest concerns was the health and nutrition of young people, but she also saw the need for children to become self-sufficient. Consequently, she included such ordinary activities as pouring water and sweeping floors in the curriculum. Montessori developed materials for her program that require fine motor coordination and taught basic skills such as counting, sequencing, and writing. Montessori schools, still popular in the United States, promote the concepts that she developed.

The first concrete research on early childhood education began in the late 1800s and early 1900s. Piaget in France and Vygotsky in Russia studied the stages of childhood thought development. Vygotsky focused on the interaction between language and thinking and the relationship between them. Vygotsky and Piaget found that the environment in which early childhood education takes place is critical to children's learning processes because considerable learning occurs in a child's early years.

Awareness and interest in early childhood education in the United States increased during World War II. With the demand for female workers in factories came the need for childcare outside of the home. Women today continue to join the work force, furthering the need for quality childcare.

In the 1960s congress' concern for disadvantaged families resulted in a proliferation of federally funded programs. Head Start is one example. Spurred by President Johnson's "War on Poverty," Head Start was established in 1965 under the Economic Opportunity Act of 1964. The centers created by Head Start promote "comprehensive child development programs and have the overall goal of increasing the school readiness of young children in low-income families" (Head Start, 2000, p. 1). Head Start programs target children ages three to five that come from disadvantaged homes as well as children with disabilities. As the programs focus on the entire family, education and support is made available to parents. The creation of Head Start increased the nation's awareness of the importance of early childhood education. Further details about Head Start are provided later in this chapter.

This chapter focuses on describing developmentally appropriate practices for early childhood education and provides some concrete examples of activities for children ages three to five, particularly for prekindergarten and kindergarten programs. Head Start Programs are discussed as well.

Program Description

Early Childhood Education Defined

Early childhood years are defined by the National Association for the Education of Young Children (NAEYC) as birth through age eight (1997). These early years of a child's life are critical to future development—from social development to academic learning. Current brain research supports earlier studies that found the first years of a child's life and early school years are critical to later development and contributes to the awareness of the magnitude of growth that occurs within the brain during the first two years of life. Research by Healy (1987) and Jensen (1998) showed that the brain begins critical development during the first months after birth. Knowledge is directly impacted during this early period as sensory messages picked up by the baby help to create synaptic connections between neurons, which is where learning begins. These findings led Healy (1987) to conclude about early childhood development that, "Active interest and mental effort by the child is key" (p. 19). Healy's conclusion highlighted the need to create environments for children that provide appropriate and ample stimulation.

A growing concern among early childhood professionals is the increasing emphasis on test scores in the United States and the consequent environments developed for young children. Environments created by an over-emphasis on testing ignores what research shows to be in children's best interests. Consequently, programs proliferate that place "undue emphasis on rote learning and whole-group instruction of narrowly defined academic skills at the expense of more active learning approaches based on a broader interpretation of children's educational needs and abilities" (Bredekemp and Copple, 1997, p. v).

Legalities

No national laws concerning early childhood exist that govern early childhood programs, although guidelines for federally funded programs such as Head Start are highly specific. States and individual districts determine how early childhood education is organized. Decisions about issues such as mandatory attendance, qualification requirements, full day versus half-day programs, and classroom size are left to state and local education agencies. The National Association for the Education of Young Children does provide guidance through numerous position statements and recommendations for early childhood education. (These guidelines are available in an edited book, *Developmentally Appropriate Practice in Early Childhood Programs* [1997] by Bredekamp and Copple or can be purchased from NAEYC.) Most of the programs that have endured the test of time are those in which the teachers understood and practiced the philosophy of developmentally appropriate practice, a philosophy described in the following section. While the focus of this chapter is primarily on the pre-kindergarten and kindergarten years, it should be noted that learning concepts appropriate to these years are also applicable for both younger and older children.

Developmentally Appropriate Practice

Developmentally Appropriate Practice (DAP) refers to professionals making decisions for children based on knowledge gleaned from research on child development. To implement developmentally appropriate programs, early childhood teachers are trained to have an understanding of how children develop:

> Human development research indicates that relatively stable, predictable sequences of growth and change occur in children during the first nine years of life. Predictable changes occur in all domains of development—physical, emotional, social, language, and cognitive—although the ways that these changes are manifest and the meaning attached to them may vary in different cultural contexts. Knowledge of typical development of children within the age span served by the program provides a general framework to guide how teachers prepare the learning environment and plan appropriate experiences. (Bredekamp and Copple, 1997, p. 10)

When teachers have an understanding of development in general they tend to view students as individuals. Even though there are predictable stages of development, each child is unique and has his/her own sequence and timing for learning. Furthermore, each child is a product of his/her own social and economic background. "Children must be considered within the context of their family, culture and community, past history and present circumstances" (Gestwicki, 1995, p. 7). While adjusting for each child's rate of learning, individualistic teaching is not mandatory and no individual child should be held to either higher or lower expectations than to which other children are held. Rigid, whole-group norms are also inappropriate. For example, expecting that all children will learn to read in their kindergarten year is unrealistic. Rather, teachers need to make adjustments for individuals within the learning environment.

NAEYC's position statements quoted in *Developmentally Appropriate Practice in Early Childhood Programs* (Bredekemp & Copple, 1997) provide twelve principles of child development and learning that delineate developmentally appropriate practice. While this list does not do justice to the complexity of these principles, it does provide an initial understanding of what is involved:

1. Domains of children's development—physical, social, emotional, and cognitive—are closely related. Development in one domain influences and is influenced by development in other domains.
2. Development occurs in a relatively orderly sequence, with later abilities, skills, and knowledge building on those already acquired.
3. Early experiences have both cumulative and delayed effects on individual children's development; optimal periods exist for certain types of development and learning.
4. Development proceeds in predictable directions toward greater complexity, organization, and internalization.
5. Development and learning occur in and are influenced by multiple social and cultural contexts.

6. Children are active learners, drawing on direct physical and social experience as well as culturally transmitted knowledge to construct their own understandings of the world around them.

7. Development and learning result from interaction of biological maturation and the environment, which includes both the physical and social worlds that children live in.

8. Play is an important vehicle for children's social, emotional, and cognitive development, as well as a reflection of their development.

9. Development advances when children have opportunities to practice newly acquired skills as well as when they experience a challenge just beyond the level of their present mastery.

10. Children demonstrate different modes of knowing and learning and different ways of representing what they know.

11. Children develop and learn best in the context of a community where they are safe and valued, their physical needs are met and they feel psychologically secure. (pp. 10-15)

Contemporary Issues

Play

"In the position on developmentally appropriate practice, play is stated to be the primary vehicle by which young children learn and show the progress in their learning in all domains" (Gestwicki, 1995, p. 7). Brewer (1998) claims that the work of Piaget, Vygotsky, Bruner, Katz, Spodek and others demonstrated that "play contributes to cognitive growth, aids social and emotional development, and is essential to physical development" (p. 114). Sometimes parents, administrators, and teachers are of the opinion that children in a kindergarten classroom are "just playing," although through play kindergarten children are capable of learning to read, acquiring basic math concepts, and gaining knowledge of science. Through "play" activities young children develop a foundation for writing, develop higher level mathematical and scientific concepts, and acquire problem solving skills. Piaget explains that young children are concrete learners who need to have hands-on activities so that they may come to their own understandings while developing their schema of the world.

Creating a learning environment based on play activities requires considerable time, commitment, and resources. Brewer (1998) talks of the many roles in which the early childhood teacher must engage—that of observer, elaborator, modeler, evaluator, and planner. The teacher as an *observer* must be able to watch children at play and notice interactions between children, interactions between children and play objects, and the amount of time each child is involved in play. Such observations enable the teacher to make better decisions about the type of play activities to use in the classroom. The teacher as *elaborator* works to help children develop their play by providing additional props, asking questions, providing vocabulary, and possibly by joining in the play for a brief time. The teacher as *modeler* deliberately joins in the play for an extended period of time. For example, if a teacher becomes aware that children are not using a block center to develop math and science concepts, the teacher might sit in the area and build with the children, adding more elaborate structures, vocabulary, and additional props. The teacher as *evaluator* carefully determines if the play is actually contributing to the cognitive, academic, social, and physical development of the children. The teacher as *planner* decides which centers to include in the classroom, what materials to place in each center, when to change materials, how much time to dedicate to play, how to move the children through the centers, how to adjust for individuals, which concepts and skills to teach, and how to teach them through play at a particular time.

Classroom Environment

As kindergarten classrooms are designed around play opportunities for learning, the physical arrangements are unlike classrooms for upper grades. Much of the space is dedicated to learning centers with a large area reserved for large group instruction—an area which is usually carpeted for the comfort of the students. Space for tables for each child or large tables that seat several children are preferable. Desks are inappropriate for young children but space where children can keep their possessions should be provided.

Most skills can be taught through center activities. Traditional learning centers include: a dramatic play center, library center, writing center, block center, science/math center, puzzles and games center, and an art center (NAEYC, 1997). Additional centers are based on the teacher's interests and access to materials. Each center should provide opportunities that help children develop socially, emotionally, physically, and intellectually. When the curriculum is planned around thematic instruction, the topic—or theme—is reflected in the centers through the choice of materials and activities. Some typical play centers are described here.

Dramatic Play Center. In the past this center was traditionally a housekeeping center with a kitchen, dress-up clothes, and dolls. Today teachers frequently alter this center transforming it into a restaurant, doctor's office, space ship, or other area of interest to children. This center allows for oral language and social skills development as the children "try on" adult roles and have some control of their world for a few minutes of the day.

Library Center. Books of high interest and those conducive to learning are placed so that children can spend time leisurely perusing literature appropriate to their age level. Teachers may add sofas, pillows, beanbag chairs, or even lofts to make this center inviting.

Writing Center. The writing center is stocked with writing materials—paper in a variety of colors and shapes, pencils, pens, markers, chalk and chalkboard, and alphabet letters. Young children are sometimes able to write before they read, making this center critical to learning to read and write.

Block Center. A large supply of unit blocks are the basic materials in this center. Various types of blocks and props such as small vehicles and toy animals may be added. The block center provides a foundation for learning mathematical concepts such as counting, proportion, geometry, and fractions. Science concepts can also be established as children work to balance blocks, make their building taller, and when their toy car travels faster on the ramp with the steepest slope. Cooperation, planning, and problem solving are other skills that children develop when they "play" in the block center.

Science and Math Center.
Here math manipulatives are housed. For example, counting cubes, scales, and measuring instruments are made available to the children. This center may also contain a sand and water table which helps children understand the different properties of substances, volume, and measurement and assist in vocabulary development in the areas of science and mathematics. Live plants and animals may also be placed in this center to assist children in learning the different concepts and responsibilities associated with keeping plants and animals alive and growing.

Puzzle and Games Center.
Board games, lacing beads, lacing cards, puzzles, and tinker toys are the types of resources that make this center an area for children to develop fine motor control, learn basic concepts like letters, numbers, and colors, and problem solving skills. Many commercial materials are available for this center although teacher-made materials are highly appropriate.

Art Center. A variety of art materials such as crayons, paint, clay, boxes, paper scraps, egg cartons, strawberry boxes, and sequins provide the basis for the art center. This is a place where children are encouraged to experiment with a wide variety of materials. (Asking children to copy a model is inappropriate at this age.) The art center helps to develop fine motor control, learn the use of space on a page, become creative, acquire problem solving skills, and increase vocabulary development. The process here is more important than the product the child creates.

Materials that assist in the child's language development can be added to any center. When the dramatic play center is a house, the teacher can add phone books, cook books, paper and pencils for messages, magazines, and catalogs. If the dramatic play center becomes a restaurant, menus and waitress order pads can be added. In the block center the teacher may provide paper and markers to make signs for the different structures and roadways and can add a journal where children can make pictures of their building structures before disassembling them. In the science/math center the teacher may make available charts for feeding and watering the plants and animals, records, and journals to complete when conducting experiments. In the art center, children can label their work or write stories to accompany their art activities. The addition of literacy activities in each center helps to reinforce one of the most important aspects of prekindergarten and kindergarten programs—the development of literacy skills.

Early childhood classrooms need to be colorful and inviting. Teachers sometimes add personal touches such as lamps, pictures, or rocking chairs to create a welcoming and comfortable atmosphere. The classroom should also be "print rich" with bulletin boards, charts, books, and labels on furniture. Even though young children may not actually be reading the daily schedule, it should be posted, and charts of the songs and fingerplays they recite should be displayed. Children may be asked to sign in for morning roll call or when moving into a center. Kindergartners need to feel that they are capable of learning to read and write long before they actually learn to read and write.

Curriculum

Many curriculum decisions are left to the classroom teacher. Published programs or kits are available but cannot cover the entire scope of judgements a teacher must make. Smith (1999) explains that

> Teaching is a social activity. Pre-designed programs cannot take the place of teachers, even when the programs are administered by teachers. Teaching involves decisions made on the spot, not decisions to move from one instructional goal to the next, but decisions about the condition of the learner. Such conditions might include the learner's (and also the teacher's) physical, emotional, and psychological state at that particular time, together with interest, comprehension, past experience, self-image, feelings about the task at hand, and feelings about the teacher (or about the student). (p. 151)

Bredekemp and Carroll (1997) emphasize that developmentally appropriate practice in the construction of curriculum should—at the very least—follow the following guidelines:

1. A developmentally appropriate curriculum provides for all areas of a child's development: physical, emotional, social, linguistic, aesthetic, and cognitive.
2. Curriculum includes a broad range of content across disciplines that is socially relevant, intellectually engaging, and personally meaningful to children.
3. Curriculum builds upon what children already know and are able to do (activating prior knowledge) to consolidate their learning and to foster their acquisition of new concepts and skills.

4. Effective curriculum plans frequently integrate across traditional subject-matter divisions to help children make meaningful connections and provide opportunities for rich conceptual development; focusing on one subject is also a valid strategy at times.
5. Curriculum promotes the development of knowledge and understanding, processes and skills, as well as the dispositions to use and apply skills and to go on learning.
6. Curriculum content has intellectual integrity, reflecting the key concepts and tools of inquiry of recognized disciplines in ways that are accessible and achievable for young children, ages 3 through 8. Children directly participate in study of the disciplines, for instance, by conducting scientific experiments, writing, performing, solving mathematical problems, collecting and analyzing data, collecting oral history, and performing other roles of experts in the disciplines.
7. Curriculum provides opportunities to support children's home culture and language while also developing all children's abilities to participate in the shared culture of the program and the community.
8. Curriculum goals are realistic and attainable for most children in the designated age range for which they are designed.
9. When used, technology is physically and philosophically integrated in the classroom curriculum and teaching (p. 20-21).

Most kindergarten teachers choose to develop the curriculum around themes so that the learning is integrated. An integrated curriculum "can help a child make sense of the world more easily [because] when children learn outside of school they learn in wholes divisible into subject-matter areas" (Brewer, 1998, p. 198). To integrate the curriculum, teachers choose a topic or a theme, and ensure that during the study of that topic all curriculum areas are covered. For example, if the theme is nutrition, students write a recipe, read a recipe, measure ingredients for a recipe, and learn about the food pyramid all while preparing a nutritious snack or when preparing ethnic foods. The teacher feels confident that in this thematic unit the subject areas of writing, reading, math, science, and social studies are all addressed.

Chard (1992) described studies and observations from Reggio Emilio, a small town in Italy, where young children were found capable of in-depth study through thematic instruction and a project approach based on children's interests. What attracted early childhood educators to Reggio Emilio was the quality of the finished products of four and five year-olds although the emphasis on the children's work in Reggio Emilio was always on process rather than product. Knowledge gained from Reggio Emilio has helped prekindergarten and kindergarten teachers check the relevance and actual learning involved in their theme studies and raised expectations for learning. (For a more comprehensive explanation of the project approach see Chard's *The Project Approach: A Practical Guide for Teachers*.)

For thematic instruction topics are taught through whole and small group interaction and with theme-related materials and activities. Additional learning occurs when children engage in centers and when they pursue interests prompted by the thematic instruction.

More On Curriculum

While development of learning experiences in centers and thematic instruction is important to child development, prekindergarten and kindergarten teachers find it critical to include art, music, movement, and physical education in early childhood programs. Current brain research lends support to this practice.

Unfortunately, due to increased pressure for academic success and budget restraints, art, music, movement, and physical education are sometimes viewed as expendable. Educators at all levels may be advised to rethink this view by examining the curricula of Japan, Hungary, and Netherlands where students rank high in math and science achievement test scores and where intensive music and art training is built into the elementary curricula (Jensen, 1998). Jensen finds that "a strong art foundation builds creativity, concentration, problem solving, self-efficacy, coordination, and values attention and self-discipline" (p. 36). Concurrently, Brewer (1998) emphasized that creativity and problem-solving are important products of a creative arts curriculum.

Research shows that the parts of the brain that are stimulated by music, art, and movement are also connected to cognitive learning. Jensen (1998) refers to the work of Carla Hannaford that demonstrates that movement education is important because movement—especially swinging, rolling, and jumping—stimulates the cerebellum which in turn activates other parts of the brain that are critical to the "attentional system which regulates incoming sensory data"(p. 84). Jensen also quotes Strick's work that makes it evident that there is a "pathway from the cerebellum back to parts of the brain involved in memory, attention, and spatial perception" (p. 84). Further, Hannaford and others "verify that sensory motor integration is fundamental to school readiness" (p. 85).

Jensen (1998) finds that daily music education is essential to every K-12 student's development. Brain research is demonstrating that "(1) our brain may be designed for music and arts, and (2) a music and arts education has positive, measurable, and lasting academic and social benefits" (pp. 36-37). Kindergarten teachers have long been aware of the value of music, using it to calm students, to get the "wiggles out," and to gain children's attention. Additionally, teachers use music to help students learn new material. For example, children sing the alphabet, the days of the week, months of the year, and sing songs to learn academic concepts. Music is also used to prompt desired behavior. For example, a particular song indicates it is time to clean up or to form a line.

Early childhood teachers also find value in recess activities. Young children need to run and play, not just for physical and social reasons, but because physical activity aids in brain development. Physical engagement can occur at designated times such as outdoor recess but can also be incorporated into many of the day's activities. For example, physical movement can accompany music class, be used for classroom management as children move from one activity to the next, and facilitate routine procedures such as cleaning up and turning in materials.

Assessment

Teachers have an obligation to measure students' progress to determine if the intended goals and objectives have been achieved. "In developmentally appropriate programs, assessment and curriculum are integrated, with teachers continually engaging in observational assessment for the purpose of improving teaching and learning" (Bredekemp and Copple, 1997, p. 21). The assessment methods most appropriate for young children are "observations of children's development, descriptive data, collections of representative work by children, and demonstrated performance during authentic, not contrived, activities" (Bredekemp and Copple, 1997, p. 21).

Due to the demand for accountability, schools are frequently under pressure to test children. Numerous assumptions and subsequent decisions about the quality of schools, teacher effectiveness, student placement, and allocation of resources are based on test scores. In *Achievement Testing in the Early Grades: The Games Grown-Ups Play,* Kamii (1990) calls for "a halt to achievement testing in grades K-2 for two reasons: These tests are not valid measures of children's learning or of teachers' accountability, and the pressure for higher test scores is resulting in classroom practices that are harmful to young children's development" (p. 15). Perrone (as cited in Kamii, 1990) points out that in early years learning is so "uneven," "idiosyncratic," and "fluid" that no one test can give an accurate measure of a child's knowledge or intelligence. Kamii describes how achievement tests are developed and demonstrates how a young child's knowledge cannot truly be measured. The current emphasis on testing too often leads teachers to spend inordinate amounts of time having children complete worksheets and encourages teachers to adopt packaged programs that are not developmentally appropriate. Morgan-Worsham (as cited in Kamii, 1990) calls for principals, as instructional leaders, to work together to educate parents, school boards, and legislators for the purpose of banning standardized testing in grades K-2.

Parent Involvement

Parents are children's first teachers. Consequently, the school's connections with parents and the connections between the school, parents, children, and the children's learning are critical. Parents care about their children, but not all know how to provide the best environment for their child to develop and learn to his or her full potential. Schools can play a key role in providing that information.

Parent involvement programs are advantageous to the school, the parents, and the children. "Involving parents when children are young has beneficial effects that persist throughout the child's academic career" (Henderson, 1988, p. 153). Some benefits to the school of having involved, caring parents are:

1. The school gains a group of supporters who are a positive voice for the school in the community.
2. The school's goals for the students are more likely to be met.
3. Teachers receive help in the classroom when parents serve as volunteers.
4. Parents themselves learn what is happening at school, how their child is progressing academically, socially, and behaviorally.

When parenting programs are truly successful, parents learn appropriate ways to interact with their own children. In turn, when parents are involved in the school the child's academic achievement and self-esteem go up (Brewer, 1998). Henderson (1988) found that "children from low-income and minority families benefit the most when parents are involved in the school, and parents do not have to be well educated to make a difference" (p. 153).

In reality some parents find it difficult to be involved in their child's school, for example, when both parents work outside the home or the family has a single parent. Others are hampered by language barriers. For those whose past experiences with schools were negative, school is not viewed a pleasant place to be. Consequently, educators become creative in finding ways to involve all parents. Following are some suggestions for involving parents of young children in school activities:

1. Conduct home visits.
2. Ask school counselors to provide parenting classes during the day as well as in the evening (for those who cannot attend during the day).
3. Encourage parents to visit school. For example, taking parents' pictures during the visit and posting them on a bulletin board can encourage others to visit as well.
4. Communicate regularly but in the language of the home.
5. Conduct parent/teacher conferences more than once a year.
6. Conduct student/parent conferences.
7. Provide translators and babysitting during parent meetings and conferences.
8. Conduct large group parent meetings at a community center, away from school and serve refreshments whenever possible.

Full-Day versus Half-Day Kindergarten

Some communities feel the need for full-day rather than half-day kindergarten. Research has not shown that academic test scores increase when kindergarten is conducted for a full day; however, test scores in these early years are not accurate indicators of the long-term effects of early education on future academic achievement, particularly if individual needs are met the first years of school. For example, language development has always been a critical component of all kindergarten programs (Brewer, 1998; Gestwicki, 1995) as such development impacts learning but language development requires time spent in a language-enriched environment. When a child's first language is not English, the focus on language development is even more critical. By spending an entire day with a certified teacher, in a language-enriched environment, children with special language needs have a greater opportunity for growth.

The real question is whether or not a truly rich kindergarten program can be achieved in a 3-4 hour program. In kindergarten if children spend time in each learning center, engage in outdoor play, enjoy music and art, and are involved in large group activities, a half-day program may not suffice.

Head Start

Head Start is a federally funded program established in 1965 to prepare young children from disadvantaged homes for entry into school and help their families become self-sufficient. Children with disabilities are included in Head Start programs as well. Head Start reaches children in all fifty states (Head Start, 2000) although the number served is not reflective of the large number of children living in poverty in the United States. The Head Start program is administered by the Head Start Bureau, the Administration on Children, Youth and Families (ACFY), Administration for Children and Families (ACF), and the Department of Health and Human Services (DHHS).

The philosophical basis for the program is that: (a) a child can benefit most from a comprehensive, interdisciplinary program to foster development and remedy existing problems, and (b) goals are better achieved if the child's entire family and the community surrounding the delivery site participate in the program. The programs are responsive to each child's and family's developmental, ethnic, cultural, and linguistic heritage and experience. The four major components of Head Start are education, health, family and community, and social services. Guidelines are specified by the government (45 CRF §1301-1308) and form the basis for regular evaluations of Head Start Centers.

Education. The objective is "to provide all children with a safe, nurturing, engaging, enjoyable, and secure learning environment, in order to help them gain the awareness, skills, and confidence necessary to succeed in their present environment, and to deal with later responsibilities in school and in life" (45 CRF § 1304.21) Developmentally and linguistically appropriate instruction is mandated.

Health. The goal is to "ensure that, through collaboration among families, staff, and health professionals, all child health and developmental concerns are identified, and children and families are linked to an ongoing source of continuous, accessible care to meet their basic health needs" (45 CFR §1304.20) Serving balanced meals, providing medical and dental care, and training parents in health-related practices are examples of the health services.

Family and Community. Head Start offers parents "opportunities and support for growth, so that they can identify their own strengths, needs and interests, and find their own solutions" (45 CFR §304.40). "Head Start believes that gains made by the child in Head Start must be understood and built upon by the family and the community. A change in one child may not last long; a change in a family does" (Parent Orientation, n.d. p. 6). Families of Head Start children are afforded social, vocational, and educational services in order to help them become less dependent on government services. In return, parents are expected to undergo the appropriate training and then serve at their child's center volunteering and participating in all aspects of the program. Parents prepare meals, work as classroom aides, serve on their Head Start's Policy Committee, and may even work as paid employees. These volunteer services are the backbone of the programs. In 2000 across the United States, 172,000 staff members were paid; volunteers numbered over 1,000,000 (Head Start, 2000).

Strong connections between Head Start Centers and parents is mandated. Consequently, workers are required to make home visits when parents permit such visits. Additionally, the Head Start staff is to develop activities to be used at home by other family members that will reinforce and support the child's total Head Start experience.

Social Services. Head Start links parents to appropriate community services and resources (45 CFR §1304.40) such as mental and physical health providers. Emergency assistance, crisis intervention, and services to pregnant women who are enrolled in appropriate programs are examples of this component.

Target Populations. The target populations of Head Start are children three to five years of age whose families are disadvantaged as well as children who are disabled. Federal regulations (45 CFR §1305.3) require that at least 90% of the children served come from families whose income falls below the poverty line. Up to 10% may be children from families that exceed the low-income guidelines but who would benefit from Head Start services. At least 10% of those enrolled may be children who are physically handicapped and require special services (45 CFR §1308.4[B]). In 2000, 35% of the children served were Black, 30% White, and 27% Hispanic (Head Start, 2000).

Funding. Federal grants for Head Start are awarded by the Administration for Children and Families (ACF) and the Head Start Bureau's American Indian and Migrant Program Branches "directly to local public agencies, private organizations, Indian Tribes, and school systems for the purpose of operating Head Start programs at the community level" (Head Start, 2000, p. 2). In 2000, over $5 billion were spent on Head Start programs and their supporting activities. The average cost per child in 2000 was $5,403 (Head Start, 2000).

Federal assistance is not to exceed 80% of the total cost of a program (45 CFR §1301.20). Matching funds in the form of in-kind contributions account for the other 20% of each center's budget. Parent volunteer hours, doctors and dentists contributed or reduced fee services, and community members' time and dollars are examples of in-kind contributions.

Staffing. At least two paid staff members must be provided for each class (45 CFR §1306.20). All staff and consultants are expected to have the knowledge, skills, and experience they need to perform their duties. Because parent participation is viewed as critical to Head Start programs, parents receive preference for non-professional staff positions.

Curriculum. Head Start serves young children with the intent of giving them the physical, emotional, and educational background necessary for success in school. The programs are designed around a developmentally appropriate curriculum. For example, one Head Start program's published goals based on Head Start Performance Standards lists their learning centers as Block and Transportation Center, Language Arts/Library Center, Music Center, and Art Center (Red River County, 1984). The intended learning goal of each center is outlined and matches the developmentally appropriate activities described earlier in this chapter.

School Leaders' Role in Early Childhood Programs

School leaders play a significant role in the success of prekindergarten and kindergarten programs. In some schools, the local Head Start program is housed in an elementary school and falls under the principal's supervision as well.

Hiring and Supporting Early Childhood Teachers. The school principal—frequently in conjunction with teachers—is responsible for hiring early childhood teachers. Those responsible for hiring should be aware of certification requirements. State law may specify a particular degree, specialization, or an endorsement. These requirements ensure that the teacher of young children has coursework in child development and understands developmentally appropriate practice, knowledge of play and curriculum development for young children.

Training. Kindergarten teachers need school leaders who understand five-year olds and how they learn. Administrators who take the time to attend workshops and staff development training on early childhood can knowledgeably support curriculum decisions that are in the best interests of the children. For example, understanding the space and material requirements for appropriate learning environments encourages the principal to provide those resources. Trained administrators are more likely to supervise and evaluate early childhood teachers in a way that encourages teacher growth. For example, a knowledgeable administrator understands that kindergartners are learning when engaged in what appears to be "play" and that teachers will not be involved in direct teaching a large percentage of the time. Such principals are aware that much of the work of an early childhood teacher occurs before and after school when they create the learning environment.

Teacher-leaders play an important role in the success of early childhood programs as well. Understanding the role the early childhood program plays in future learning and modeling that understanding, encouraging new teachers to learn about early childhood development, and dispelling myths about very young children are ways teacher-leaders promote the interests of children. Sergiovanni (2001) encourages school leaders to operate their schools as communities rather than as organizations. He describes such schools as places where "people come together because they share common commitments, ideas, and values" and encourages developing caring communities "where members make a total commitment to each other" (p. 74). Schools develop into such communities when teacher-leaders take responsibility for the school's climate and understand that commitment includes all programs, including prekindergarten, kindergarten, and any other early childhood program housed in the school.

A Glimpse of a Successful Program

The principal walks into the kindergarten classroom and sees the children sitting on a rug, listening to the teacher read. The principal is aware of the value of this activity, knowing that by reading aloud to the children the teacher is increasing: (a) the students' receptivity to reading, (b) their language development, (c) their knowledge of book language, and (d) their listening, prediction, and comprehension skills. After reading and asking questions to check for comprehension, the teacher allows the children to retell parts of the story. The teacher then dismisses the children to centers. The principal notes that the children know a procedure for choosing a center and that they immediately become engaged in center activities. A wide variety of centers are available for the children to choose from, all equipped with materials that are developmentally appropriate and supportive of age-appropriate learning. The teacher is carefully observing the entire classroom, monitoring the children's activities. She makes written notes as she moves about the room. The principal notices that the noise level rises and falls, but the children remain engaged in productive activities and conversations.

By moving the children from the rug area to the centers the principal realizes that the teacher balanced whole group and small group activities and equalized the amount of time between projects that engage the children actively and time spent on more subdued activities. The principal hears the children discussing their activities as they play and notices that the teacher joins a group to provide some direction, encouraging a productive learning experience for the children. The principal is aware of the printed materials in all of the centers as well as around the classroom.

The classroom is colorful with furniture built to the children's size. All materials are organized for easy access. Each center has clear boundaries and a selection of materials that keep the children engaged. The centers that encourage quieter activity are on one side of the room, the noisier centers are on the other. There is evidence that a theme study is in progress. Pertaining to the theme are projects made by the children, some displayed on the walls, some on tables, and others hang from the ceiling. Vocabulary words and facts are posted around the room. Books associated with the theme are in evidence and make up a large portion of the library center. Some of the center activities are related to the theme study. The principal leaves the room, knowing that these young children are engaged in productive activity in an enriched learning environment.

Applying Your Knowledge

Mr. Stone, the principal of an elementary school, is listening to the complaints of Mrs. Krebs whose son, Joe, is in kindergarten. Mrs. Krebs says that all Joe does in class is play and explains that her child is very bright and needs to be getting ready for first grade. She feels Joe's year in school is being wasted. "After all," she says, "Joe played in preschool and now it is time to do serious schoolwork." She says that Joe's cousin who is in kindergarten at another school is bringing home paperwork every day and has an hour of homework every night. When questioned, Mrs. Krebs says that she visited Joe's class on several occasions and all Joe was doing was building blocks. She states firmly that this approach will not lead to learning the necessary skills of reading and writing.

Questions:

1. Can Mr. Stone reassure Mrs. Krebs that her child is learning and is being prepared for first grade? If so, what approach should he use?
2. In explaining the differences between the kindergarten program in this school and Joe's cousin's kindergarten program, what major points should Mr. Stone make?
3. What could Mr. Stone and the teacher have done to avoid this confrontation?
4. What should the teacher-leaders in this building do to prevent this type of misunderstanding about their school's programs? What resources would they need from the principal?

Questions for Thought

1. In what ways do developmentally appropriate practices for early childhood programs affect curriculum decisions? What impact do such practices have on budget decisions and judgements about testing?
2. Would full-day or half-day prekindergarten and kindergarten programs better serve your population? Why?
3. Plan a program to educate parents about developmentally appropriate early childhood programs.
4. How can you facilitate more parent involvement and education in your school?

For Additional Information Online

The National Association for the Education of Young children **www.naeyc.org**
ERIC database for elementary and early childhood education **www.childrensdefense.org**
The Childrens Defense Fund **www.highscope.org**
Information for early childhood educators **www.earlychildhood.com**

References

Administration for Children and Families, Head Start Bureau. (1970). *Head Start policy manual 70.2: The parents*. Washington, D.C.: U.S. Department of Health & Human Services.

Bredekamp, S., & Copple, C. (Eds.). (1997). *Developmentally appropriate practice in early childhood programs*. Washington, D.C.: National Association for the Education of Young Children.

Brewer, J. (1998). *Introduction to early childhood education*. (3rd ed.). Boston: Allyn and Bacon.

Chard, S. (1992). *The project approach*. Alberta, Canada: University of Alberta. (Order copies from: Instructional Technology Centre, Faculty of Education, University of Alberta, B117 Education Building North, Edmonton, Alberta, T6G 2G5, Canada.)

Eliason, C., & Jenkins, L. (1994). *A practical guide to early childhood curriculum*. (5th ed.). New York: Merrill.

Gestwicki, C. (1995). *Developmentally appropriate practice: Curriculum and development in early education*. Albany, NY: Delmar Publishers Inc.

Head Start (2000). [Online]. ,http://www.acf.dhhs.gov> [2001, Jan. 28].

Healy, J. (1987). *Your child's growing mind*. New York: Doubleday.

Henderson, A. T. (Oct., 1988). Parents are a school's best friends. *Phi Delta Kappan, 70*, 148-153.

Jensen, E. (1998). *Teaching with the brain in mind*. Alexandria, VA: Association for Supervision and Curriculum Development.

Kamii, C. (Ed.). (1990). *Achievement testing in the early grades: The games grown-ups play*. Washington, D.C.: National Association for the Education of Young Children.

Morgan-Worsham, D. (1990). The dilemma for principals. In C. Kamii (Ed.). *Achievement testing in the early grades: Games grown-ups play* (1-13). Washington, D.C.: National Association for the Education of Young Children.

Parent orientation handbook. (No date). Head Start of Greater Dallas, Inc. Dallas, TX: author.

Perrone, V. (1990). How did we get here? In C. Kamii, (Ed.). *Achievement testing in the early grades: Games grown-ups play*. Washington, D.C.: National Association for the Education of Young Children.

Red River County Head Start (1984). *Red River County Head Start handbook*. Clarksville, TX: Clarksville Center.

Sergiovanni, T. J. (2001). *The principalship: A reflective practice perspective*. (4th ed.). Boston: Allyn and Bacon.

Smith, F. (1999). Why systematic phonics and phonemic awareness instruction constitute an educational hazard. *Language Arts, 77*(2), 150-155.

Chapter 8

Programs for Gifted and Talented Students

Carol S. Anderson and Beth Anne Dunavant

For every gifted child who is not allowed to reach his or her potential,
there is a lost opportunity. That child might eventually have composed
a concerto, found a cure for a hitherto terminal disease, or developed a
formula for world peace. Wasting the potential of a gifted mind is
reckless for a society in desperate need of creativity and inventiveness.

Carl Rogers

Objectives:
- **Provide an understanding of the historical underpinnings of gifted programs.**
- **Identify the major components that make up an effective program.**
- **Consider various issues that currently impact students who are gifted.**

Many American educational institutions make some provision for educational programs for gifted students. Some programs meet the needs of these students; others fall short. "Despite sporadic attention over the years to the needs of bright students, most of them continue to spend time in school working well below their capabilities" (O'Connell, 1993, p. 5). While all children deserve a stimulating and challenging education that includes provisions for diversity and standards of excellence, the unique needs of those with exceptional abilities cannot be overlooked. Following an historical overview of programs for gifted students, the major issues surrounding such programs today are addressed.

Historical Background

Historically, American educational systems' treatment of gifted education is fraught with disagreement. Proponents of gifted programs argue the need for providing opportunities for all children to develop their talents and contribute to the betterment of society. Consequently, the modern concepts of differentiated curriculum and program models were created. Those that differ claim that labeling children "exceptional" leads to the creation of an elite population within schools—a system that does not provide the best possible education for all. Despite the debate within educational circles, nations as a whole have recognized the need to identify and educate gifted citizens for centuries.

Education for the gifted probably began with Plato. He recognized that human abilities varied and believed that young men who showed promise of great mental aptitude should be given special education and training. His goal was to produce leaders for the state. The Romans embraced some aspects of Plato's plan, including them in their educational system for more than 500 years (Ellis, 1991).

In China, child prodigies were sent to the imperial court for special training by the Tang Dynasty as early as 618 A.D. Their custom of valuing and honoring those with exceptional talents has continued throughout history (Colango, 1991).

Interest in the gifted spawned an entire period of European history. During the Renaissance individuals whose creative talents lay in many different areas were encouraged and given the freedom to make their contributions to society while being underwritten by wealthy individuals or governments (Colango, 1991).

Binet and Simon, two French scientists, developed the first test to measure intelligence, paving the way for a more scientific means to identify gifted students (Gold, 1965). This test was later modified by Terman and titled The Stanford-Binet Intelligence Scale (Colango, 1991) and would play a significant role in further development of gifted education in America.

In America, Thomas Jefferson believed that gifted individuals existed in all segments of the American population, a belief that was firmly imbedded in his argument for publicly funded education for all (Law, n.d.). Prior to the 1950's, education for the gifted consisted of accelerating the progression of a student through the existing system. After the development of the Stanford-Binet test, enrichment rather than acceleration became the preferred practice. Enrichment fostered multiple tracking systems and various forms of individualized instruction (Law, n.d.). World War II, though, brought about a decline in gifted education. The Industrial Revolution increased the need for mass training and teaching of new skills (O'Connor, 1980) and support for gifted education decreased. Interest in programs for the gifted was further eroded by fear of elitism brought about by the world's discovery of the horrors inflicted upon those deemed "less worthy" by Hitler's regime.

In 1957, renewed interest in the education of gifted children was sparked when Russia launched Sputnik but revealed American shortages in the fields of math and science. The United States' desire to win the "space race" led to identifying individuals who might have potential in the natural sciences. Public and private funds became available for classes for promising students. Educators began designing and implementing enrichment activities; however, few programs were available for students possessing talents in non-academic areas and few provisions were made to include the disadvantaged and those with physical disabilities.

America's attention shifted away from gifted education during the 1960s as the Vietnam War focused national interest on civil rights, racial integration, and the need for education to address contemporary concerns (Long, 1984). Thus the earlier surge of interest in funding and concern for gifted programs brought about by Sputnik floundered. At the conclusion of the 1960s, *The Education Index of 1970* contained only half the number of entries under "Gifted Children" than did the 1960 volume that covered the 1950s period (Johnsen & Corn, 1992).

Congress' passing of the Elementary and Secondary Education Act of 1970 (ESEA) renewed efforts by America's schools to provide programs for gifted students. Titles III and V of ESEA included funding for serving identified students. The establishment of the Office of the Gifted and Talented in 1974 temporarily increased interest in gifted education but the office was dissolved in the 1980s (Sayler, 1997).

Support was once more renewed with the enactment of the Jacob Javits Gifted and Talented Students Education Act of 1988 that provided funding for and leadership in the implementation of gifted education nationwide. Accompanying this funding was encouragement to include minority, disabled, and disadvantaged children in gifted programs (O'Connell, 1993). This increased interest in gifted education in this century led to some general guidelines for gifted programs. The specifications include:

- A comprehensive identification process.
- Programs that foster higher-level thinking skills.
- Opportunities for students to demonstrate advanced-level understanding of stated objectives.
- A differentiated curriculum that emphasizes a multitude of areas in which identified students exhibit the ability to excel.

These standards support the learning needs of students and provide the basis for gifted education in America today. The specifications are directed at improving strategies, services, and teacher training. High expectations are imbedded in these standards as students are expected to compete at a global level.

Legal and Regulatory Guidelines

Gifted programs in the United States have very little protection under state and federal law. States implement programs for the gifted entirely at legislative discretion and all fifty states passed legislation to provide some financial assistance for these programs by 1997, although funding is minimal in some cases. Consequently broad differences in educational opportunities exist in school districts for students with identified gifts and talents.

Thirty-three states mandate programs requiring identification and services for gifted students. These generally are written state policies and regulations that include definitions of gifted students, identification procedures, curriculum and programming descriptions, and professional development requirements. Yet both policies and funding levels are widely divergent from state to state (Willard-Holt, 1997). The remaining states have permissive legislation which provide for discretionary state-supported gifted and talented programs. In these states the local school districts make decisions about identification and programming (Snyder, 1998).

The Marland Report of 1972 sparked interest in federal funding for gifted programs. This endeavor was temporarily suspended in 1981 but was reestablished in 1988 with the creation of the Jacob K. Javits Gifted and Talented Education Act (O'Connell, 1993). This act was amended in 1992 and currently provides the only federal funds for gifted programs. Funds derived from this grant are used to design and implement model programs and projects for gifted students in underserved populations and subsidize research on the needs of gifted and talented students through a National Research Center (U.S. Department of Education, 1998). With less than ten million dollars allocated for this act, a 1990 federal government document reported that only two cents of every $100 was spent on special programming addressing gifted education in the United States (O'Connell, 1993).

Program Descriptions

Gifted education program development involves setting criteria for several key areas. The definition of giftedness set forth by each school district determines the initial direction of the program. Standards for program design, student identification, curriculum and instruction, guidance and counseling, professional development, and program evaluation guide the course of action. Attention to gender bias and underachievement of gifted students are additional issues addressed when setting standards. The National Association for Gifted Children publishes standards for gifted programs (National Association for Gifted Children, 1998) that are worth attention.

Some states have written state plans for the management of their state gifted education programs. For example, Texas and Virginia have progressive gifted education plans. The state of Virginia includes in its goals for gifted education the grade levels of students targeted for services, the personnel at the state level to oversee such programs, funding for the program, and local district administrative responsibility (Virginia Department of Education, 1997).

Definitions

The term *gifted* describes individuals with special talents or aptitudes. With regard to children, gifted is generally used to describe those with talents or abilities beyond their years and includes those who perform at or show potential for performing at a remarkably high level of accomplishment in a particular area of interest (TEC §29.121, 1995). These children are best served by the use of special teaching methods and practices and the provision of opportunities that allow for their full development.

In a 1972 report to Congress, U.S. Commissioner of Education Sidney P. Marland, Jr. (1971) described "gifted" students, a definition that many districts have adopted:

> Children capable of high performance include those with demonstrated achievement and/or potential ability in any of the following areas, singly or in combination: general intellectual ability, specific academic aptitude, creative or productive thinking, leadership ability, visual or performing arts, and psychomotor ability. (p. 9)

Under this definition, the gifted population should include a minimum of 3% to 5% of the general student population.

The Texas Association for the Gifted and Talented provides a brief description of each of the areas of giftedness listed by Marland and serves as an example here.

1. General intellectual ability or talent is often recognized by a wide-ranging fund of general information, high levels of vocabulary, ease and speed in acquiring new information, and persistent questioning.
2. Specific academic aptitudes or talents are indicated by a student's ability to perform at a level beyond that considered age appropriate.
3. Creative or productive thinking is seen as the ability to produce new ideas by bringing together elements usually thought of as independent or dissimilar. Characteristics of creative and productive thinkers include openness to experience, ability to play with ideas, willingness to take risks, preference for complexity, positive self-image, and the ability to become submerged in a task.
4. Leadership ability can be defined as the ability to direct individuals or groups to a common decision or action and negotiate in difficult situations. This ability is usually demonstrated by a keen interest and skill in problem solving and can include displays of self-confidence, responsibility, cooperation, dominate personalities, and the ability to adapt to new situations.
5. Ability in the area of visual and performing arts include talents in art, music, dance, drama, and other related studies. Students who exhibit special talents in one of these categories are considered to be gifted in that area.
6. Psychomotor abilities are considered to include practical, spatial, mechanical, and physical skills. Indicators include advanced understanding of or achievement in any one or combination of these areas. It should be noted that these behaviors are seldom used as criterion for placement in gifted programs (Sayler, 1997).

Research indicates that students considered to be gifted usually display common intellectual, emotional, and social traits regardless of the area of giftedness in which they are identified. Intellectual traits may include advanced vocabulary, creative problem solving abilities, and passionate and focused interests. Other characteristics may include the ability to retain information in great detail, boredom with repetition, high energy levels, keen observation and questioning skills, unusually long attention spans, and preference for complexity over simplicity. Emotional and social traits indicating giftedness are a keen sense of humor, empathy for others, highly developed sense of fairness, high expectations, and few, but focused, friendships.

Program Design

Designs for gifted programs insure that students are provided learning experiences that reinforce students' strengths, needs, and interests. Some established practices for program design include a continuum of services, adequate funding, flexible grouping of students, and adequate time scheduled for instruction during the school day. Additionally, students need time to work independently, with other gifted students, and with regular education students during the school day (Texas Education Agency, 1996).

Gifted programs can be formatted in a variety of ways. Alternatives include magnet or residential schools, pull out programs, cluster grouping, and dual enrollment. In some school districts, options differ from grade to grade or campus to campus.

Some school districts designate magnet schools to serve a particular population of identified gifted students. Sometimes these populations are actually sub-populations of gifted students, for example when a magnet school serves only gifted performing arts students or gifted math and science students. Still others serve regular education students along with the gifted students. Generally, students must apply and audition before being accepted to a magnet school. Some states have gone so far as to establish residential schools for advanced instruction in several disciplines (O'Connell, 1993). Many states offer summer camps and Governors' Schools for qualifying students.

In "pull out" programs, identified gifted students are removed, or "pulled out" from their regular class for a specific period of time, either daily or weekly. Teachers with specialization in gifted education conduct these classes. During pull out classes students have a chance to work with a mentor, explore an individual research project, or work together with other gifted students.

Cluster grouping occurs when gifted students are served in general education classrooms but are grouped with other gifted students within the classroom for projects, enrichment activities, or cooperative learning. In most cases the regular classroom teacher attends to the cluster group, although some districts employ a gifted and talented specialist who moves from class to class to work with the gifted students.

Many districts offer dual or concurrent enrollment. In this situation students co-enroll in secondary and college level classes, earning credit for both courses. This dual arrangements allows gifted students to enter college having already accrued college credits. The College Board Advanced Placement (AP) courses allow students to be challenged by a college level curriculum while still in high school. Upon completion of an AP course, students can take the appropriate tests and earn college credit.

Identification

Both qualitative and quantitative measures should be taken into consideration when determining which students will be included in a gifted program. Factors to consider are:

- Whether or not to include all students—kindergarten through high school.
- If testing is to be done on an as-needed basis or simply once a year.
- What assessments are to be used.
- What arrangements will provide for non-English speaking students and those with disabilities.
- What professional development will provide for staff members who are involved in the final selection process.

Throughout the identification process, though, careful attention is paid to state or district guidelines as these take precedence over local decisions.

The inclusion of children of diverse cultural, ethnic, and economic backgrounds in gifted education remains a challenge for educators. Although gifted children can be found throughout all segments of the population, identification of children from cultural and ethnic minority groups in gifted programs is disproportionate to their numbers as a whole. Research indicates English-based assessment tools, limited allowance for differences in learning styles and life styles, and limited nominations of students by teachers all contribute to the low numbers of program participants from these populations (St. Jean, 1996).

While attempts to identify gifted and talented children are increasing, some misconceptions have developed. Not all gifted children like school or thrive in an academic setting. Some gifted children have trouble learning due to boredom, perfectionism, or other obstacles. Many gifted children do not read early or perform well in mathematical computations. Some gifted children have learning disabilities. No one is gifted in all areas. However, true "gifts" are lasting. The challenge for educators is to identify children free of these misguided beliefs.

Curriculum and Instruction

The curriculum taught in gifted programs is designed to maximize learning for the "whole" child. Gifted children—like all children—should be well rounded in their education. Social skills, creativity, and activities involving higher-level thinking skills are included. Such a curriculum promotes "concept" teaching and provides choices for the student both in activities and the products they turn out. The curriculum for the gifted program follows the general school curriculum with modifications for depth, complexity, and pacing. Various ways to deliver an appropriate curriculum include differentiated curriculum, curriculum compacting, Renzulli's enrichment triad, and mentor relationships.

When components of the curriculum "differ" from the regular instructional practices usually employed in a classroom, the curriculum is referred to as "differentiated." Specifically, differentiation occurs when teaching environments and practices combine to create appropriately altered learning experiences for students. Such teaching practices include (a) a variety of methods for students to investigate content, (b) several options for students to apply what they learn, and (c) an array of assessment tools (Tomlinson, 1995).

Some common elements inherent in a differentiated curriculum are:

Deletion of mastered material. Gifted students should not be expected simply to "do more." Completion of tasks that do not require application of new knowledge does little to increase learning.

Addition of new content, process, or product expectations. Concepts taught are organized around the learner. They add to the depth of the content. Varying learning styles are addressed along with the inclusion of intrinsic motivational activities. Additionally, gifted students are offered the option of completing an advanced level product that supports creativity, fluency, and flexibility (Dinnocenti, 1998).

Extension. Students learn best when they are curious. Extension activities are offered to those who grasp the intended objective and are ready to learn more. These activities are "learner friendly" so that a student is stimulated to increase his or her knowledge base. Extension encourages students to learn new strategies for constructing knowledge and is accomplished when the student is able to demonstrate advanced understanding of a concept.

Enrichment. Enrichment offers the child a more "in-depth" look at concepts they are already studying in their current academic areas or investigation of a discipline that is outside of the school's regular curriculum. For example, enrichment may include providing experiences in leadership skills or in the arts. The goal of enrichment activities is to allow the gifted student the freedom to apply old or new knowledge in a variety of settings.

Acceleration. Acceleration refers to altering content already learned or providing new content. This practice strengthens the student's ability to make connections between concepts already learned and those that are newly introduced. Acceleration may involve more rapid movement through a specific content area or instruction in an area determined to be a student's strength. Options include: (a) flexible pacing programs that offer advanced placement courses or dual enrollment in grade levels (Daniel & Cox, 1989), (b) credit by examination, and (c) instruction not normally included in the child's educational plan in a given area of aptitude such as fine arts or social skills.

Another approach to acceleration is described in Renzulli's book, *Five Dimensions of Differentiation* (Dinnocenti, 1998). Renzulli described the process for delivering a differentiated curriculum and includes goals for the classroom and the teacher. (It should be noted that teachers need to understand this process before attempting to use this delivery method.) In describing differentiation, Renzulli stated that depth is added to the curriculum by organizing curriculum by concepts and structure of knowledge. The process is enhanced when teachers use various teaching techniques and materials to accommodate various learning styles, and products are improved by students' ability to express their ideas through improved cognitive development. The classroom environment should contain options for flexible grouping such as learning centers, computer stations, and adequate room for free movement. If space is limited, the student can be allowed an alternative learning site such as the library, gym, or lab. Renzulli suggested that teachers should be models for learning, providing personal experiences, opinions, or beliefs that invite students to join in the process.

Curriculum compacting is another approach to teaching gifted students, one that can be used to motivate students. The advantage of curriculum compacting is that it reduces the amount of redundant work required of students. In some learning situations, gifted students have already mastered a skill or concept being introduced. The sensible approach is to provide gifted students with alternate learning experiences. Three major phases of compacting should be considered.

1. The goals or outcomes of the particular unit are defined and the teacher determines which content is new to the students.
2. The students are assessed to determine their knowledge and mastery of the new content (most often done through pre-testing).
3. Replacement activities are provided for those students that have previously attained mastery of the new content. Some examples are self-directed projects, activities focused on particular thinking skills, individual research projects, and group research projects. Management of the replacement activities is a critical component and is most often managed through a student-teacher compact (Reis, Burns, & Renzulli, 1992).

Another approach to teaching gifted students is offered by Renzulli's triad model of giftedness, composed of three clusters of human traits. This model is frequently the basis for enrichment programs. The traits Renzulli identified are (a) above-average ability, (b) task commitment, and (c) creativity. Gifted and talented students generally demonstrate high ability in all three areas (Johnsen, 1992). Three types of activities are developed to fit these traits. The first type of activity focuses on process skills and is used with select groups of students, addressing higher thinking levels, creativity, and communication. Lessons are delivered in a regular or special classroom. The second type of activity focuses on situations that pique a student's curiosity about a topic. Examples are guest speakers, hands-on projects, and field trips to investigate topics of study. The last type of activity is student driven projects. Here a student-teacher contract is helpful and completed projects are usually presented to outside audiences (Renzulli, 1999).

The use of mentors also enhances gifted students' educational acceleration. Mentors are people willing to share their time, knowledge of a specific area, and experience. A mentor can greatly impact the life of a gifted student by instilling passion, attitudes, or values through a meaningful relationship. Mentors are invaluable resources for some gifted students. Those students who have mastered all essential aspects of the curriculum and possess an aptitude and interest in many areas may have a difficult time setting priorities or long term goals such as college or career planning. For them, mentors often have a maturing effect and may even help a student develop a personal vision. Other groups of students who benefit from mentoring are students from disadvantaged populations and gifted females. These students have been shown to possess more self-confidence and have higher aspirations after being paired with a mentor (Berger, 1990). Mentoring relationships afford students a sense of what is necessary to achieve personal and professional goals. Steps that facilitate mentoring are:

1. Identify what a student needs.
2. Make certain that the student really wants to be mentored.
3. Identify prospective mentors and interview them.
4. Prepare the one to be mentored for the mentoring process.
5. Monitor the relationship (Berger, 1990).

Guidance and Counseling

Some gifted learners are better served when offered appropriate counseling. Gifted children tend to be more introverted than their peers (Freedman & Jensen, 1999). Many gifted students characterize themselves as perfectionists, a condition that may lead to stress, depression, and feelings of anxiety. Educators are cautioned to remember that gifted students are not always "good students" and may be even at risk for failure. Consequently, they require the same care and concern afforded any other student who is at risk.

Counseling for college and career guidance begins early in the school program for gifted students. Students who accelerate their studies in elementary and secondary classes need to consider college options at a younger age than most. Optimally, college and career considerations are discussed between the student, a secondary counselor with knowledge of college options, and the student's parents. Because many gifted students have several career path options, the ultimate selection may be more complex than it is for other students (Kerr, 1990). Not uncommon is a gifted student's deep interest in a career at an extremely young age.

Professional Development

A national survey conducted in 1998 indicated that a very small portion of professional development funds were used for gifted education training (Westburg, Burns, Gubbins, Reis, Park, & Maxfield, 1998). Educators at all levels are wise to take the time to obtain the skills and expertise to deliver appropriate curriculum and program options for gifted students. This training should include the nature of gifted students, their needs, innovative approaches to curriculum and instruction, and how gifted students are best assessed. Glickman, Gordon, and Ross-Gordon (1995) examined studies of effective staff development and found some common characteristics.

Common characteristics of effective staff development are:

- Involvement of administrators and supervisors in planning and delivering the program.
- Training experiences differentiated by teachers.
- Placement of the teacher in an active role (generating ideas, materials, etc.).
- Teacher choice of goals and activities.
- Teacher self-initiated and self-directed training activities.

Successful staff development programs that Glickman et al. (1995) examined showed these common themes:

- An atmosphere of collegiality and collaboration.
- Experimentation and risk taking.
- Time to work on staff development.
- Leadership and sustained administrative support.
- Designs built on adult learning principles and the change process.

In Texas, staff development is viewed as so necessary to successful gifted programs that not only are teachers required to engage in on-going training but building principals are also obligated to attend staff development on issues related to the gifted.

Program Evaluation

Evaluation of a school's gifted program is a critical piece and includes both formative and summative strategies. The results of an efficient and economical evaluation should be shared with all stakeholders and conducted on an annual basis. Stakeholders include students, teachers, administrators, and parents as well as other parties when necessary.

Contemporary Issues

Gender Bias

Research indicates that gifted girls often experience a drop in IQ scores during adolescence, do not receive recognition for their achievements, and attend less prestigious colleges than highly gifted boys. Studies have also shown that fewer females than males are considered to be gifted in science and math. Differential treatment by both parents and educators alike may contribute to this phenomenon (Rose, 1999).

Underachievement

Gifted students sometimes perform far below their ability level. Underachievement is generally defined as a discrepancy between academic performance and indicated potential; however, such behavior is case-specific and may involve subjective variables such as attitude and expectations. Underachievement is often linked to issues of self-esteem but students may underachieve in one area and overachieve in another, confounding such assertions. If underachievement is a behavior, it should be reversible with proper attention. Ultimately, the challenge is to determine the basis for this phenomenon and find ways to allow students to effectively overcome the problem (Delisle & Berger, 1990).

Ability Grouping

One of the most controversial issues in education centers on ability grouping students. Educators who favor ability grouping believe that student achievement is increased by reducing the difference in ability levels of students in a given class. High achieving students are believed to benefit from the increased pace and level of instruction as well as from the competition between peers of similar abilities. Lower achieving students are believed to receive more individual attention, repetition, and teacher review of their coursework (Hollifield, 1987).

Those who oppose ability grouping and favor homogeneous grouping often argue that ability grouping does not allow low-achieving students the stimulation and challenge offered them by higher achieving students. Furthermore, lower-achieving students, when grouped, sometimes receive low quality, "watered down" instruction. Consequently, "low-achieving" becomes a self-fulfilling prophesy (Hollifield, 1987).

Slavin (1986), on the other hand, argued that ability grouping creates academically elite groups of students within a school. He conducted a comprehensive review of research on ability grouping and recommended the following practices be applied when grouping students by ability:

- Students are identified primarily within a heterogeneous class.
- Students are grouped to be taught specific skills, not by IQ or achievement levels.
- Frequent assessment and reassignment based on progress is practiced and commonplace.
- The level and pace of instruction is dependent upon the regrouped students' levels of readiness and learning rates.

Separation of Gifted Students

Commonly used gifted "pull out" programs are one of the various ways schools meet state and local gifted requirements. Advocates of this arrangement have witnessed programs with well-trained teachers and coordinated curriculums. Often the small amount of time spent in a "pull out" program is not adequate to make a difference in the learning of most students (Tomlinson, 1999). Problems may also arise from the time of day or subject the student is removed from to attend the "pull out" gifted class. Consequently, general education teachers and gifted specialists are urged to communicate regularly.

Magnet programs also separate gifted students from the general education classroom. Commonly, magnet programs are offered to broaden a student's field of study in a specific areas such as science, math, or the performing arts. Large school districts are able to create magnet schools for gifted students, even at the elementary level. Admission criteria are generally rigorous.

While magnet programs can advance students at a faster pace and use an enriched curriculum with all students in the school, the same arguments used against ability grouping exist. Additionally, funding for such programs can be a major hurdle, particularly for poor or small districts.

School Leaders' Role in Gifted and Talented Programs

In order to develop and guide an exemplary program for gifted students, school leaders and program directors must attend to key issues. Some examples follow.

Students. The academic and emotional needs as well as the interests of gifted students sometimes differ from those of other students. These need to be understood. For example, when a gifted student threatens to drop out of school, leaders might explore boredom as a possible cause.

Parents. Parents of gifted students often have questions about their child and sometimes make unusual requests. Keeping lines of communication open between parents and the school staff is particularly important. One area that can be particularly sensitive is when a student is tested for the gifted program but does not qualify under the particular guidelines of that district. Explaining to the parents why their child does not qualify or why one child qualifies but his or her sibling does not often is a task that often falls to a teacher-leader or the principal. Conferences with parents should be handled professionally and with tact. Placing blame on the process used or on the gifted program director does little to establish working relationships with school personnel or with parents.

Instruction. Principals, together with teachers, make decisions about teaching assignments. Teachers of gifted students need appropriate training and should be current on instructional issues. In some states, teachers in the gifted program are required to have a graduate degree or specialization in gifted education. Since teacher certification and training varies from state to state, the Department of Education in the state should be consulted for requirements (Friedman-Jenkins, 1983). Because gifted students often present unique challenges, teachers who are willing to adapt to individual student needs and abilities should be selected for such positions. Effective principals maintain dialogue between gifted specialists, themselves, and other staff.

Teachers who are willing to take leadership roles in the school have unique opportunities to promote the success of gifted programs. Teacher-leaders can serve as mentors to teachers beginning their work with gifted students, can promote staff development that encourages all teachers to become skilled in teaching the gifted, and become advocates for gifted students in various situations. Teacher-leaders can also help dispel myths about gifted students. For example, a general education teacher may oppose placing an academically failing gifted student in a gifted and talented program because such a placement "rewards undesirable behavior" and should be reserved for "more deserving students." The teacher-leader has the opportunity to explain that academic failure is not uncommon behavior for gifted students.

Management of Gifted Programs. Management concerns arise when leaders work to meet the needs of gifted students. Some examples follow.

- Scheduling students into classes specifically designated for gifted students requires students and staff to make difficult choices when options are limited.
- Intervention may be needed if teachers experience conflict about work that is missed in the general education class when students are "pulled out" of their classes.
- Scheduling College Board Advanced Placement courses may be difficult, particularly in small and rural schools.
- Principals and teachers need to remain current in their knowledge of state and district gifted education guidelines. Scheduling training is a management issue.
- Program evaluations and training records must be updated regularly as many states have requirements for monitoring their gifted programs, including how funds are spent.

Summary

Education of the gifted has undergone many changes in the past 50 years. Currently, the legal and regulatory guidelines differ from state to state because there is no federal mandate for gifted programming. Some of the contemporary issues facing school districts include: defining and identifying giftedness, designing a program, planning the curriculum and instruction, and appropriately handling the challenges surrounding gifted students. Principals and teacher-leaders play key roles in insuring the success of programs for the gifted.

When education is strengthened for gifted students, society benefits. Gifted artists, authors, and musical composers enlighten us and bring us joy. Gifted scientists, inventors, and mathematicians broaden the world's horizons and make possible the seemingly impossible. Gifted statesmen and orators challenge social conscience and invite people to believe in one another. Those whose gifts or talents exceed the ordinary will continue to impact people's hopes, dreams, and lives. The responsibility of the education system is to nurture students who are gifted and cherish what they have to offer.

Applying Your Knowledge

Jack is a bright thirteen year-old eighth grade student in a small rural junior high school. His grade average is 74% in his core classes. Jack lives with his mother who is single and who quit school after the tenth grade. Jack has few friends, sometimes having to live in a homeless shelter. The few friends he does have are often in trouble with the law. Jack's special interests are magic and science experiments.

Jack easily qualified for the gifted program in his school when he was in the fifth grade. As a seventh grader he was identified as a Duke Scholar and scored high enough on the ACT to receive national recognition. Many of his teachers describe him as lazy and not inspired enough to complete his class assignments. The only teacher Jack trusts is his science teacher, Mr. Hale, who describes Jack as attentive and one of the best science students he has ever taught. Jack says that he does not have any idea what he will do with his life although he told Mr. Hale that he would like to attend college. Jack's mother is not supportive; she would like for him to get a job upon his graduation from high school and help support the two of them.

Jack obviously has the intellectual ability to attend college. The counselor is asking the eighth graders to make their course selections for the ninth grade. Jack is looking at the list of courses, wondering what to select.

Questions:

1. What are the key issues in this situation?
2. Can the school or the community help Jack academically and personally? If yes, provide some examples.
3. What level of courses should the counselor advise Jack to take, given his grade average? Who should be involved in this decision?
4. Should Jack be afforded special counseling services by the school? If so, on what should the counselor focus?
5. How much responsibility should be placed on Mr. Hale to help Jack?

Questions for Thought

1. Historically, world events and social change have impacted education for the gifted. Do you think that the Internet will change the course? If so, how?
2. Should the federal government be more involved in setting standards and providing funds for the gifted population?
3. How should elementary school gifted programs be designed? How should those at the secondary level be designed? How can they be implemented?
4. What actions can an administrator take to guard against gender bias in the identification and serving of gifted students?

For Further Information Online

Hoagies' Gifted Education Page **www.hoagiesgifted.org**
The Gifted Development Center in Denver **www.GiftedDevelopment.com**
The Hollingworgh Center for Highly Gifted Children **www.Hollingworgh.org**

References

Berger, S. (1990). *Mentor relationships and gifted learners.* ERIC Digest No. E486. Reston, VA: The Council for Exceptional Children. (ERIC Document Reproduction Service No. ED 321 491)

Colango, N., & Davis, G. (1991). *Handbook of gifted education.* New Jersey: Prentice Hall.

Daniel, N., & Cox, J. (1989). *Meeting the needs of able learners through flexible pacing.* ERIC Digest No. 464. Reston VA: The Council for Exceptional Children. (ERIC Document Reproduction Service No. ED 314 916)

Delisle, J. R., & Berger, S. L. (1990). *Underachieving gifted students.* ERIC Digest No. E478. Reston VA: The Council for Exceptional Children.

Dinnocenti, S. T. 1998, Winter). Differentiation: Definition and description for gifted and talented. *The National Research Center of the Gifted and Talented 1998 Winter Newsletter* [Online]. <www.sp.uconn.edu/~nrcgt/news/spring98/sprng985.html> [2000, Nov.].

Ellis, A. (1991). *An introduction to the foundation of education.* Boston: Allyn & Bacon.

Freedman, J., & Jensen, A. (1999). *Joy and loss: The emotional lives of gifted children* [Online]. <www.kidsource.com/kidsource/content4/joy.loss.eq.gifted.html> [2000, Nov.].

Friedman-Jenkins, R. (1983). *Professional training for teachers of the gifted and talented.* Reston, VA: ERIC Clearinghouse on Handicapped and Gifted Children. <http://www.kidsource.com/kidsource/content2/professional.gifted.html>[2000, Nov.].

Gold, M. (1965). *Education of the intellectually gifted.* Columbus, OH: Merrill Books.

Hollifield, J. (1987). *Ability grouping in elementary schools.* Urbana, IL: ERIC Clearinghouse on Elementary and Early Childhood Education. (ERIC Document Reproduction Service No. ED 290 542)

Johnsen, S. K. & Corn, A. L. (1992). *Screening assessment for gifted elementary students (primary) Examiner's manual.* Austin TX: PRO-ED.

Kerr, B. (1990). *Career planning for gifted and talented youth.* ERIC EC Digest No. E492. Reston VA: The Council for Exceptional Children. (ERIC Document Reproduction Service No. ED 321 497)

Law, K. (No date). *Strengthening instruction for gifted students using outstanding teaching strategies.* Bellevue, WA: Bureau of Education and Research.

Long, R. E. (Ed.). (1984). *The Reference Shelf: American Education, 56*(5). New York: The H. W. Wilson Company.

Marland, S. P., Jr. (1971). *Education of the gifted and talented,* Vol. 1 & 2. Washington, DC: U.S. Government Printing Office.

National Association for Gifted Children. (1998). *Pre-K - Grade 12 Gifted Program Standards* [Brochure]. Washington, DC: Author.

O'Connell, R. P. (1993). *National excellence: A case for developing America's talent.* Washington, DC: Office of Educational Research and Improvement.

O'Connor, E. (1980). *Education.* St. Paul, MN: Greenhaven Press.

Reis, S. M., Burns, D. E., & Renzulli, J. S. (1992). *Curriculum compacting: The complete guide to modifying the regular curriculum for high ability students.* Mansfield, CT: Creative Learning Press.

Renzulli, J. S. (1999). What is this thing called giftedness, and how do we develop it? A twenty-five year perspective. *Journal for the Education of the Gifted, 23*(1), 3-54.

Roets, L. F. (1995). *In-service manual for gifted & talented.* Des Moines, IA: Leadership Publishers, Inc.

Rose, L. (1999, Spring). Gender issues in gifted education. *The National Research Center of the Gifted and Talented 1999 Spring Newsletter* [Online]. <http://sp.uconn.edu/~nrcgt/news/spring99/sprng994.html> [2000, Nov.].

Sayler, M. (1997). *Raising Champions: A parent handbook for nurturing gifted children* (2nd ed.). Austin, TX: Texas Association for the Gifted and Talented.

Slavin, R. E. (1986). *Ability grouping and student achievement in elementary schools: A best evidence synthesis.* Baltimore, MD: Center for Research on Elementary and Middle Schools.

Snyder, T. D., & Plisko, V. (2000). Chapter 2 - Elementary and secondary education. In *Digest of Education Statistics, 1999.* [Online]. Washington, DC: National Center for Education Statistics. <http://nces.ed.gov/pubs2000/digest/d99t055.html> [2000, Nov.].

St. Jean, D. (1996, Spring). Valuing, identifying, cultivating, and rewarding talents of students from special populations. *The National Research Center of the Gifted and Talented 1996 Spring Newsletter* [Online]. <www.sp.uconn.edu/~nrcgt/news/spring96/sprng965.html> [2000, Nov.].

Texas Education Agency Division of Advanced Academic Services. (1996). *Texas state plan for the education of gifted/talented students.* [Online]. Austin, TX: Texas Education Agency. <www.tea.state.tx.us/gted/> [2000, Nov.].

Texas Education Code. §29.121 (September, 1995)

Tomlinson, C. A. (1995). *Differentiating instruction for advanced learners in the mixed-ability middle school.* ERIC Digest No. E536. Reston, VA: The Council for Exceptional Children. (ERIC Document Reproduction Service No. ED 389 141)

Tomlinson, C. A. (1999, October). Leadership for differentiated classrooms. *School Administrator* [Online]. <http://www.aasa.org/sa/oct9901.htm> [2000, Nov.].

U.S. Department of Education. (1998). *Javits gifted and talented students education program.* [Online] <www.ed.gov/prog_info/Javits/brochure.html> [2000, Nov.].

Virginia Department of Education Office of Programs for the Gifted. (1997). *The Virginia Plan for the Gifted.* Richmond, VA: Virginia Department of Education. <www.pen.k12.va.us/VDOE/Instruction/Gifted/gftpln.html> [2000, Nov.].

Westberg, K. L., Burns, D. E., Gubbins, E. J., Reis, S. M., Park, S., & Maxfield, L. R. (1998). *Professional Development Practices in Gifted Education: Results of a Nation Survey.* Storrs, CT: National Research Center of the Gifted and Talented.

Willard-Holt, C. (1997). *Gifted education and the law. PAGE Bulletin.* Norristown, PA: PAGE, Inc. (ERIC Document Reproduction Service No. ED 425 599)

Chapter 9

Counseling Programs

Richard E. Lampe, Jerry Trusty, and Reba J. Criswell

Ideally, counselors operate as part of the educational team in an early childhood through twelfth-grade counseling program that is planned and organized to meet the needs of all students.
Richard Lampe

Objectives:
- Provide the historical background of school counseling.
- Describe a role for the school counselor that works to benefit students.
- Outline the scope of counseling services.
- Specify the legal guidelines under which school counselors operate.
- Illustrate how guidance services can be organized and delivered.

Of the various services and programs for which educational administrators have responsibility, counseling programs may be one of the least well-defined. In some states, a model for an organized, comprehensive counseling program with specified services is provided (Sink, 1998). In other states, local administrators have varying dominion over the roles and responsibilities of school counselors. Whereas this may at first glance seem desirable for administrators, without research-based guidelines and administrative understanding of how counseling services can be effectively organized and orchestrated, students are less likely to receive the services they need.

Ponec and Brock (2000) described the relationships between school counselors and principals as crucial, yet principals and counselors sometimes see things differently. Summarizing the perspectives of students in counseling and in educational leadership departments at their university, Shoffner and Williamson (2000) wrote that principals-in-training focus on tasks, results, and legal liabilities, while counselors-in-training focus on process, dealing with the dilemma, and the importance of confidentiality. Shoffner and Williamson also described 14 points of conflict between counselors and principals including, for example, formal authority versus shared leadership, discipline, and evaluation of the counselor. These points of conflict and different opinions may be due to insufficient reciprocal understanding of the roles of counselors and principals. For example, in a nationwide survey of 376 department heads in administrator preparation programs, over 40% of the respondents held that preparation in guidance was insufficient at their universities, and over 13% of the respondents said no training about guidance whatsoever was available to future school administrators at their universities (Lampe, 1985).

In this chapter we will include a brief history of school counseling, definitions of related terms, and descriptions of appropriate roles of school counselors. We will also present contemporary views on how counselors' services can be integrated into an organized guidance program and discuss several ethical and legal guidelines related to school counselors. Finally, we will offer suggestions regarding counselors', administrators', and teacher-leaders' responsibilities for enhancing the counseling program's contributions to overall school effectiveness.

History of School Counseling

Although many pertinent events and conditions occurred earlier, the beginnings of the school counseling movement (or school guidance, as the concept has commonly been called) are often said to have taken place in the early 1900s (Gysbers & Henderson, 2000; Picchioni & Bonk, 1983). Societal changes during and following the Industrial Revolution, such as immigration and migration from agrarian to urban areas, resulted in concentrations of population in urban industrial centers. This led to an increasingly divergent population in the schools (Schmidt, 1999), concentrations of poverty, and masses of unskilled laborers (Picchioni & Bonk, 1983). With the increasing availability of public education to students from varying economic backgrounds, the resulting student population's needs expanded well beyond preparation for professional positions in areas such as law, medicine, and the ministry (Schmidt, 1999; Smith & Gideon, 1929). Subsequently, several schools began to provide guidance in areas of concern such as moral development and vocational choice.

Because of the expanding needs of students and the broadening expectations placed on public schools, guidance outgrew its vocational focus to include a broader range of services such as interpreting standardized tests and counseling students with personal/social/educational problems. Today, counselors provide an even wider range of services (adding, for example, consultation with parents and teachers, coordination of various activities, referral for specialized assistance, and teaching age-appropriate guidance curriculum to foster the personal, social, educational, and career development of all students). Ideally, counselors operate as part of the educational team in an early childhood through twelfth-grade counseling program that is planned and organized to meet the needs of all students.

Definitions of Related Terms

Guidance is sometimes used as the "umbrella" term that encompasses all of the services that counselors and others provide to promote student development. These services collectively are organized into *guidance programs* (albeit, some more organized than others). In current terminology, *counseling program* is sometimes used instead of *guidance program*. It is also popular to use the term *guidance curriculum* to refer to age-appropriate and planned goals, objectives, and activities related to personal, social, educational, and career development that counselors (and sometimes teachers) provide, often in the classroom. *Counseling* in schools historically has denoted a process involving a special relationship in which a trained professional (the counselor) directly assists students with personal problems and concerns. *Therapy* (also *psychotherapy*) is usually differentiated from school counseling in that therapy is more often associated with treatment of deep-rooted, long-standing psychological problems of clients or patients in clinical or medical settings (Myrick, 1997). In non-school settings (in community agencies and hospitals, for example), distinctions between counseling and psychotherapy are less delineated.

Counselor Roles

Although the duties of specific school counselors vary according to grade level assignment, student and community needs, expectations of school administrators, and governmental regulations, there are several broad categories of activities and services that describe appropriate counselor roles. These characteristically include, but are not limited to, counseling, consultation, coordination, assessment, large-group guidance, and program management—each of which will be summarized in this section. How these different yet interdependent roles can be incorporated into an organized program will be presented in the subsequent section.

Counseling

When used in school settings to describe a specific activity (as opposed to a program or to the profession) *counseling* refers to a process that involves helping students deal with problems of a personal, social, academic, or career development nature (Starr, 1996; Texas Education Agency, 1998). Counseling is provided to students on an individual basis or through small groups. If provided on a small group basis, the group is small enough to allow the counselor to monitor and incorporate the interactions of the group members. Whether individual or group based, counseling usually relates to students' problems and goals. Involving a relationship between the student and the counselor and theory-based techniques, counseling per se is not equated with advising or providing information.

Definitions of counseling vary, sometimes extending the domain of counseling beyond developmental and situational concerns into the area of addressing pathology as well. For school children, treatment of pathology, if necessary, is likely provided by specialists other than the school counselor, possibly through a referral to a resource such as a psychologist, psychiatrist, or community mental health agency counselor.

Consultation

Although school counselors sometimes use consultants to secure information or to discuss options for dealing with certain situations (perhaps the counselor needs the assistance of a qualified professional regarding how to proceed in an unusual case, how to address an ethical or legal concern, etc.), counselors also provide consultation as a service. In the role of being a consultant (as opposed to using a consultant), the school counselor provides service to the student indirectly—usually through direct contact with teachers, parents, and/or school administrators (Starr, 1996). For example, a teacher (called the consultee) who is having difficulty with a student might contact the school counselor (the consultant) for assistance. In their interactions, the counselor and teacher share information, discuss options, and perhaps jointly generate a plan of action for the teacher to implement (Myrick, 1997).

In consultation, although the direct contact is between the counselor and the consultee, the focus of their interaction is on the student—on how the consultee might interact directly with the student for the benefit of the student. In providing consultation, the counselor should guard against focusing on resolution of a personal problem the consultee might introduce. For example, the parent may seek assistance from the counselor for his/her alcoholism. Although this parent would probably benefit from personal counseling, provision of such for the parent is generally not within the role of the school counselor (American School Counselor Association, 1998).

Sometimes consultation is provided by the counselor on a group basis. For example, the counselor could work with a group of parents regarding parenting techniques, or the counselor could conduct professional development activities for teachers regarding interpretation of test results. In both instances, the ultimate beneficiaries are the students.

Coordination

As a counselor intervention, Myrick (1997) defined coordination as "the process of managing different indirect guidance services to students, including special events and general procedures" (p. 303). In providing this service, counselors are called upon to collect and disseminate information and to develop and maintain positive working relationships with other school professionals and outside resources in the community (Texas Counseling Association, 1992). As a coordinator, the counselor may also plan and arrange meetings, develop and operate special programs, supervise others, and provide leadership (Myrick). Examples of specific activities that counselors sometimes coordinate include Career Day, financial aid workshops, referrals of students to outside community agencies or practitioners, maintenance of student records, peer helper programs, orientation, scholarships, and student awards ceremonies.

It is possible for coordination to become a "catch-all" for quasi-administrative duties that are assigned to the counselor, leaving insufficient time and resources for the counselor to adequately serve students in ways more aligned with the counselor's professional qualifications. Coordination of the school's testing program is one example. Although often done by a school counselor, coordinating testing involves a large amount of time counting, packaging, and manipulating test materials—activities not requiring the qualifications of a professional counselor yet limiting the counselor's availability to provide more direct services (Burnham & Jackson, 2000).

Assessment

Assessment (sometimes called appraisal) refers to collecting and interpreting data to facilitate more-informed decisions. Assessment of students is accomplished by using standardized instruments (usually measuring achievement, aptitude, interest, or personality) and by less standardized techniques such as interviews, surveys, and observations. School counselors may also participate in the assessment of various environments affecting students such as school climate, home environment, and peer groups (Drummond, 2000).

In schools, assessment results are commonly used for purposes of student description (achievement level, educational diagnosis), placement (courses, special programs), prediction (educational or career planning), or to provide information for the school (curriculum planning and program effectiveness). To serve these purposes, school counselors interpret assessment results as needed to students, parents, teachers, and school administrators. Administration and interpretation of specialized assessments may require the services of the school diagnostician, school psychologist, or school psychometrist.

Large-Group Guidance

Counselors can provide information for and lead discussions with large groups of students. Often referred to as classroom guidance, the focus of this activity is on involving students as a group with information that is designed to meet their developmental needs. Commonly, large group guidance has instructional objectives related to personal and social skills, educational development, and career planning. Although instructional in nature, delivery of large- group guidance is not restricted to a lecture format—discussions, multi-media, panels, guest speakers, and other means of involving students in learning are frequently involved. As described, large group guidance is differentiated from group counseling, wherein a smaller and more cohesive group of students interact with each other and a counselor "for more intense and private assistance" (Myrick, 1997, p. 223).

A planned sequence of large group guidance objectives is often outlined in a *guidance curriculum* with content and delivery methods that are age-appropriate. A school's guidance curriculum should be planned with the overall needs of the students in mind. Some states provide guidance curriculum guidelines that can be useful in forming an individual school's (or district's) plan. Sink and MacDonald (1998) reported that 11 of 41 states they reviewed provided guidance curriculum models, with more states having models being developed.

The school counselor often delivers large group guidance, although classroom teachers also teach guidance-related curriculum. In such cases, counselors can assist teachers with planning and resource materials (Texas Counseling Association, 1992). According to Starr (1996), the guidance curriculum and guidance program should not be seen as ancillary to the school curriculum and school activities. Rather, it should be viewed as an integral component of the total curriculum and school.

Program Management

Whether viewed from the perspective of a lone counselor trying to serve all students in a rural area, or of a group of counselors serving a particular school, or of a central-office director of guidance for an entire district in a large city, the counselor should be involved in management of the guidance program. This is not to say that all counselors have an equal role, but all share some responsibilities. Viewed broadly, program management includes four components: planning, implementation, evaluation, and educating stakeholders (Texas Education Agency, 1998). Planning encompasses assessing needs, establishing realistic goals and objectives, setting priorities, and designing activities. The implementation component includes actuating and carrying out activities to meet objectives. Evaluation consists of judging the value or worth of both individual counselor activities and the overall program in terms of meeting desired objectives. Finally, educating stakeholders involves informing the school staff, parents, and the broader community about the guidance program (Texas Counseling Association, 1992).

Organization of Services

Although the roles described in the preceding section comprise many of the services provided by counselors, an effective guidance program is more than a loosely connected, unplanned, or hit-or-miss collection of counselors' efforts. Gysbers, Lapan, and Jones (2000) described a contemporary approach to guidance programming as involving the counselor in an "organized, sequential, structured, district-wide program of guidance and counseling K-12" (p. 349). Several resources (e.g., Campbell & Dahir, 1997; Gysbers & Henderson, 2000; Myrick, 1997; Starr, 1996) described how effective programs could be organized. Counselors and administrators should check with their particular state education agencies and/or state counseling associations regarding the availability of additional models.

Having an organized model to follow, or even having a written guidance program plan for a school, does not guarantee that an effective guidance program will be fully implemented. Gysbers, Lapan, and Blair (1999) summarized several studies in which it was found that students in schools with more fully implemented guidance programs were more likely to report higher grades, better preparation for the future, more positive school climate, higher scores on the ACT examination, and so forth; yet counselors are often asked to perform non-guidance duties that reduce the time available for guidance tasks (Burnham & Jackson, 2000).

In this section, we will summarize the Gysbers and Henderson (2000) comprehensive model. This model interrelates three broad elements: (a) content, which outlines what students should be able to do, or competencies, as a result of experiencing the guidance program; (b) organizational framework that addresses the what, why, and assumptions underlying the program as well as the program's major components; and (c) the resources needed.

Content

According to Gysbers and Henderson (2000), an organized, comprehensive guidance program specifies student competencies that are distinct and developmentally appropriate for different grade levels. These age-appropriate competencies are grouped into domains such as academic development, interpersonal skills, responsible choices, and knowledge of self and others; and it is common to use the same list of domains for all grade levels. Several resources are available for administrators and counselors to assist with the identification of age-appropriate competencies and with grouping these into domains, including models from the American School Counselor Association (Campbell & Dahir, 1997), the state of Missouri (Gysbers, Starr, & Magnuson, 1998), the state of Texas (Texas Education Agency, 1998), and the state of New Hampshire (Carr & Hayslip, 1989).

Organizational Framework

Gysbers and Henderson (2000) proposed that it is important to provide stakeholders with clear statements that (a) define the guidance program and identify its importance in the overall educational process, (b) explain the rationale for the program, perhaps including community/student needs, state guidelines, and so forth, and (c) clarify assumptions—the premises underlying the program's success such as administrative support, availability of professionally qualified school counselors, and commitment to serve all students across all grade levels. Sample statements of definition, rationale, and assumptions are provided in the literature (Gysbers & Henderson, 2000; Texas Education Agency, 1998), although individual schools or districts should develop their own in accordance with local situations.

In addition, Gysbers and Henderson (2000) delineated the organizational framework through identification of four major guidance program components. These components, briefly introduced in the paragraphs below, include guidance curriculum, responsive services, individual planning, and system support.

Guidance Curriculum. Earlier in this chapter, guidance curriculum was defined as referring to age-appropriate and planned goals, objectives, and activities related to personal, social, educational, and career development. The guidance curriculum is often implemented through classroom units taught by counselors, by counselors and teachers on a team basis, or by teachers with counselor support and consultation. Other vehicles for implementing the guidance curriculum involve larger group activities such as Career Days, college/technical school nights, financial aid workshops, and orientations of students to a new school level. Through the guidance curriculum, many of the desired student competencies mentioned above in the content section are addressed. Examples of age-appropriate curricular goals, objectives, and activities related to guidance are available in the literature (e.g., Gysbers & Henderson, 2000), but these are samples only—to provide a starting place for the evolution of a locally appropriate guidance curriculum.

Responsive Services. Whereas the guidance curriculum component provides guidance-related content to all students for everyday life skills, the responsive services component is designed to provide prevention and/or intervention related to immediate concerns of a smaller number of students (Texas Education Agency, 1998). According to Starr (1996), these services should be available to all students, and students often initiate services in this component. These students are in situations where (a) preventive action is called for because of threats to healthy development or (b) remedial intervention is necessary to resolve a problem that is already interfering in a student's life. Counselors' responses to either of these situations often involve the earlier described roles of consultation, counseling (including crisis counseling), and/or referral.

Individual Planning. A third component of a comprehensive guidance program is individual planning (Gysbers & Henderson, 2000). This component focuses on helping each individual understand self-development and formulate and monitor plans that are goal oriented. Planning courses to be taken in high school to reach one's goals is an example. In assisting students with their individual planning, counselors attempt to help students understand and maneuver through viable alternatives and to help them avoid premature and irrevocable decisions. Although plans regarding personal/social development are included, much of the individual planning component is related to educational and career domains. Even though titled *individual planning,* a portion of this component is accomplished through group guidance—particularly with regard to awareness and exploration of educational and career opportunities. An individual's plan that is made in secondary school is grounded in developmental guidance curriculum activities carried out in elementary school.

System Support. The fourth guidance program component, system support, is necessary to sustain the other three. System support activities include, for example, conducting research regarding program effectiveness, providing for continuing professional development of counselors, promoting the program through public relations, organizing and managing the program, educating parents, and consulting with teachers (Gysbers & Henderson, 2000). Because the guidance program is an integral part of the larger school program, counselor activities that support the school as a system, such as serving on academic curriculum committees, serving on community committees and boards, and assessing student needs also provide relevant system support. Many system support activities are carried out through the earlier mentioned counselor roles of consultation and program management.

Component Balance. The four guidance components are integrated in different proportions based on the needs of the students. This is particularly evident as one compares and contrasts time spent in each component at elementary, middle, and high school levels. In general, counselors and administrators should expect more emphasis on guidance curriculum than other components at the elementary level, and this focus usually decreases at the upper grade levels. On the other hand, individual planning usually involves less time in the program at the elementary level, but it increases significantly in high-school programs. Responsive services maintain a steady and significant portion of the time balance at all three levels. The fourth component, system support, also maintains a fairly steady emphasis through all levels, generally involving less time than the other components throughout (e.g., Gysbers & Henderson, 2000; Texas Education Agency, 1998). These typical component ratios are not rigid, however, and should be adjusted as student needs change.

Program Development

School counseling literature provides several models for developing a program (e.g., Gysbers & Henderson, 2000; Schmidt, 1999; Texas Education Agency, 1998). Among these, various authors have chosen different labels for the steps in the program development process, and some variations exist in the order of proposed actions to be taken. However, similarities are more common than differences and in many program development models follow this order:

- An assessment is made of the current program.
- Organizing for change occurs.
- Needs are assessed.
- Planning and designing the new or revised program is done.
- The program is implemented.
- The implemented program is evaluated.

Also, using a committee (steering committee, guidance committee, advisory committee) is commonly recommended to facilitate the process throughout its steps (e.g., Gysbers & Henderson, 2000; Myrick, 1997; Schmidt, 1999).

Assessing the Current Program

Assuming that some form of counseling or guidance activities exist, an informal determination that the current counseling program is not as effective as it could or should be is often the spur for change. Once change is being considered, a more formalized assessment of the current program is in order. This might begin with a review of the current written program plan with regard to adequacy and extent of implementation. Potential indicators of the level of program adequacy could include reviews of counselor logs; program budgets; student records; job descriptions and actual involvement of counselors and other personnel; feedback from students, parents, teachers, and administrators; and adequacy of facilities, materials, and equipment (Schmidt, 1999; Texas Education Agency, 1998).

Organizing the Support Needed for Change

Moving a school from the situation of having guidance as a bare collection of services to having a comprehensive and organized counseling program involves a level of change that often raises anxiety and sometimes evokes resistance. Having commitment from all staff, including administrators, is important. The process of change itself should not overwhelm, and time and budget must be set aside for assessing, organizing, planning, implementing, and evaluating. Mitchell and Gysbers (as cited in Gysbers & Henderson, 2000) emphasized that an effective organized change process is incremental rather than abrupt.

Appropriate leadership for the change process should be identified. Gysbers and Henderson (2000) proposed (a) that a steering committee be formed to manage the overall change process and (b) that a school-community advisory committee be formed to provide recommendations and advice as a liaison between the school and community. The advisory committee does not form policy or make decisions. The steering committee must be small enough to manage its charge and large enough to be representative of counselors, administrators, teachers, parents, special school personnel (such as the special education coordinator and the school nurse), and perhaps community leaders. The steering committee in this stage would work with the administration and meet with the school board to inform and to seek support and authorization to proceed with the change process.

Assessing Needs

Gibson, Mitchell, and Higgins (1983) described needs assessment as the foundation of program development. They describe processes for assessing the needs of the community, the school, and the target populations (primarily students, but also teachers and parents). A variety of techniques are available ranging from surveys, interviews, focus groups, and Delphi studies to examination of school and public records. Russo and Kassera (1989) described a comprehensive needs-assessment package effectively used in a large high school. In addition to providing a useful needs-assessment model, they pointed out that needs may vary depending on sub-groupings in the student population (such as grade level, gender, ability group, racial, and ethnic differences), and that this lack of homogeneity suggests that needs particular to certain groups must not fall victim to pressures to identify only overall needs.

Designing the Program

A general program model, such as the model described above consisting of guidance curriculum, responsive services, individual planning, and system support, is adopted and studied thoroughly by the steering committee. The model should be publicized along with statements of rationale and fundamental assumptions that are made. The content areas to be infused in the comprehensive guidance curriculum are determined. In designing the program, the assessed needs should be considered on the bases of both frequency and intensity before they are prioritized to form the basis for overall program goals, particular curriculum content areas, program balance (relative emphasis on the four components at different grade-levels), and specific program objectives. Gysbers and Henderson (2000) suggest an alternative—that the formal needs assessment (see preceding section) be conducted *after* the program is designed in order to use desired student competencies established in the program designing stage as items in the formal needs assessment.

Implementing the Program

Implementing the program involves carrying out the designed improvements and using the school counselors in accordance with job descriptions that properly utilize counselors' competencies. Carefully designed and prioritized activities, provision of staff development for counselors and others involved in the program, and acceptance of a fitting model for the evaluation of school counselor performance facilitate implementation (Texas Education Agency, 1998).

Evaluating the Program

Broadly defined, evaluating the counseling program involves gathering data about the program, and it also involves using the data to draw conclusions about the value of the program. As such, evaluation forms the basis for changing a program to increase its effectiveness, for demonstrating accountability (i.e., responsiveness) to needs, and for counselors' professional development and growth. Proper program evaluation requires clearly stated goals that are agreed upon by those involved in the evaluation procedure. As one would find in many fields, program evaluation is a continuous process, not an outcome goal itself. Subsequent to evaluation, requirements for change are recognized, and the cycle of organizing, assessing, designing, and implementing becomes continual.

Evaluating the counseling program entails using data about the (a) delivery of services and (b) the outcomes related to those served. Schmidt (1999) clarifies that delivery of services can be evaluated by reporting how many times the services were provided, by how many people received the service, and by surveying recipients to assess their degree of satisfaction with the service(s) provided. Services-oriented evaluations may also focus, for example, on the balance of time allocated to the different program components, availability of the counselors, timely delivery of services, and relationships between counselors and other school personnel. Program evaluation may also be approached by assessing outcomes. This aspect of evaluation centers on assessing the development and/or improvement of competencies in areas such as study skills, decision-making strategies, academic grades, career awareness, and school attendance—either on a school-wide basis or as needed on an individual student basis. Schmidt points out that if such assessments are limited to school-wide data, the program runs the risk of not addressing the needs of individual students or of small groups of students.

Inherent in program effectiveness is the effectiveness of the counselors in performing their roles. Therefore, an effective means of evaluating individual counselor performance should be incorporated into program evaluation (Texas Education Agency, 1998). Regardless of the evaluative procedures or databases used, evaluation of individual counselor performance should be based on the job description that the counselor is expected to follow, the procedures should be understood by the evaluator and counselor in advance, and the model should be flexible enough to reflect variations agreed upon by the counselor and evaluator. Schmidt (1999) and the Texas Counseling Association (1992) provide general and specific models, respectively, for counselor performance evaluation. Evaluations should be based on data gathered through a variety of means such as observations (live or taped), interviews, self-reports, input from those receiving services, products developed by counselors, records of activities, and outside expert review.

If observations of counselors performing activities are being used as a database, guidelines regarding such observations should be agreed upon. Several resources (e.g., Gysbers & Henderson, 2000; Henderson & Lampe, 1992; Texas Counseling Association, 1992) are available to assist with developing guidelines for using observation as a database in counselor performance evaluation.

Ethical and Legal Guidelines

Ethical and legal considerations affect principals and counselors daily. School counselors have two major sources of ethical guidelines: (a) the *Ethical Standards for School Counselors* (American School Counselor Association, 1998) and (b) the *ACA Code of Ethics and Standards of Practice* (American Counseling Association, 1995). In order for the administrator to better understand the counselor's role and decisions, it is important for school administrators and teachers to be aware of several ethical issues addressed in these codes. Although ethical standards are not in themselves laws, they often relate to legal issues. Administrators must be familiar with federal and state laws that affect education and counseling in particular. These relate to many issues such as release of records, discrimination, documentation, academic requirements, testing, staffing, reporting child abuse, credentials, and special populations. Two general ethical issues drawn from the *Ethical Standards for School Counselors*, both with possible legal ramifications, are presented in the following paragraphs.

Ethically, the school counselor's primary obligation is to the counselee, and information obtained by the counselor is kept confidential unless there is clear and imminent danger to the counselee or others or legal requirements for disclosure. In clear and imminent danger situations, the counselor is ethically called upon to inform appropriate authorities. An ethical dilemma is presented to the counselor when an administrator or teacher demands confidential information that does not fall into the above categories. Confidentiality also applies to counseling records, which are to be released only according to prescribed laws and school policies (American School Counselor Association, 1998).

Another ethical issue that school counselors and the rest of the school staff sometimes see differently involves dual relationships, wherein the counselor and the client have a relationship outside of counseling that might impair the counselor's impartiality and/or the willingness of the student to participate in counseling. Obvious examples include sexual contact with clients, counseling family members, and counseling one's own students if the counselor is also a teacher of record. A dual relationship problem occurs when the counselor is called upon to administer or witness punishment or is placed in a potentially disciplinary "spotlight" such as hall monitor. In small communities, some dual relationships are impossible to avoid (e.g., children of family, children of friends, or members of the same church), and the ethical standards provide guidelines for reducing the potential for harm if dual relationships are unavoidable (American School Counselor Association, 1998).

Counselor Roles in Promoting Counseling Program Effectiveness

In addition to effectively carrying out the counselor roles described earlier in this chapter, the counselor has responsibility for doing so in a professional manner. (Texas Counseling Association, 1992). This requires a commitment to following ethical standards, carrying one's load, being timely and available, maintaining collegiality, advocating for students, and modeling service. The counselor should demonstrate and promote teamwork among school professionals and keep administrators informed (within ethical limits of confidentiality). The school counselor also is obligated to engage in professional development to stay knowledgeable of current social conditions, techniques, ethical standards, and laws.

School Leaders' Roles in
Promoting Counseling Program Effectiveness

School leaders' roles in promoting the formation and effectiveness of a comprehensive counseling program are varied. These may differ some by staff or administrative level (e.g., teacher-leader, principal, and superintendent), but regardless of the level, the roles at different levels often parallel each other.

For example, at all levels, the teacher-leaders and the principal play an important role of supporting program development/improvement efforts in house (among faculty and staff) and in the community. Formal and informal (and frequent) public relations activities, whether spoken or written, can have substantial impact. The administrator must promote a budget that allows for the necessary resources, clerical assistance, facilities, information resources, assessment tools, equipment, and supplies. Also in the budget, the administrator must address funding for professional development activities to better meet the needs of the district by improving the competencies of the counselors (Gysbers & Henderson, 2000).

The superintendent and school board play an important role in hiring an adequate number of properly qualified professional counselors. This is particularly crucial given the shortages of counselors in some areas and the calls for lowering the ratio of school counselors to students, both of which could force administrators to hire less than qualified counselors (Towner-Larsen, Granello, & Sears, 2000).

Teacher-leaders play an important role in determining the degree to which the school counselors' time is spent with students and teachers who need their services. Teacher-leaders serve as models for the rest of the staff by sending students in need of guidance for counseling, by seeking advice on student issues from the counselor, by working collaboratively with the counselor on behalf of a troubled student, and by letting new and uninformed teachers know of the counseling services available.

Assuming properly qualified counselors are hired, the administrator, particularly the building principal, exercises a central role in determining whether or not counselors are involved in non-guidance activities. Burnam and Jackson (2000) reported that although counselors do perform the functions described in contemporary program models, there are discrepancies and wide variations. They further suggest that assignment of non-guidance duties to counselors remains a most troublesome practice and that involvement of administrators is vital in determining who best should carry out these non-guidance tasks. Gysbers and Henderson (2000) echoed this problem, arguing that it is necessary to streamline counselor involvement in non-guidance activities. Myrick (1997) pointed out that coordination, an appropriate role of counselors, can become a "catch all" source of overload, and that coordination of activities should be shared with other personnel to give counselors time for more direct services.

If a lead counselor in a school is not available to do so, the principal is often responsible for evaluating the effectiveness of individual counselors. This requires an understanding of the proper roles of counselors, a commitment to using counselors fittingly, and knowledge of suitable standards and databases upon which to base the evaluations (Texas Counseling Association, 1992). Closely related to evaluation is supervision, or overseeing the work of others to improve performance and professional development (Borders & Leddick, 1987). Henderson and Lampe (1992) described an effective model of supervision of counselors in a large school district, with particular emphasis on clinical supervision involving feedback regarding counselor activities observed in progress.

Summary

Roles and responsibilities of school counselors vary, based on the needs of constituencies served and the understandings and expectations of principals who are ultimately responsible for guidance operations in their schools. In this chapter, we have attempted to describe varying roles of counselors, define commonly used counselor-related terms, and explain how counseling and guidance services can be organized, improved, and evaluated. Several ethical situations that counselors and principals might see from different perspectives were presented, and the importance of the counselor and the principal working as a corps for the benefit of students was emphasized. The following case study and questions were constructed to help pull together the information and ideas presented in this chapter.

Applying Your Knowledge

During the first few weeks as principal of a school, you have observed with much dissatisfaction, the manner in which the school counseling program is being conducted. The two school counselors in your building appear overburdened and preoccupied with administrative tasks and clerical work. What is worse, you recognize that many students' needs are not being met or even being considered. There appears to be a lack of support and involvement from within the school system as well as from the community and parents. You have some knowledge of the organization of a comprehensive guidance program, as this was how the school counseling program was designed at your previous school. You decide to approach both school counselors individually to ask their opinion of their roles and duties as school counselors.

You first approach Jan, as she has been with the school the longest period of time. After expressing your concerns, particularly in the area of students' needs, she quickly becomes defensive. She comments that she has tried to meet all the demands placed on her at this school, but there just isn't enough time to comply with everyone. She also states she feels resentful that she has been subjected to roles and functions that were not in her area of training. You attempt to reassure her that it is not your intent to condemn, but that you are looking for ways to improve the program so everyone benefits. Jan negatively responds, "I tried to convince the previous principal that things were not working smoothly; however, she didn't appear to care. So, I feel it will be a miracle if anything significant changes around here."

Your next visit is with Susan, a second-year school counselor. She shares that she feels very distressed over the roles and functions expected of her. The counselor-student ratio is approximately 1:500 students. Overwhelmingly, she comments that she feels caught up in administrative tasks totally inappropriate to her specific training; as a result, students' needs are neglected. Given the fact that last year she was new to the school, she did not feel comfortable approaching the principal about her concerns. She indicated that she welcomed any ideas the principal may have to improve the program.

Questions:

1. What do you think may be contributing to Jan's resistance and negative attitude?
2. What steps would you take to build cooperation, trust, and support from staff regarding the implementation of a comprehensive guidance program?
3. What approaches could you take to elicit support from students, parents, and the community?
4. What role could teacher-leaders in the school play in changing the guidance program?
5. Do you anticipate a counselor-student ratio of 1:500 students a barrier to the effective implementation of a comprehensive guidance program? If so, what are some suggestions for dealing with these challenges?

Questions for Thought

1. What are the major advantages of a comprehensive guidance program? What might be some disadvantages?
2. When implementing change, what are the benefits of a master plan of action?
3. What is the importance of program evaluation? What is the importance of individual counselor evaluation? How often should these processes occur, and what might be done to lessen the overwhelming task?
4. In what ethical and legal aspects of counselor functioning should an administrator seek professional development?

For Further Information Online

The American Counseling Association **www.counseling.org**
The American School Counselor Association **www.schoolcounselor.org**

References

American Counseling Association. (1995). *ACA code of ethics and standards of practice*. Alexandria, VA: Author. [Online].
<http://www.counseling.org/resources/codeofethics/htm> [2001, January 5].
American School Counselor Association. (1998). *Ethical standards for school counselors*. Alexandria, VA: Author. [Online]
<http://www.schoolcounselor.org/ethics/standards.htm> [2001, January 5].
Burnham, J. J., & Jackson, C. M. (2000). School counselor roles: Discrepancies between actual practice and existing models. *Professional School Counseling, 4*(1), 41-49.
Borders, L. D., & Leddick, G. R. (1987). *Handbook of counseling supervision*. Alexandria, VA: American Association for Counseling and Development.
Campbell, C. A., & Dahir, C. A. (1997). *National standards for school counseling programs*. Alexandria, VA: American School Counseling Association.
Carr, J. V., & Hayslip, J. B. (1989). Getting unstuck from the 1970s: New Hampshire style. *The School Counselor, 37*, 41-46.
Drummond, R. J. (2000). *Appraisal procedures for counselors and helping professionals*. (4th ed.). Upper Saddle River, NJ: Merrill.
Gibson, R. L., Mitchell, M. H., & Higgins, R. E. (1983). *Development and management of counseling programs and guidance services*. New York: Macmillan.
Gysbers, N. C., & Henderson, P. (2000). *Developing and managing your school guidance program* (3rd ed.). Alexandria, VA: American Counseling Association.
Gysbers, N. C., Lapan, R. T., & Jones. B. A. (2000). School board policies for guidance and counseling: A call to action. *Professional School Counseling, 3*(5), 349-355.
Gysbers, N. C., Lapan, R. T., & Blair, M. (1999). Closing in on the statewide implementation of a comprehensive guidance program model. *Professional School Counseling, 2*(5), 357-366.
Gysbers, N. C., Starr, M., & Magnuson, C. (1998). *Missouri comprehensive guidance: A model for program development, implementation, and evaluation*. Jefferson City, MO: Missouri Department of Elementary and Secondary Education.
Henderson, P., & Lampe, R. E. (1992). Clinical supervision of school counselors. *The School Counselor, 39*, 151-157.
Lampe, R. E. (1985). Principals' training in counseling and development: A national survey. *Counselor Education and Supervision, 25*, 44-47.
Myrick, R. D. (1997). *Developmental guidance and counseling: A practical approach* (3rd ed.). Minneapolis, MN: Educational Media Corporation.

Picchioni, A. P., & Bonk, E. C. (1983). *A comprehensive history of guidance in the United States.* Austin, TX: Texas Personnel and Guidance Association.

Ponec, D. L., & Brock, B. L. (2000). Relationships among elementary school counselors and principals: A unique bond. *Professional School Counseling, 3*(3), 208-217.

Russo, T. J., & Kassera, W. (1989). A comprehensive needs-assessment package for secondary school guidance programs. *The School Counselor, 36,* 265-269.

Schmidt, J. J. (1999). *Counseling in schools: Essential services and comprehensive programs* (3rd ed.). Boston: Allyn & Bacon.

Shoffner, M. F., & Williamson, R. D. (2000). Engaging preservice school counselors and principals in dialogue and collaboration. *Counselor Education & Supervision, 40,* 128-140.

Smith, L. W., & Gideon, L. B. (1929). *Planning a career.* New York: American Book Company.

Sink, C. A., & MacDonald, G. (1998). The status of comprehensive guidance and counseling in the United States. *Professional School Counseling, 2*(2), 88-94.

Starr, M. F. (1996). Comprehensive guidance and systematic educational and career planning: Why a K-12 approach? *Journal of Career Development, 23,* 9-22.

Texas Counseling Association. (1992). *Texas evaluation model for professional school counselors (TEMPSC).* Austin, TX: Author.

Texas Education Agency. (1998). *A model developmental guidance and counseling program for Texas public schools: A guide for program development pre-K – 12th grade.* Austin, TX: Author.

Towner-Larsen, R., Granello, D. H., & Sears, S. J. (2000). Supply and demand for school counselors: Perceptions of public school administrators. *Professional School Counseling, 3*(4), 270-276.

Chapter 10

Accessing Central Office Resources

Anita Pankake

Administering special programs in a school is one among many areas for which principals and teachers need the help and support of central administration. Taking full advantage of the resources that exist in the district's central office is a responsibility as well as an opportunity for school leaders.

Anita Pankake

Objectives:
- **Provide an understanding of the role of central office staff in regard to schools.**
- **Present a model that promotes collaboration and cooperation between the school and central office staffs.**
- **Demonstrate how school leaders can best access the persons and resources available at central administration.**

Almost every special program in a school district is accompanied by one or more specialists, consultants, directors, coordinators, or assistant superintendents who function external to the classroom delivery of that program. Often, though not always, the individuals who occupy these positions are located at the school district's central office. According to the National Center for Educational Statistics (May 1995) over 31,000 positions comprise some aspect of central office operations other than the superintendent. Robinson (1992) estimated that approximately 4.3% of an average school district's budget is allocated to support these central office positions.

Traditionally, the purposes of such positions have been to monitor and control decisions and resources related to specific programs and administrative functions. Additionally, responsibility for support, assistance and coordination of program efforts for the district as a whole often appear in the formal job descriptions for such positions. Unfortunately, these central office positions have not always been viewed as particularly helpful by the intended audience, i.e., individuals at the school. The perspective of principals and teachers regarding the responsibilities and practices of these various administrators is often less than positive. Rather than seeing the superintendent and the central office administrators as individuals whose roles are to serve and support, the individuals operating at the delivery points of these programs (principals and teachers) see people in these positions as creators of complications, confusion, and massive paperwork. Sarason (1996) offers a particularly poignant description of such perceptions:

> The dominant impression one gains is that school personnel believe that there is a system, that it is run by somebody or bodies in some central place, that it tends to operate as a never ending source of obstacles to those within the system, that a major goal of the individual is to protect against the baleful influences of the system, and that any one individual has and can have no effect on the system qua system..." (p. 163).

Whitaker & Moses (1994) point out that within the TQM philosophy proffered by W. Edwards Deming, the most important job of leaders is to find and remove barriers in the organization that might be preventing people from being successful. Whitaker & Moses, then, transfer this perspective to the school superintendent by stating that, "It is up to the superintendent to remove the hurdles faced by principals and teachers as they initiate change. Central office personnel must begin to view themselves not as regulators, but as leaders who help initiate improvement efforts and involve others in those efforts" (p. 166). They go on to assert that, "One thing is certain, school level changes are near impossible without the help and support of central administration"(Whitaker & Moses, 1994, p. 166).

Administering special programs in a school is one among many areas for which principals and teachers need the help and support of central administration. Taking full advantage of the resources (human and non-human) that exist as district's central office is a responsibility as well as an opportunity for school leaders. Central office, no matter how large and complex or small and overworked, can provide information, technical assistance, legal advice, networking with programs in other districts and regions, clerical support, and myriad other essentials for the quality operations of special programs at the building level. This chapter will give an overview of central office in terms of definition and design and some information regarding significant changes that are being initiated and/or being thrust upon central office administrative operations because of efforts to decentralize and increase site-based decision-making for school improvement efforts. The last section offers some specific ways in which school leaders can access and utilize central office services and support. A tone of advocacy is evident throughout the chapter. Neglect of or inappropriate use of the resources available to school leaders—in this case, those at central office—result in missed opportunities to do our best for the children we serve.

A Brief Overview of Central Office

Today, the fact that there is a central office staff in a school district is taken for granted. Now and then there may be some grinching about the organization being "top heavy" or "having too many people 'over there'", but, according to English (1992), administrative roles other than the principal and superintendent have become a fixed part of our thinking regarding school district administration. The general development of central office is described by Knezevich (1984). He marks the beginning of central office administration with what he refers to as the "one-person-office-of-the superintendent." During this time an individual in the position of superintendent often taught one or two classes, coached, and/or did the district's clerical work. Other duties at the central office were formed as assists to the initial administrative position of school superintendent. Knezevich (1984) divides the development of central office into three phases:

- Phase one began when superintendents were relieved of non-administrative functions such as teaching and coaching.
- Phase two occurred when personnel were hired to assume the clerical and non-professional administrative responsibilities of the school district.
- Phase three was initiated when enrollments in elementary and secondary units became large enough to merit their own full-time administrators.

As might be expected, large districts were the first to move through these phases and actually develop a central office team. As various federal and state initiatives have been implemented, new and different needs for specialized administrative positions have developed. Many larger districts have one or more central office administrative or supervisory positions devoted each to special education, guidance and counseling program, migrant education, bilingual and ESL programs, programs for the gifted and talents, vocational education, tech prep, and myriad others. The number and focus of specialized management positions at the district level varies between and among school districts and can change with any federal or state legislation or state department initiative.

Orlosky, McCleary, Shapiro, & Webb (1984) claim that "To understand the configuration of administrative and supervisory positions of a district central office, one can subdivide the responsibilities of the superintendent as required by the number, complexity, and size of tasks into a range of positions occupied by specialists. This configuration is referred to as the superintendency" (p. 50). Central office management for the district is created when a function or set of functions is divided into specific tasks and delegated to a specialist. Depending on the nature of the tasks delegated, the administration will be structured into levels with assistant superintendents in charge of one or more functions. Major tasks under the responsibility of an assistant superintendent may be assigned to directors. Although titles may differ, two- and three-level hierarchies of administrative specialists are not uncommon.

Little uniformity exists in titles and the commensurate responsibilities of central office positions from one district to another. Such variation in these positions exist to the extent that a study by the Association for Supervision and Curriculum Development completed in the 1980s concluded that the roles of central office supervisors were so unique from one district to another that they were "non-comparable" (Snyder, Giella, & Fitzgerald, 1994). Knezevich (1984) demonstrates this vividly in the following statements, "Members of the administrative team include personnel with such diverse titles as deputy, associate or assistant superintendent; director; supervisor; administrative assistant; coordinator; and consultant, all of whom are attached to the office of the superintendent of schools" (p. 312). However, the distinguishing characteristic of central office administrators is that they, "...are charged with responsibilities that are system-wide in scope but limited in range within the institutions. Thus, the supervisor of music's functions are system-wide in scope but confined to music; the assistant superintendent in charge of elementary education is responsible for elementary education only, but in all parts of the system" (p. 312).

An important distinction to make between and among central office administrators is related to knowing the hierarchical power and authority of their roles. English (1992) differentiates the two types of positions, "line" and "staff." He defines line positions as those "directly concerned with implementation" and staff positions as "those who support, but do not directly deliver instructional programs" (p. 147). Perhaps even more important for our purposes in this chapter is the contrast between the two types of positions offered by Wiles and Bondi (1983). They describe line personnel as the "formal leadership" in the schools and school districts and staff personnel as those "who advise and consult others of the organization, formally and informally, but have no authority" (pp. 113-114). Position titles sometimes help in revealing the line or staff authority of central office administrative positions, but they are no guarantee.

Central office administrators working with special programs or in other areas may also differ in the focus of their positions responsibilities, i.e., "generalists" or "specialists" (Campbell, Cunningham, Nystrand, & Usdan, 1985, p. 226). Generalists, such as superintendents and principals, have a wide range of responsibilities encompassed in their positions. Individuals in positions that have a focus on one area or single group of functions are specialists. Some of these positions are advisory (i.e., staff) positions, others have line authority. School districts need both kinds of positions to operate; generalists need advice and information from a variety of specialists to make good decisions and someone needs to see the "big picture" of the school system operation which goes beyond any one specialty area.

An understanding of the traditional perspectives helps one to appreciate the monumental changes being proposed (and in some places implemented) regarding the purpose and practice of central office administration (Pankake & Boyter, 1998). According to Whitaker & Moses (1994), "Historically, the superintendent and central administration have assumed the roles of primary decision makers and enforcers of school board policies. Although the roles of central administration still include being accountable for decisions, they are gradually changing from enforcing ones to supporting ones" (p. 166). These changes provide important opportunities for school leaders to use and even help develop central office resources as supports for rather than barriers in the administration and delivery of special programs.

Major reform and restructuring efforts have influenced the roles and responsibilities of central office personnel as well as the individuals in the school sites. A shift from the traditional control and monitoring roles toward roles more focused on services and supports that assist with improved student performance generally in the school is occurring in varying degrees in districts across the nation (Hord & Smith, 1993). Thus, "Central staff are no longer the sole authority figures, distributing directives and monitoring compliance" (Hord & Smith, 1993, p, 23). Rather, in the "new central office, staff members must learn to operate without the crutch of hierarchy and have only themselves to rely on" (Hanna, 1988, cited in Tewel, 1995, p.66). Accordingly, Tewel (1995) admonished that "...success [in central office positions] now depends on figuring out whose collaboration is needed to act on good ideas. In short, the new work implies very different ways of obtaining and using power and influence" (p. 66). School systems, like businesses and government agencies, are trying to create flatter organizations, or as Tewel (1995) described it, to "become leaner, less bureaucratic, and more entrepreneurial" (p. 65). Certainly some school districts' central office administration would fit perfectly in one or more of the traditional schemes described earlier. Others, however, are in the midst of trying to implement the new roles, relationships, and responsibilities that accompany the system restructuring. As with any system, making a change in one area of the system results in associated changes in other areas of the system. Consequently, as changes occurred in the structure and operations at central office, changes will be enabled and required in response at the school level.

Proposed changes in central office administrative operations are numerous. They include:

1. More channels for action created, especially, cross-department projects, inter-agency ventures, and collaboration with various professional associations.
2. Creation of "more potential centers of power" to provide "the opportunity for greater flexibility" (Tewel, 1995, p. 66).

To accomplish these changes, central office administrators and supervisors must

- Shift to being facilitators and sources of technical expertise to help the school in their efforts to change (Hord & Smith, 1993).
- Begin sharing and in some instances relinquishing decision-making authority in many areas of school operations (Hord & Smith, 1993).
- Start thinking cross-functionally and building multiple networks (Tewel, 1995, p. 67). According to Tewel (1995), surving and thriving for central office administrators will depend on finding knowledge and services of value to individuals at the building sites. This will happen only if these individuals spend more time working across boundaries with peers and other staff members over whom they have no direct control but need their interpersonal and negotiating skills. Power will evolve from personal strengths of the individuals, not from organizational structure (Tewel, 1995).

An important point made by Tewel (1995) and one to be kept in mind as these various concepts of the traditional and contemporary operations regarding central office administration are linked is that, "While the old organization no longer exists on paper, . . . it continues to haunt the minds, habits, and performance of staff." (p. 76). School leaders need to assess the situation in their district and take advantage of both the old and/or the new in terms of leadership opportunities. Obviously not all districts will have made the transition from the traditional, more centralized structure to the more decentralized, autonomous site operations. Being able to analyze how a district actually is operating (whether or not that is what's described in the organizational chart and/or the operational philosophy) will be important in taking advantages of the resources available.

Accessing and Using What's Available

As the new ways of operating become embedded in the central office, school leaders will need to respond appropriately. In order to take full advantage of the collaborative, facilitative, shared decision making, support, and assistance perspective developing at the central office, similar perspectives need to be developed at the school sites.

Sarason (1996) points out:

"More than any other single position in the American School hierarchy, the principalship represents the pivotal exchange point, the most important point of connection between teachers, students, and parents on the one hand and the educational policy-making structure—superintendent, school board, and taxpayer —on the other. Through the principal's office pass both the needs, problems, and issues of the local community and the problems and issues that accompany the implementation of policies flowing downward from the top of the school bureaucracy" (p. 180).

This statement emphasizes the importance of the school leadership in making use of all resources that may improve the quality of programs. Following are some ideas on how school leaders can take advantage of the new opportunities developing as the restructuring at the central office occurs or how to take better advantage of the existing opportunities if restructuring of the central office is yet to be initiated in the current situation.

One of a number of consequences from reform efforts at the central office is that personnel and other program resources are being decentralized and located at the school rather than at the central office. The relocation of specialized positions from central offices to schools is one of the recent changes being observed across the country. An attempt to move the resources as close to he point of instructional impact for students as possible is an assumption driving decisions egarding central office restructuring. According to Delehant (1990), "The traditional, centralized district organization is being replaced with a structure that directs all resources that bear upon student performance to be the work of the schools. The responsibility and accountability for decisions that affect student performance are shifting from central management to the schools" (p. 17). This reallocation is an effort to assist improved student performance in the school generally, not just in the specific special programs. Locating human and non-human resources where the programs are happening allows some authentic on-site technical assistance to be afforded to students, teachers, and building administrators alike.

Delehant (1990) notes that as the restructuring occurs in Rochester, NY, "Central office staff are being asked to review services and methods of delivery to ensure they are compatible with and support the schools' new roles" (p. 17). Conversely, such changes require that school leadership become good customers. What can this mean for school's leaders?

Knowing Your Priorities. As central office administrators offer support and assistance, they will need to know what the priorities are in order to make the best use of their time, knowledge, and skills in addressing the needs at the various school sites. Central office resources will be limited. To get the best service and assistance school leaders need to be clear about what they need, when, and how they perceive it might best be delivered.

Offering Feedback on the Quality of Services and Assistance. As Hunter (1982) noted, everybody likes to have an answer to the question, "How am I doing?" In fact, it is necessary to have some sense of this in order to know to adjust and improve the quality of services. The only ones who have the information on how well those at central office are meeting needs will be individuals at each building site. Therefore it is incumbent on the building leadership to set up various means of collecting feedback on the services and assistance provided

143

and convey this information to those at central office. Without such information, whether or not activities are truly resulting in quality services will be a best guess on the part of the central office personnel (Pankake, 1998).

Getting Information about Who Can Do What for Whom. Depending on the size and complexity of the central office staff, there may be several sources of information available. Knowing who has the information and services needed will increase the efficiency and accuracy with which the central office can respond to any request. Representatives from the school site may find it helpful to both themselves and their central office administrators and supervisors to spend some time learning about who knows what and who can do what regarding the various special programs operating in the building. This may well be a point at which knowing who are the generalists and who are the specialists in the central office will become quite useful. It will also be helpful for the school leadership to understand the line and staff divisions at central office. This will prevent them from asking for a decision from someone who does not have the authority to make it, and will lead to asking for advice from those who truly have the expertise in that particular area.

Some of the resources available at the central office may not be encompassed in personnel specifically allocated to the administration of special programs. For example, the central office unit dealing with staff development may be of great assistance in a variety of areas. While they may not have specific information about a particular program, they may well be able to locate who does. If there is a particular knowledge base needed by the school staff to implement new strategies, the staff development personnel can find it, organize its presentation, and maybe even fund it.

Another central office unit that may be helpful to school leaders as they look to make quality improvements are the administrators in the central office who work with personnel matters. Generally, these people are experts in certification requirements and can be most helpful in identifying applicants who meet the paper requirements as well as the practice requirements. Personnel office administrators and staff may also be involved in the allocation of time for individuals who serve more than one school, i.e., the "traveling teachers" or "shared personnel." Staying informed about who makes these assignments and in turn, keeping those individuals informed about the school's needs for the services of these staff members will make it more likely that staff allocations are based on needs, not just numbers.

Another opportunity for building level access to central office resources that is presenting itself more frequently is participation in district level planning. Many districts are implementing vertical teams in their planning processes to ensure that a variety of perspectives are being considered at the planning stages of all operations and of any new initiatives. School leaders need to have personnel ready and willing to take part in these activities as the opportunities arise. Full participation in these opportunities requires that school leaders know the interests, skills, and talents of their staff members. School leaders would do well to get acquainted with everyone in their organization to discover what talents and areas of expertise exist (Pankake, 1998). Knowing who has had special training in a particular area, who may be bilingual but not working in the bilingual program, who has some community connections and involvement that might assist on a school or district project, who is looking to pursue a school administration career, and who is looking to accept some leadership responsibilities but does not wish to leave their classroom assignment can help assure that when central office extends an invitation to participate, the school is ready to respond.

"Specialists" at central office can be a wealth of information regarding the rules, regulations, and reports that seem to be part and parcel of every special program. The role of school leader is much more of a generalist than a specialist. "Generalists" have a wide range of responsibilities included in their jobs, while "specialists" usually have their responsibilities focused on one area or group of functions operationally or programmatically (Campbell, et al, 1985). Individuals with specialized information related to various school and district programs are often located at the district level. However, their specialized knowledge is only a phone call, e-mail or office visit away. They know the latest in their area. School leaders who access this specialized knowledge can help ensure quality programming for students and help avoid complaints and litigation situations for everyone.

Specialists may also have established contacts and working relationships with individuals in external agencies that provide needed services and support to students and/or their families. School leaders can work through the central office specialists to move more quickly and effectively in accessing personnel and information located in these external agencies. Taking advantage of the bridges and communication networks already in place through central office specialists can facilitate interagency cooperation in providing services for students and reduce bureaucratic frustrations for everyone.

Closing Comments

"With a decades-long drive to push reform to the school level, the central office has too frequently become the bad guy in these efforts. The accusations of central office 'interference' in reform are many..." (Richardson, 2000, p. 1). It is time to end the traditional blame game of "them" and "us" when considering school reform with a focus on quality programming for all students. Schools and school systems won't improve with leaders spending their time waiting for each other to change. If the oft used term "systemic change" has any real meaning for quality education, surely it is that all levels and all individuals working at those levels in the educational system have some responsibilities for making changes. Leaders at both the central office and school sites have important roles to play in the school improvement process and the implementation of special programs. The central office's efforts to become less bureaucratic and dominating and more service and support oriented are taking hold in many systems throughout the country; other systems are likely to follow. However, when the efforts to change toward this decentralized service and support structure are initiated, school leaders must simultaneously reciprocate by recognizing this and taking action to access the information and services offered. This can be done in q myriad ways, only a few of which have been offered here.

Applying Your Knowledge

The new superintendent has expressed a desire for some major changes in the roles, relationships, and responsibilities for all leadership personnel throughout the district. She has asked that you and three of your colleagues from other schools serve as members of a restructuring task force (RTF). Other members of the task force are: the Director of Staff Development, the Assistant Superintendent for Non-Instructional Support Services, one of the Bilingual Instructional Facilitators, the Early Childhood Education Services Coordinator, the Director of Social, Psychological, and Psychometric Services, the Administrative Assistant for Business and Purchasing, two parents, and a Program Administrator from the Educational Service Center for the region.

To get things underway, the superintendent has hosted a continental breakfast and now everyone is seated at the conference table. The superintendent calls the meeting to order and repeats her desire for the RTF to explore some of the major issues that may be preventing quality delivery of instructional and support services to the children enrolled in the district. She reinforces that it is her intent to determine ways in which positions, procedures, and resources can be reallocated and restructured to increase the quantity and quality of services for all children. She has provided two individuals from her office to serve as scribes for the meeting. Her goal for this session is to have everyone offer ideas on what they perceive to be problems or issues that should be explored by the RTF.

You are feeling optimistic about this effort and the leadership of the superintendent. In a variety of informal meetings with your school leadership colleagues, you have been openly critical of operations at central office, especially as they relate to services for special needs students and the quality and relevance of teacher inservice offerings. Suddenly you are jogged from your satisfied reflection when you realize that the superintendent has just spoken your name. All eyes at the conference table are on you and the scribes have their markers in hand, as the superintendent says to you, "...let's have you start us out. Have you experienced any difficulties in securing the assistance you need from those of us at central office?"

Questions:

1. How will you respond to the superintendent's question with honesty but in such a way that it keeps the discussion positive and open?
2. What do you think about the make-up of the task force membership? Is there anyone you believe should be added to the group? Anyone currently on the group that you believe probably shouldn't be? Explain.
3. Will you share information about the work of the RTF with others in your school? Will you seek their input? Why? How?

Questions for Thought

1. How might knowing which central office administrators are in "line" positions and which are in "staff" positions impact building leaders in their work with special programs?
2. Give a brief history of the development of the central office. Discuss what you believe will be the future of the central office given the current climate.
3. What are some professional development issues related to the delivery of quality special programming with which the central office might offer support? What forms would this support take?
4. If a decision were made to reallocate the resources and responsibilities of one central office position to your building, what position would you request? Why? How would you put the resources to work? What responsibilities would you give the person in this position?

For Further Information Online

*American Association of School Administrators (AASA) **www.aasa.org**
*National Staff Development Council (NSDC) **www.nsdc.org**
*Association for Supervision and Curriculum Development (ASCD) **www.ascd.org**
Education Week **www.edweek.or/ewhome.htm**
Also many universities and private agencies have policy analysis units that could be helpful.

*Each of these organizations has affiliate organizations in most states. State affiliates could be sources of information more specific to the unique information requirements of a particular area.

References

Campbell, R. F., Cunningham, L. L., Nystrand, R. O., & Usdan, M.D. (1985). *The organization and control of American schools* (5th ed.). Columbus, OH: Charles E. Merrill.
Delehant, A. M. (1990). A central office view: Charting a course when pulled in all directions. *The School Administrator, 47*(8), 14, 17-19.
English, F. W. (1992). *Educational administration: The human science.* New York: HarperCollins.
Hord, S., and Smith, A. (1993). Will the phones go dead? *Insight,* (winter), 23-26.
Hunter, M. (1982). *Mastery teaching.* El Segundo, CA: TIP Publications.

Knezevich, S. J. (1984). *Administration of public education: A sourcebook for the leadership and management of educational institutions* (4th ed.). New York: Harper & Row.

National Center for Educational Statistics (May, 1995). *Statistics in brief.* Washington, DC: U.S. Department of Education OERI, NCES-95-213.

Orlosky, D. E., McCleary, L.E., Shapiro, A., & Webb, L.D. (1984). *Educational administration today.* Columbus, OH: Charles E. Merrill.

Pankake, A. M., & Boyter, G. A. (1998). Central office career choices for women. In B. J. Irby & G. Brown (Eds.), *Women Leaders: Structuring Success* (pp. 168-179). Dubuque, IA: Kendall/Hunt Publishing Co.

Pankake, A. M. (1998). *Implementation: Making things happen.* Larchmont, NY: Eye on Education.

Pankake, A. M. & Fullwood, H. L. (1999). "Principals of inclusion": Things they need to know and do. *Catalyst for Change, 28*(2), 25-26.

Parsley, J. F. (1991). Reshaping student learning. *The School Administrator, 48*(7), 9, 11,13, & 14.

Richardson, J. (2000, October). Central office guidance strengthens the whole district. *NSDC Results,* 1& 6.

Robinson, G. (1992). *School administration under attack: What are the facts?* Arlington, VA: Educational Research Service.

Sarason, S. B. (1996). *Revisiting "The culture of the school and the problem of change."* New York: Teachers College Press.

Scambio, E. J., & Graber, J. (1991). Reform through state intervention. *The School Administrator, 48*(7), 8, 10, 12, & 14.

Snyder, K. J., Giella, M., & Fitzgerald, J. H. (1994). The changing role of central office supervisors in district restructuring. *The Journal of Staff Development, 15*(2), 30-34.

Tewel, K. J. (1995). Despair at the central office. *Educational Leadership, 52*(7), 65-68.

Whitaker, K. S., & Moses, M. C. (1994). *The restructuring handbook: A guide to school revitalization.* Boston, MA: Allyn and Bacon.

Wiles, J. & Bondi, J. (1983). *Principles of school administration: The real world of leadership in schools.* Columbus, OH: Charles E. Merrill.

Chapter 11

Teachers as Leaders in Special Programs

Leeann Moore

Teacher leadership is viewed by some as the only way in which genuine and lasting change will take place in schools.

Leeann Moore

Objectives:
- **Demonstrate the need for teachers to share in the school's leadership responsibilities.**
- **Show the leadership opportunities teachers have in the day-to-day operations of special programs.**

Preface

The previous chapters in this book detailed the various special programs that teachers and administrators may encounter in a school. For each program, such issues as historical backgrounds, the populations served, funding, and how students are identified are provided. While school principals are ultimately responsible for the school's success, special programs cannot operate in the best interests of students without a high rate of involvement, care, and concern on the part of teachers. Each chapter in this book contains a section on the school leaders' role in the program under discussion. The intent is that the suggestions offered apply to teacher-leaders as well as to administrators. This chapter on teacher leadership is included to highlight an important point—that teachers play a key role in the success of each and every program. In the first section of this chapter, the argument is made that teachers need to take leadership positions in schools. The second part of the chapter offers some concrete avenues teachers can take should they choose to take that active leadership role.

Teachers as Leaders

The call for teachers to become leaders in their schools and districts has increased in the past two decades (Darling-Hammond, 1990; 1997; Goodlad, 1990; Fullan, 1991; Hargreaves & Fullan, 1992; Senge, 1990; Sergiovanni, 1990, 1995, 1999; Walling, 1994). In 1996 the National Commission on Teaching and America's Future released its report: *What Matters Most: Teaching for America's Future* which issued a challenge to the American public, policymakers, and educators. The report advocated restructuring the teaching profession and for a greater level of teacher leadership through collegiality and a higher—and deeper—level of professional development. In response, leaders in school districts, at individual school sites, and in professional associations are stepping forward.

Why Teacher Leadership?

Teacher leadership is viewed by some as the *only* way in which genuine and lasting change will take place in schools. Armstrong, Henson, and Savage (2001) insist that decentralizing decision-making is a means for sharing authority with those professionals most aware of the needs of the school. Duke (1994) declares, "The traditional emphasis on individual rather than collective accountability in schools has….served as a deterrent to an expanded concept of teacher leadership" (p. 270).

In favor of teacher leadership, Glickman (1993) described successful schools as places where:

- Faculty members supervise and guide one another….and work in coordination.
- Faculty members are not treated as subordinates, but instead are regarded as the colleagues of administrators and others involved in decisions and actions.
- Faculty members, administrators, and others….have established norms of collegiality for discussions and debating (p. 16-17).

Proponents of teacher leadership see decentralization as an important way to increase teachers' ownership in school decisions. The need for an increased sense of ownership as well as the need for accountability are ways to address "drift" and "detachment" of individuals in the organization. Duke (1994) defines "organizational drift" or "loose coupling" as a prevalent condition in which "little relationship appears to exist between the efforts of individuals and units in the organization…" (p. 256). The disconnection between individuals within the school organization is sometimes referred to as "teacher detachment." Duke explains,

"Detachment" refers to situations from which individuals withdraw psychologically while remaining physically present. No longer fully engaged, they are said to "go through the motions," doing just enough to get by. The symptoms of detachment vary. …stress and burnout…denial of evidence of diminishing effectiveness, depersonalization of blame, excuse-making, and feelings of helplessness and hopelessness may be associated with detachment. (p. 258)

Schools can address detachment by making the work environment a place that provides meaning to teachers' lives. "Meaning refers to that which makes lives seem significant and worthwhile"(Duke, 1994, p. 260). Meaning can occur when teachers are provided opportunities for personal growth, when they are made to feel valued, and when they are able to influence their surroundings. Developing teacher leadership is one way of providing meaning. Duke (1994) states, " . . . leadership helps bring meaning to the relationship between individuals and greater entities, such as communities, organizations, and nations….In the presence of leadership, for instance, individuals often sense movement and purpose" (p. 262). Moreover, teachers are in a position to take the lead in long-term change because they are "likely to remain for relatively long periods of time in a particular school" where administrators come and go through transfers and reassignments. Furthermore, "parents typically only remain involved for the duration of their children's school attendance" (p. 265).

"Organizational drift" or "loose-coupling" can be addressed by involving teachers in making decisions surrounding the school's goals, priorities, and policies. The sense of purpose that comes with involvement is "embraced and internalized, not dictated, and enforced" (Duke, p. 269).

To change the problems of detachment and organizational drift, some tried-and-true practices must be challenged. Glickman (1993) called for removing the "traditions of isolation" in schools and making them places that are "without hierarchical status." To accomplish this, teachers and administrators will have to be willing to discard some of the structure and traditions of the past. The physical organization of the school, for example, keeps people apart. With an "egg crate structure," one teacher is provided for one group of students, classrooms are boxed off from others, and people are unable to see the others at work. Another tradition that Glickman claims must go is the "legacy of the one-room schoolhouse"—the notion that teaching is an autonomous act. He urges moving from the traditional hierarchy of decision making and "restricted dialogue" toward involving teachers as a vital part of the decision-making body with access to communication and professional dialogue.

Sergiovanni (1999; 1995) urges educators to view schools as communities. He states:

> Communities are not defined by instrumental purposes, rationally conceived work systems, evaluations schemes designed to monitor compliance, or skillfully contrived positive interpersonal climates. Communities are defined by their centers. Centers are repositories of values, sentiments, and beliefs that provide the needed cement for uniting people in a common cause. Centers govern the school values and provide norms that guide behavior and give meaning to school community life. (p. 102)

Fullan (1994) advocates teachers attaining "knowledge of collegiality." He explains that:

> Today's teachers must be committed to, skilled at, and involved in collaborative work cultures….[c]reating collaborative work cultures is incredibly complex. Yet this is a large part of the agenda for teacher leadership. [This challenge is critical to getting past 'just' restructuring schools and getting to] 're-culturing' schools, requiring a wholesale transformation of the teaching profession. *Teacher leadership is not for a few; it is for all* [emphasis added]. (p. 246)

Sources of Authority and Power

In order to better understand better the concepts of teacher leadership, authority and power need to be understood. Three types of authority are appropriate for this discussion on teacher leadership: legitimate, referent, and expert.

Legitimate power is "the authority granted by the organization to the formal management position a manager holds" (Daft, 1994, p. 404). The principal of a school traditionally holds this type of power by virtue or her/his title. When teachers are encouraged to become leaders as well, that power is *shared* between the principal and the staff.

Referent power or personal power is "based on the leader's expertise in providing leadership in human relations, in using motivational techniques, and in artfully practicing other interpersonal skills" (Sergiovanni, 1999, p. 49). In the context of teacher leadership, referent power is present in a teacher who has strong interpersonal skills, can work as a valuable member of the team, inspires the best effort in other team members, and is able to collaborate with others.

Expert power "is the power of information and knowledge. People who have important information, people who know how to do things and how to get things done, can use their expertise as a source of power" (Bolman & Deal, 1985, p. 116). Sergiovanni (1999) terms this "professional authority" and explains that it "comes from the context itself and from within the teacher" (p. 52). A teacher who is recognized by peers, administrators, and parents as an expert in instruction, classroom management, and curriculum would possess "expert power."

Leaders are sometimes described as those "with authority" and those "without authority." "Leadership with authority" comes in a formal capacity with a role or a title resulting from an election, an appointment, or contracted employment. The nature of the role or title bestows that person with authority and responsibility. For example, the principal is said to have leadership with authority at the campus.

While certain roles and titles carry with them the expectation of leadership— legitimate authority—there are many instances when individuals who are in subordinate positions exercise authority as well. An example is the teacher who takes on the role of informal leader in a school without the benefit of a title. Heifetz (1994) describes another form of leadership which is temporary in nature and comes from within the ranks. For example, a teacher may speak out in a meeting on behalf of several colleagues or chair a committee. Heifetz explained, "The scarcity of leadership from people in authority...makes it all the more critical to the adaptive success of a polity that leadership be exercised by people without authority...[and leaders without authority may be able to] provide the capacity within the system to see through the blind spots of the dominant view point" (p, 183).

Types of Leadership

Leadership is often described as being either transactional or transformative. Sergiovanni (1999) describes the traditionally accepted form of leadership, transactive, as "focus[ing] on basic and largely extrinsic motives and needs of followers...." (p. 69) This type of leader looks for ways to meet the needs of the individuals and the leader's own self-interests; she or he looks for ways to reward at the extrinsic level and leadership comes from carefully planned strategies.

In contrast is transformational leadership about which Sergiovanni (1999) said, "[It] focuses on higher-order, intrinsic, and moral motives and needs of followers" (p.68). He explained that transformational leaders have the ability to lead in a capacity to make decisions beyond their own individual desires, but instead lead in such a capacity that they "advance the common good as defined by group commitments" (p. 68). Daft (1994) describes transformational leaders as having the ability to use their interpersonal skills to share their vision, to motivate followers toward the vision, and to thereby bring about innovation and institutional change. Burns (1978) explaines that transformational leadership, "occurs when one or more persons engage with others in such a way that leaders and followers raise one another to higher levels of motivation and morality. Their purposes, which might have started out as separate but related...become fused" (p. 263).

Heifetz (1994) described a third, and new, style of leadership that is desirable for these times of great complexity—adaptive leadership. Here the concern is with sharing leadership with workers in the organization to help support an adaptive system, to mobilize people to tackle tough problems. The adaptive leader is focused on integrity and on issues and sees the value of disclosing information to all workers. Furthermore, the adaptive leader understands that conflict in a group is not a negative state to be avoided, but the adaptive leader allows for the exposure of conflict in order for the group to move toward a solution or resolution that advances the group.

Skills for Leading

Effective leadership exhibits certain characteristics in virtually any context and at any level within an organization. Leadership skills are widely discussed in the literature (Bolman & Deal, 1991; Schein, 1992; Senge, 1990; Covey, 1990; Fullan 1994; Sergiovanni, 1990, 1995; Short & Greer, 1997; Kouzes & Posner, 1987; Wheatley, 1994; Heifetz, 1994). Leadership skills mentioned include the ability to:

- Listen and to gather information.
- Analyze, synthesize, and conceptualize.
- Empower others within the organization—building human capital.
- Be sensitive to human needs and human behavior.
- Understand group processes.
- Think both critically and creatively.
- Display intellectual capacity.
- Communicate.

- Take risks and "think outside the box."
- Respect others.
- Know when to lead and when to follow.
- Commit to continuous learning.
- Hold personal values that are aligned with behavior.

In *Rethinking Leadership* (1999) Sergiovanni adds a new dimension to leadership by calling for leaders to behave substantively and with moral foundation. He explains, "School leadership is about connecting people morally to each other and to their work. …[It] involves developing shared purposes, beliefs, values, and conceptions themed to teaching and learning, community building, collegiality, and character development" (p. 96).

It is Sergiovanni's call for educators to behave morally that links teachers to responsible behavior. Ensuring that special programs are operating smoothly and that students are receiving the care they need requires teachers to take on leadership responsibilities.

Some recommendations for leadership action on the part of teachers in regard to special programs are listed in the previous chapters. More structured approaches are offered here. These include (a) teachers as mentors, particularly to inexperienced teachers, (b) teachers as peer coaches, and (c) teacher leadership that influences the entire school's climate and culture. Each approach offers opportunities for teachers to ultimately provide attention to students who have more than the ordinary array of needs.

Leadership Through Mentoring

One avenue for adopting a leadership role in the school is through the mentoring process. The optimal time to develop positive attitudes regarding special programs and the students served by them is during a teacher's early career years, sometimes termed the "induction" period. Beginning teachers frequently bring fresh energy and provide experienced teachers with new and innovative ideas and teaching methods. Experienced teachers, on the other hand, have the opportunity to take on leadership responsibilities and, as mentors, considerably influence others' attitudes about students with disabilities, those who move frequently, the gifted, the disadvantaged, and the limited English proficient. Mentors model how the curriculum should be modified, help identify special needs students, and teach what it means to show personal concern for students.

The term *mentor* takes on different interpretations; however, the role is usually agreed to mean someone who "teaches, counsels, guides, and develops a novice in an organization or profession" (Alleman, 1986, p. 45). The mentor is a person who holds knowledge and expertise in his/her field and is able to communicate and transmit those pieces of content and process that assist the protégé with his/her progress toward desirable standards. For example, a mentor teacher can guide a new teacher through the special education referral process, provide councel about challenging gifted students, and share strategies for helping non-English speaking students.

The mentor must have the ability to develop positive relationships and foster trust. Successful mentors have good communication skills, flexibility, enthusiasm, the ability to express care and concern, knowledge of how adults learn, and the ability to *teach* adult learners (Allerman, 1986; Anderson & Shannon, 1988; Haensly and Edlind, 1986; Schein, 1978; Zimpher & Rieger, 1989). Anderson and Shannon (1988) describe a mentor as a sponsor who is able to protect, support, and promote:

> Teacher mentors can protect their protégés from something in the environment …or by helping protect protégés from themselves….Teacher mentors can support their protégés when they participate in an activity assigned to them….As sponsors, teacher mentors can promote their protégés both within the instructional and social systems of the school program. (p. 40)

Mentoring is a very sophisticated form of working *with* people. The mentor serves as a career advisor, a counselor, and a confidant as he/she guides the person through professional growth. Anderson and Shannon (1988) describe and illustrate how these mentoring functions would be played out in a school setting: "Examples of basic mentoring activities...include: demonstrating teaching techniques to a protégé, observing the protégé's classroom teaching and providing feedback, and holding support meetings with the protégé" (p. 41). All of these examples include opportunities to demonstrate teaching students enrolled in special programs, particularly those with special classroom needs.

Asked to describe their first years of teaching, most experienced teachers will recall their personal struggles with such issues as classroom management, time constraints, pacing instructional time, and motivating reluctant students. Developing working relationships with colleagues, administrators, and students are likely to be remembered as well. Despite the importance, the experienced teacher will likely recollect less about how students were referred for special education, how Upward Bound or gifted students were identified, or the process for placing students in a Title 1 program. Yet this is critical information for beginning teachers and crucial to student success. Mentors can make the difference here by ensuring that teachers obtain this critical information.

Mentoring and Special Programs

Mentors' influence focuses on giving information and shaping others' attitudes and beliefs about the school and the students. Mentors also impact what others believe about their ability to impact their surroundings. Consequently, mentors have considerable power to shape the culture and norms of their school in the best interests of students. Some examples of what mentors can do that will ultimately affect students in special programs are:

- Encourage others to attend staff development on special program issues.
- Remain current on legal issues.
- Show others how to identify students who have needs that are out of the ordinary, e.g., the gifted or those who should be referred to special education.
- Educate others on the special education referral process.
- Inform others of the services offered by the school counselor(s).
- Share knowledge of TRIO programs and how students qualify.
- List for others the various resources available for teaching students in special programs.
- Provide information on contact persons in the district or education service centers who can be of help when problems arise.
- Share this book with other teachers who are new to the profession.

Peer Coaching

Teacher leadership through peer coaching is an opportunity for teachers to break the isolation of their classrooms and collaborate for meaningful change. The literature on staff development has led to increased interest and implementation of coaching as a form of professional development (Lortie, 1975; Huberman & Miles, 1984; Hargreaves, 1989; Fullan, 1991, Lieberman, 1986). Showers (1985), an early proponent of coaching, explains, "Coaching appears to be most appropriate when teachers wish to acquire unique configurations of teaching patterns and to master strategies that require new ways of thinking about learning objectives and the processes by which students achieve them" (p. 44). Working with the disadvantaged, disabled, and other students with unique needs challenges teachers to explore alternate teaching strategies. While some innovative ideas are gleaned from workshops and staff development, many are simply shared, one teacher to another. Peer coaching encourages that exchange.

The term *coaching* comes from the long-standing practice in athletics in which a coach or a mentor is "one who instructs or trains a performer...." (Webster's Ninth New Collegiate Dictionary). In the "coaching of teaching" is implied a similar relationship or partnership between two teachers working closely together to achieve the goal of improving the "performance" of teaching. In this practice, teachers visit and observe one another, each learning from watching the other. Following the observation, the teachers, discuss how to help the students and how to improve teaching skills to increase student achievement. No evaluation is inherent in this partnership. In other words, *no one person holds any evaluative power over the other*. No criticism is given or expected. The observed teacher uses the de-briefing session to determine a method to increase effectiveness. The entire tone of the coaching partnership is one of support and reflection (Joyce and Showers, 1982; Showers, 1985; Hargreaves & Dawe, 1990; Hargreaves & Fullan, 1992; Glickman, Gordon, & Ross-Gordon, 2001).

Peer coaching has several purposes. It breaks teachers out of their isolated existence in day-to-day school life and provides opportunities to build relationships with colleagues. It allows teachers an opportunity to discuss their "craft" and to participate in reflection for better instruction. It encourages the implementation of innovations that positively impact students.

Peer Coaching and Special Programs

Peer coaches can help teachers with identifying effective instructional strategies. Some examples of what peer coaches can do that will ultimately affect students in special programs are:

- Demonstrate how instruction can be enriched, modified, and organized to address students' academic and emotional needs.
- Introduce new teaching techniques and methods.
- Encourage student interaction and collaborative learning techniques.
- Promote high expectations for students.
- Emphasize higher level thinking skills in all students.
- Promote developmentally appropriate instruction at all levels.
- Share and address concerns about individual students.
- Ask the peer to observe for bias and discrimination.

Broad-based Teacher Leadership

While mentoring and peer coaching can successfully impact teachers one by one, an avenue for teachers to impact the entire school is through more formal decision-making councils that determine policies and procedures for the entire organization. The educational reform movement in the past decade has promoted the use of site-based management as an answer to the traditionally highly centralized form of decision–making. Armstrong, Henson, and Savage (2001) state, "The idea of site-based decision making is to trust critical decisions to the people who will actually be delivering educational services to learners" (p. 371).

The central component of site-based decision making is shared power. Leadership teams, or site-based councils, usually are composed of teachers, administrators, parents, and representatives from the community. Some site councils in secondary schools also include representatives from the student body. These councils are given authority over a broad array of decisions depending on the school district or state. Decisions may include issues of curriculum, budgeting, policy-making, staff development, community relations, and even staffing.

A teacher can well expect to have the opportunity to serve on a site council. Teacher leaders on site councils are often expected to commit to a length of service of one or more years. Site council representatives are expected to be available to those whom they represent, to be an active member of the council, to make decisions that support the common good and not come from a personal agenda, and to maintain an open line of communication.

Parent and community representation on site councils offer the unique avenue for council members to seek formal feedback from parents on their perceptions of how the school is meeting their obligations to students, particularly those students with special needs. Persons outside the school sometimes are aware of issues about which those within the organization are less aware. For example, community members may know of employment opportunities for students who have difficulty finding jobs, be able to approach parent involvement from a new viewpoint, work to enlarge the pool of parent volunteers, provide enrichment for gifted students, and find translators for parents who do not speak English.

Site Councils and Special Programs

Site-based councils have considerable power to influence and change the total school program. Site councils can impact special programs specifically by:

- Encouraging innovative approaches to solving problems.
- Providing training for teachers and parents on issues where bias and discrimination exist.
- Supporting school-wide approaches to serving students with special needs.
- Encouraging parent partnerships and high parent involvement in the school.
- Encouraging teachers to learn the language of the students.
- Sharing in the hiring process so teachers who take a personal interest in students are employed.
- Observing the scheduling process so that students are placed according to their needs.
- Supporting training that keeps teachers abreast of the changing legal guidelines surrounding special programs.
- Advocating that counselors' time be used to aid students with a minimum of their time spent on clerical duties.

Summary

Earlier in this chapter referent power and transformational styles of leadership were discussed. Referent power is based on leaders' expertise. Where the needs of students in special programs are concerned, teachers hold considerable referent power as their expertise increases year by year. Teachers who decide to shoulder leadership roles make optimal use of their referent power when, in regard to students with special needs, they focus on what Sergiovanni (1995) describes as transformational leadership. These teachers utilize higher-order, intrinsic, and moral motives to do what is best for students. Armed with a high degree of knowledge about special programs, a transformational teacher-leader can be a powerful force within a school. The challenge to all teachers is to find and fit their own particular area of expertise to the matching area of need in the school. Students can only benefit when all teachers choose to make a difference in their own school.

Applying Your Knowledge

Mrs. Jones, a teacher in Terrance Middle School, walks into the teachers' lounge where three of her colleagues are eating lunch and discussing their problems. One teacher says, "I just can't hold class when six students can't even speak English. Those students just sit there or get in trouble. I don't know what to do with them." Another answers, "Yes, and how am I supposed to teach all these students who aren't even reading on grade level. I need help and nobody seems to care." The third teacher chimes in, "You're right. We have too many students who need extra time, time that we don't have to give and we have too many we don't even know how to help. What do they expect us to do? Perform miracles?"

Mrs. Jones understands the frustration of these teachers as she has similar problems. She is aware that, while other teachers in the building have the same complaints, she knows of a few teachers who are successful despite the students' wide variety of needs. As Mrs. Jones ponders the issues, she realizes that the teachers are unhappy because they feel unable to provide what the students need but she also knows that the students are the ones who are suffering the most. Mrs. Jones leaves the lounge, unsure whether she, as a teacher, should or can do something about the problem.

Questions:

1. What are the main issues in this situation?
2. What changes might be in order for this school and who is responsible for making them?
3. Should Mrs. Jones have talked to these teachers rather than leaving the lounge?
4. How do you suppose students feel in this school?

Questions for Thought

1. If teachers want to change attitudes and beliefs about students, what can they do?
2. Can first and second-year teachers take leadership roles in schools?
3. How long does it take to make lasting changes in a school?
4. To what degree should parents and community members become involved in school problems?

References and Bibliography on Teacher Leadership

Alleman, E. (1986). Measuring mentoring—frequency, quality, impact. In Gray & Gray (Eds.). Mentoring: Aid to excellence in career development, business, and the professions (pp. 44-51). Vancouver, B C: International Association for Mentoring.

Anderson, E. M., & Shannon, A. L. (1988). Toward a conceptualization of mentoring. *Journal of Teacher Education, 39*(1), 38-42.

Armstrong, D. G., Henson, K. T., & Savage, T. V. (2001). *Teaching today: An introduction to education.* (6th ed.) Columbus, OH: Merrill- Prentice-Hall.

Beyer, L. E. (1984). Field experience, ideology, and the development of critical reflectivity. *Journal of Teacher Education, 35*(3), 36-41.

Blair, T. R. (1984). *Clinical indicators of effective cooperating teachers.* (ERIC Documentation Reproduction Service No ED 263 064)

Blomenkamp, J. L. (1996). A survey of selected elements of the student teaching program. Unpublished doctoral dissertation, University of Nebraska.

Bolman, L. G., & Deal, T. E. (1985). *Modern approaches to understanding and managing organizations.* San Francisco: Jossey Bass.

Burns, J. M. (1978). *Leadership.* New York: Harper & Row.

Clift, R. T., & Say, M. (1988). Teacher education: Collaboration or conflict. *Journal of Teacher Education, 39,* 2-7.

Cortez, A. T. (1995). Cooperating teachers' perceptions of the student teaching experience. Unpublished doctoral dissertation, University of Illinois at Urbana-Champaign.

Covey, S. R. (1989). *The seven habits of highly effective people.* New York: Simon Schuster.

Cruickshank, D. R., & Armaline, W. D. (1986). Field experiences in teacher education: Considerations and recommendations. *Journal of Teacher Education 37,* 34- 40.

Daft, D. L. (1994). Drift, detachment, and the need for teacher leadership. In D. R. Walling (Ed.) *Teachers as Leaders: Perspectives on the Professional Development of Teachers.* Bloomington, IN: Phi Delta Kappa.

Darling-Hammond, L. (1990). Instructional policy into practice: The power of the bottom over the top. *Educational Evaluation and Policy Analyses, 12,* 233-241.

Darling-Hammond, L. (1997). *Doing what matters most: Investing in quality teaching.* New York: National Commission on Teaching and America's Future.

Duke, D. L. (1994). Drift, detachment, and the need for teacher leadership. In D. R. Walling (Ed.) *Teachers as Leaders: Perspectives on the Professional Development of Teachers.* Bloomington, IN: Phi Delta Kappa.

Evans, R. (1993). The human face of reform. *Educational Leadership, 51*(1), 19-23.

Fullan, M. G. (1991). *The new meaning of educational change.* New York: Teachers' College Press.

Fullan, M. G. (1994). Teacher leadership: A failure to conceptualize. In. D. R. Walling (Ed.). *Teachers as Leaders: Perspectives on the Professional Development of Teachers.* Bloomington, IN: Phi Delta Kappa.

Glickman, C. D. (1993). *Renewing America's schools.* San Francisco: Jossey-Bass.

Glickman, C. C., Gordon, S. P., & Ross-Gordon, J. M. (2001). *Supervision and instructional leadership: A developmental approach.* Boston: Allyn-Bacon.

Goodlad, J. L. (1990). *Teachers for our nation's schools.* San Francisco: Jossey-Bass.

Guyton, E., & McIntyre, D. J. (1990). Student teaching and school experiences. In W. R. Houston, M. Haberman, & J. Sikula (Eds.). Handbook of research on teacher education (pp. 514-534). New York: Macmillan Publishing.

Haensly, P. A., & Edlind, E. P. (1986). A search for ideal types in mentorship. In W. A. Gray & M. M. Gray (Eds.) Mentoring: Aid to excellence in education, the family, and the community (pp. 1-8). Vancouver, B.C.: International Association for Mentoring.

Hargreaves, A. (1989). *Curriculum and assessment reform.* Toronto: OISE Press.

Hargreaves, A., & Dawe, R. (1990;). Paths of professional development: Contrived collegiality and the case of peer coaching. *Teaching and Teacher Education, 4* (3).

Hargreaves, A., & Fullan, M. G. (1992). *Understanding teacher development.* New York: Teacher's College Press.

Heifetz, R. A. (1994). *Leadership without easy answers.* Cambridge, MA: Belknap.

Hoy, W. K., & Woolfolk, A. E. (1990). Socialization of student teachers. *American Educational Research Journal, 27*(2), 279-300.

Huberman, M., & Miles, M. (1984). *Innovation up close: How school improvement works.* New York: Plenum.

Joyce, B. R. (1988). Training research and preservice teacher education: A reconsideration. *Journal of Teacher Education, 39*(5), 32-36.

Joyce, B., & Showers, B. (1982). *Student achievement through staff development.* New York: Longman.

Kets de Vries, M. F. R., & Miller, D. (1984). *The neurotic organization.* San Francisco: Jossey-Bass.

Kouzes, J. M., & Posner, B. Z. (1987). *The leadership challenge: How to get extraordinary things done in organizations.* San Francisco: Jossey-Bass.

Lambert, L. (1998a). *Building leadership capacity in schools.* Alexandria, VA: Association for Supervision and Curriculum Development.

Lambert, L. (1998b). How to build leadership capacity. *Educational Leadership,55*(7), 17-19.

Lieberman, A. (1986). Collaborative work. *Educational Leadership, 44*(1), 4-8.

Lieberman, A. (1995). Practices that support teacher development. *Educational Leadership, 53,* 591-596.

Little, J. W., & McLaughlin, M. W. (1993). *Teachers' work: Individuals, colleagues, and contexts.* New York: Teacher's College Press.

Lortie, D. (1975). *Schoolteacher.* Chicago: University of Chicago Press.

Moore, L. (2000). *An Organizational Grounded Theory of the Structural and Political Dynamics of the Student Teacher Placement Process. An Executive Summary.* (ERIC Document Reproduction Service No. ED 439 104)

Sarason, S. (1990). *The predictable failure of educational reform*. San Francisco: Jossey-Bass.

Schein, E. H. (1978). *Career dynamics: Matching individual and organizational needs*. Reading, MA: Addison-Wesley.

Senge, P. M. (1990). *The fifth discipline*. New York: Doubleday.

Sergiovanni, T. J. (1990). Adding value to leadership gets extraordinary results. *Educational Leadership, 48*, 23-27

Sergiovanni, T. J. (1995). *The principalship: A reflective practice perspective.* (3rd Ed.) Boston: Allyn & Bacon.

Sergiovanni, T. J. (1999). *Rethinking leadership: A collection of articles.* Arlington Heights, IL: Sky Light.

Short, P. M., & Greer, J. T. (1997). *Leadership in empowered schools: Themes from innovative efforts* Upper Saddle River, NJ: Merrill.

Showers, B. (1985). Teachers coaching teachers. *Educational Leadership, 42* (7), 43-48.

Smith, S. D., Reinhartz, J., Oshima, L., & Smith, W. (1983). A study of student teacher discipline. *Journal of Professional Studies 9*(4), 23-42.

Steffy, B. E. (1989). *Career stages of classroom teachers*. Lancaster, PA: Technomic.

Uhlenberg, D. M., Fuller, M. L., & Slotnick, H. B. (1993, Fall). Differing beliefs about classroom management: Student to professional. *Teacher Education Quarterly, 20*(4), 115-127.

Walling, D, R. (Ed.). (1994). *Teachers as leaders: Perspectives on the professional development of teachers*. Bloomington, IN: Phi Delta Kappa.

Whaley, C. R., & Wolfe, D. M. (1984). Creating incentives for cooperating teachers. *Journal of Teacher Education, 35*(4), 46-48.

Wheatley, M. J. (1994). *Leadership and the new science*. San Francisco: Berrett-Koehler.

Wiles, J. W. (1993). *Promoting change in schools: Ground level practices that work*. New York: Scholastic.

Young, A., & Copenhaver, R. (1993). When teachers and administrators are asked: Improving teacher education through collaboration. East Lansing, MI: National Center for Research on Teacher Learning. (ERIC Document Reproduction Service No. ED 378 160)

Zeichner, K. M. (1980). Myths and realities: Field-based experiences in preservice teacher education. *Journal of Teacher Education, 31*(6), 45-55.

Zeichner. K. M., & Tabachnick, B. R. (1981). Are the effects of university teacher education "washed out" by school experience? *Journal of Teacher Education, 32*(3), 7-11.

Zimpher, N. L., & Rieger, S. R. (1989). Mentoring teachers: What are the issues? *Theory into Practice, 27*(3), 175-182.

Index

Counseling Programs

Early Childhood Programs

Gifted and Talented Programs

ability grouping 120
acceleration 112, 117, 118
Cluster grouping 118
curriculum compacting 116-117
differentiated instruction 111-112, 116-117, 119
Elementary and Secondary Education Act of 1970 112
enrichment 112, 115-117
Jacob Javits Gifted and Talented Education Act of 1988 112-113
magnet schools 115, 120
Marland Report 113-114
pull out programs 115, 120
Renzulli 116-117
staff development 113, 119, 121
Stanford-Binet Intelligence Scale 112
student identification 113
traits
       emotional 114, 121
       intellectual 114, 122
       social 114, 116-117, 122-123
Triad model 117
Underachievement 113, 119

Migrant Education

agricultural worker 38-39, 50
dairy worker 38
dropouts 39, 43, 49
eligibility 37, 42, 45, 49, 51
ESEA (Elementary and Secondary Education Act) 38-40, 43-44
fishing 37-38, 43
identification (see recruitment)
immigrants 38
Improving America's Schools Act 40-41, 43, 50
limited English proficiency 39, 42
Migrant Education Even Start Program (MEES) 43
migrant funding 38-39, 41, 48-50, 52
Migrant Student Records Transfer System 50
New Generation System (NGS) 44
Office of Migrant Education (OME) 37-38
Parent Advisory Council (PAC) 42, 44
parental involvement 42, 49
Reauthorization Act of 1994 40
Recruitment 39, 44-45, 49, 51
social services 38
Title One 39-43

Special Education

Teachers as Leaders in Special Programs

Title One Programs

Upward Bound and Other Trio Programs